Strategies for Landscape Representation

Strategies for Landscape Representation discusses a variety of digital and analogue production techniques for the representation of landscape at multiple scales. Careful consideration is required to represent time, and to ensure accuracy of representation and evaluation in the landscape.

Written as a guide for making appropriate selection of a wide variety of visualisation tools for students and built environment professionals with an interest in landscape, the book charts emerging technologies and historical contexts while also being relevant to landscape legislation such as Building Information Modelling (BIM) and Landscape Assessment. This book is an innovation-driven text that encourages readers to make connections between software, technology and analogue modes. The management, choice and combination of such modes can arguably narrow the unknown of landscape character, address the issues of representing time and change in landscape and engage and represent communities' perceptions and experience of landscape.

Showcasing international examples from landscape architecture, planning, urban design and architecture, artists, visualisers, geographers, scientists and model makers, the vitality of making and intrinsic value of representational work in these processes and sites is evidenced. An accompanying companion website provides access to original source files and tutorials totalling over 100 hours in mapping and GIS, diagrams and notation, photomontage, 3D modelling and 3D printing. Visit www.routledge.com/cw/cureton.

Paul Cureton is a Senior Lecturer in Architecture and Unit Leader for Future Cities at the University of Hertfordshire, UK, Member of the Herts UAV Group, Researcher for the International Garden Cities Institute and Researcher for HS2LV at Birmingham City University, UK. He holds a PhD in Landscape Architecture Representation from the Manchester School of Architecture, UK. Primary research interests include GIS, UAVs, mapping, modelling and digital fabrication.

"This book negotiates a careful balance between genuine scholarly inquiry and practical usability for the reader. Drawing on sources across the built environment disciplines as well as social, philosophical and critical theories, the book is comprehensive in its scope. The rigour of the research allows the author to demonstrate the importance of representational strategies to the discipline of landscape architecture, drawing on a wealth of beautifully illustrated historical and contemporary examples. What is crucial is that such academic research is presented in an accessible and usable manner: the clear intention is for the reader to mobilise the knowledge presented within the book, making it extremely valuable to practitioners, students and academics alike."

Ray Lucas, Head of Architecture, University of Manchester, UK

"Investigations into how urban and territorial landscapes are represented are essential endeavours for landscape architecture and urban design disciplines. Paul Cureton's approach of working between practical methods of drawing and mapping and philosophical conceptions of representation make this a unique book and a significant development of landscape discourses."

Ed Wall, Academic Leader Landscape, University of Greenwich, UK

"Paul Cureton brings an expansive and important account of various techniques for the representation of landscape. Informative and insightful, the book brings sharp focus on key concepts including: agency, valence and the temporal aspects of landscape, whilst opening up the intellectual debate for future landscapes in order to provide a strong case for designers to make a considered approach from the increasingly wide range of representation and evaluation tools and methods available."

Nick Dunn FRSA, Chair of Urban Design, Research Director: Lancaster Institute for the Contemporary Arts and Associate Director: Institute for Social Futures, Imagination Lancaster, Lancaster University, UK

"Contributing to the important task of filling in the conceptual void that lies at the heart of design education, Dr Cureton expands our knowledge of the scope and role of representation in landscape architecture. This fresh approach, capturing the energy and depth of graphic possibilities, explores the purpose and intent of a wealth of representational methods and techniques. Setting out a new and expanded field of design practice, connecting ideas and form, art and design, this book will contribute significantly to the resurgence of interest there is in landscape architecture around the world, helping students and practitioners alike to acquire new skills at the analogue/digital interface and to realize the full communicative potential of visual, graphic expression in design."

Kathryn Moore, IFLA President

Strategies for Landscape Representation

DIGITAL AND ANALOGUE TECHNIQUES

Paul Cureton

LONDON AND NEW YORK

First published 2017
by Routledge
2 Park Square, Milton Park, Abingdon, Oxon OX14 4RN

and by Routledge
711 Third Avenue, New York, NY 10017

Routledge is an imprint of the Taylor & Francis Group, an informa business

© 2017 Paul Cureton

The right of Paul Cureton to be identified as author of this work has been asserted by him in accordance with sections 77 and 78 of the Copyright, Designs and Patents Act 1988.

All rights reserved. No part of this book may be reprinted or reproduced or utilised in any form or by any electronic, mechanical, or other means, now known or hereafter invented, including photocopying and recording, or in any information storage or retrieval system, without permission in writing from the publishers.

Trademark notice: Product or corporate names may be trademarks or registered trademarks, and are used only for identification and explanation without intent to infringe.

British Library Cataloguing-in-Publication Data
A catalogue record for this book is available from the British Library

Library of Congress Cataloging in Publication Data
Names: Cureton, Paul.
Title: Strategies for landscape representation : digital and analogue techniques / Paul Cureton.
Description: New York, NY : Routledge, 2017. | Includes bibliographical references and index.
Identifiers: LCCN 2016027952| ISBN 9781138940987 (pbk. : alk. paper) | ISBN 9781315673936 (ebook)
Subjects: LCSH: Landscape architectural drawing. | Landscape architecture—Simulation methods. | Landscapes—Models.
Classification: LCC SB472.47 .C87 2017 | DDC 712—dc23
LC record available at https://lccn.loc.gov/2016027952

ISBN: 978-1-138-94098-7 (pbk)
ISBN: 978-1-315-67393-6 (epub)

Typeset in Univers
by Florence Production Ltd, Stoodleigh, Devon, UK

Printed and bound
by Bell and Bain Ltd, Glasgow

*For Sarah & Alana
With Love Forever*

CONTENTS

Acknowledgements   ix

INTRODUCTION: REPRESENTATION, AGENCY AND VALENCE   1

Structure   5
Summary   19

1 WORKING WITH DATA (MAPPING)   23

Common data sets   32
Types of data capture   32
Map data outputs, design and strategies   48
Unmanned aerial systems and unmanned aerial vehicles   52
Summary   57

2 LANDSCAPE, PARTICIPATION, NOTATION AND FIELDWORK (NOTATION AND DIAGRAMS)   61

Diagrams of landscape   81
Diagram types   81
Movement notation   88
Understanding Motion   92
Summary   93

3 TIME IN LANDSCAPE (COMPOSITES)   97

Collage/composites   103
Principles of perspective   123
Strategies for time-based 2D imagery   124
Summary   128

4 STRATEGIES FOR REPRESENTATION (3D MODELS)   131

Layering complexity   138
Workstages and strategies   149
Summary   164

5 LANDSCAPE MODELLING AND FABRICATION (MODELS)   169

Layering interactivity   173
3D printing models and augmentation   179
Digital fabrication   199
Landscape architecture and urban design model types   201
Summary   205

6 CONCLUSION: FUTURE LANDSCAPES   209

Landscape imaginaries   211
Future scales   219
Future metabolisms   227
Summary   237

Index   *241*

ACKNOWLEDGEMENTS

I would particularly like to thank my wife for her support and encouragement in the writing of this book, which could not have been achieved without her. I would like to thank my daughter Alana for her input, particularly the bashing of my computer screen and the high level of annotation of my drawings. I would also like to thank friends and family who provided an incredible support network throughout this process, particularly Peter and Juliet Storey, Susan Cureton and Gillian Clark.

I would like to thank Louise Baird-Smith and Sadé Lee at Routledge for their careful advice, guidance and production of this book. I would also like to thank Ed Gibbons for production and Gary Smith for copy-editing. The early chapters of the manuscript were kindly reviewed by Silvio Carta and Nick Dunn, and I would like to highlight their editorial work and quality of advice in the early draft stages. I would like to acknowledge some of the special contributions in particular: the drawing, mapping and masterplan collaboration with Kathryn Moore; the data and workflow typologies by Serena Pollastri; the diagramming of Sophie Parker-Loftus; the composites of Rich Miller; and the Space Syntax collaboration with Laurens Versluis. I would like to thank Steven Adams at SSAHRI, University of Hertfordshire for the ongoing support of my research work and Ben Davis for the assistance with image permissions. I would like to thank Tom Landell-Mills for his professional landscape practice advice and the team at Groundworks, Hertfordshire. Much of my work is future thinking and I would like to thank Nick Dunn for the continuing dialogue and collaboration on future cities that has provoked futures thinking in the course of my work.

I would like to thank Ed Wall, the Environment Agency, Agnes Denes, MKDC Library and Archive, Lawrence Halprin Archives, Vitaly Komar, Olin, SCAPE, Atelier Bow-wow, Karolis Janulis, Swiss Topo, Frac Centre, Bill Rankin, NASA, Satellite Imaging Corporation, David Watson, Historic England, Jarlath O'Neil Dunne, Drone Air, Thomas Lennon, CyberCity 3D inc., Ray Lucas, SWA, OMA, Michel Paysant, Lien Dupont, Isabel Griffiths, Karl Kullmann, JJ Watters, Randolph Hester, Magic Leap, Iona Meldrum, Noël van Dooren, Stoss Landscape Urbanism, Mark Tansey, Taktyk, Turenscape, Groundlab, Hassell, Sasaki Associates, MAUD, West8, Gross Max, Denali National Park & Preserve, Giona Andreani, Byron Wolfe & Mark Kleet, Aecom, Aerometrex, Computer History Museum, Arup, Atelier Crilo, Sanford Museum, Atelier Crilo, ASPECT

Studios, Colour, Alexandra Bergin, Karl Kullmann, Marijn Raeven, Tom Beddard, Lee Griggs, Zaha Hadid Architects, Przemyslaw Prusinkiewicz, British Antarctic Survey, Space Syntax, Terreform 1, British Geological Survey, Pipers Model Makers, Fosters & Partners, Palmbout, Martha Swartz & Partners, Tinker Imagineers, Gensler, Mcor Technologies, Daisy Ginsberg, RIBA, Common Wealth Association of Architects, Helen Mayer Harrison and Newton Harrison, Civic Systems Lab, MVRDV, Newton Fallis and Ecologic Studio.

INTRODUCTION
Representation, agency and valence

> The old falls down, times change, and new life blossoms out of ruins.
>
> (Taylor and Schiller, 2011, Act IV, sc. ii)

Strategies for landscape representation develop a variety of production techniques, both digital and analogue, for the representation of landscape at multiple scales. Strategy is termed as a plan of action; to achieve a number of aims as well as the direction and scope of this action. To represent landscape requires careful consideration to representing time in landscape, accuracy of representation, participation and evaluation. Representation is for one thing to stand for something else, i.e. a drawn design image functions as a message of what a place is like or what the drawing will do to transform a landscape. As such; this work must act as an agent.[1] This agency means communicating landscape analysis and design ideas from representation to production. This function is not linear. Representation filters through the process of realising a space, working with media from design perception of site to the public perception of place; what the place stands for at any such time, and then how it changes in time. As such, representation is a vital generative issue for landscape architecture in time, as Agnes Denes writes: 'time is the scale upon which we lay the sequence of events' (Denes, 2008, p. 56). The recognition of this time, cycle and function is imperative for the landscape of tomorrow, given worldwide resource and climate issues. As Diana Balmori has asserted, 'landscape's role for our time must be redefined. Now. The need is urgent' (Balmori and Conan, 2010, p. 1). Balmori's assertion is challenging; alongside other scholars a growing number of voices have called for a reconceptualisation of landscape, a rebalancing or disciplinary alignment.[2] *Strategies for Landscape Representation* discusses the various actions and responses to design decisions and processes and also aims to map the cause and effect of these fluid representations of landscape. This book is not intended as a technical manual nor a theoretical treatise, technological biased or tied to the discussion of the cannons of landscape architecture, but aims to move in many circles. Many sources used here offer innovative solutions or novel approaches from a variety of professions, all of a standing in their respective fields. These works on face value could seem unstructured and outside the landscape architectural discipline, which can lead to dismay or an

FIGURE I.1 John Czaky, National Bowl Concert Venue, Milton Keynes, United Kingdom; photographs taken by John Donat, images courtesy of MKDC Archive. In 1973, a large earth mound was envisaged to create a 60,000 capacity performance and event space using sub-soil excavated from adjacent rail works. The road building for the grid structure of the city and the soil surplus from construction was used as infill for the pit due to the extensive cut-and-fill of realising the grid network on Buckinghamshire topology, creating vast savings in transportation costs and disposal. This project is indicative of the drawing and the valence of design, with the site celebrated a premier music venue, and the city being championed as the preferred urban form for new towns in the United Kingdom (Walker, 1981).

anxiety about what landscape *is*. Landscape representation is dynamic, fluid, contradictory, conflictual and social. The recognition of these qualities is important. Lawrence Halprin suggested that landscape architecture was a discipline capable of grasping the whole sphere of environments.[3] This grasp I would argue can only emerge from a plurality of pragmatic design representation which determines our strategic choices for and of landscape in time.

The image has agency, it has an impact, an influence, and it translates from its surface to something else, i.e. it becomes built. The image may be creatively generated from an individual, but become a collective social image, a representation of a place with shared values. This is an important fundamental idea and is argued in architecture by the late Robin Evans when he states: 'the subject matter (the building or space) will exist after the drawing, not before it' (Evans, 1996, p. 165). This mode Evans terms 'reverse directionality' of the projection of drawing. The artwork is purposed generally for the gallery space, the design work is purposed for production into something else, and this is a remarkable condition often overlooked (Moore, 2009). Landscape representation is an agent between the material space (paper, digital, etc.) of the designer and a physical assemblage. Such a principle can be evidenced with construction drawings which purport to translate exactly the design on a paper surface to reality (or 'as built' drawings at the end of a contract).

This agency does not stop at this stage, the habitation and use of the spaces from everyday practices and rituals in landscape/urban spaces forms representations of what the design space is; it reflects back and this could be understood as valence – the term in this case means the capacity of a design to unite, react or interact with something else. Representation therefore has agency and both negative and positive valence; for example, the propagation of urban blight or the design of new cultural icons.

In contemporary landscape architecture visualisation – a small part of the wider representational term – what are the impacts of visualisations based on Evan's 'reverse directionality' principle? What does it say about the designer's connection with and understanding of the landscape space? With the vast array of tools at the designer's disposal, what should be selected and what is the reasoning behind this selection? In order to address this question, it is more helpful to discuss visualisation as part of a cycle of representation of landscape. This locates and maps the visual within the wider social, political and cultural space in which it plays a part. This book covers maps, diagrams and notations, composites, 3D models and physical model making, discussing theoretical underpinnings, practical steps and strategies in the creation of these works in relation to wider representational fields of landscape. The book will summarise with a concluding chapter on landscape futures.

Arguably in current landscape representation, there exists a dominant paradigm of visualisations which have been subject to economic and educational constraints, resulting in prosaic homogeneous images which little describe site specificity, but present themselves as ultra-real. This is particularly evident in presentational works.

FIGURE I.2 Komar and Melamid, America's Most Wanted, 1994; oil and acrylic on canvas; photo: D. James Dee, courtesy of Ronald Feldman Fine Arts, New York. Employing market research by Marttila & Kiley, Inc. of 1,001 adults on various nationalities' pictorial preference, the artists produced the most wanted and least wanted paintings for each country (Komar, 1997). In America's Most Wanted, George Washington stands contemplatively across a lush mountainous landscape and lake joined by a hippo to the left and deer that can walk on water to the right. The aesthetic results from a generalisation from the consolidation of data, and a painterly landscape and water body take the majority of the pictorial plane. Such work likely reflects the landscape aesthetics of the public that may be radically different from the designer's aesthetic.

These works differ from analytical approaches which develop site specifics and landscape science. This kitsch is most evident in perspective presentations. This observation is repeated by James Corner, who suggests such perspectival schemes 'overlook the ideological, estranging, and aestheticising effects of detaching the subject from the complex realities of participating in the world' (Corner, 1999a, p. 156). The book aims to establish a number of emergent workflows that can adjust this paradigm and make visualisations part of a wider representational cycle. *Strategies for Landscape Representation* seeks to present a practice and workflow which borrows historically significant representational practices, while blending this with contemporary and emergent technological possibilities. This is not an exhaustive exploration, but the establishment of pragmatic principles of assimilation of a variety of visualisation tools and emphasis of continual experimentation by designers, while also being embedded with strict data sets and analyses. The book's purpose is not to advance discrete modes of working, promote certain landscape practices, nor function as a light picture book, but to discuss the interdependency needed to represent landscape and provide exercises for the reader to strategise and utilise in practice, build upon and reflect.

FIGURE I.3 Environment Agency, Geomatics Group, Olympic Park, Point Cloud Data, October 2013. © Environment Agency copyright 2014. All rights reserved. The process is called LiDAR (laser imaging, detection and ranging). The technology has been around for 30-odd years, though this is slowly democratising and its application in landscape architecture is not as pronounced. Accuracy can vary, in this case the digital model has a horizontal ±25 cm and vertical ±5 cm accuracy. LiDAR data are shown here using a colour ramp, a gradient of single or multiple colours referencing specific heights of natural and human forms, in this case the grey and white colour band being the uppermost height above sea level. In these clouds as seen in the millions of points are allocated a colour depending on height (dark green lowest, white highest etc. . . .). This can be combined with digital terrain models (DTM) which have been traditionally used in 3D modelling to create a large, accurate picture of the landscape site. This was previously an expensive and specialist area of expertise, though Chapter 1 shows a number of ways to gather this information and evaluate its uses. These uses include evaluating vegetation, identification and health, flood risk, topology and many others.

All sections of the book contain chapter summaries, strategies for working with data, as well as further reading. Accompanying files and tutorials can be found at: www.routledge.com/cw/cureton.

STRUCTURE

The relationship between landscape design representation and the everyday experience of spaces is sometimes located on two completely different vectors. This poses a question about methods for design professionals about where this public 'experience' can be incorporated within the scope of landscape architectural representation and environmental assessment. In addition to this, the variety and complexity of available data sets means that appropriate choice and processing may limit and discourage designers.

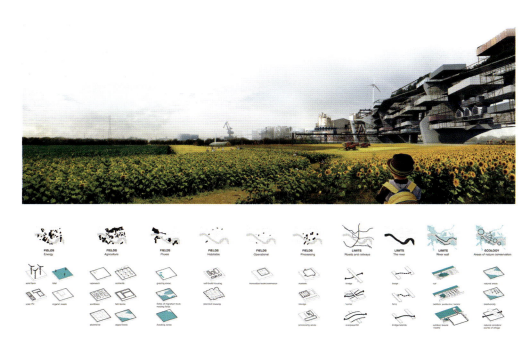

FIGURE I.4 The Eastern Ranch, Lubricity, London As It Could Be Now (Architecture Foundation / Royal Academy); Ed Wall, Helena Rivera, George Wade, Kate Priestman, Chris McCarthy and Alex Malaescu. The Lubricity proposal identified the various intersections, edges and patterns along the east of the Thames, proposing new forms of urban living.

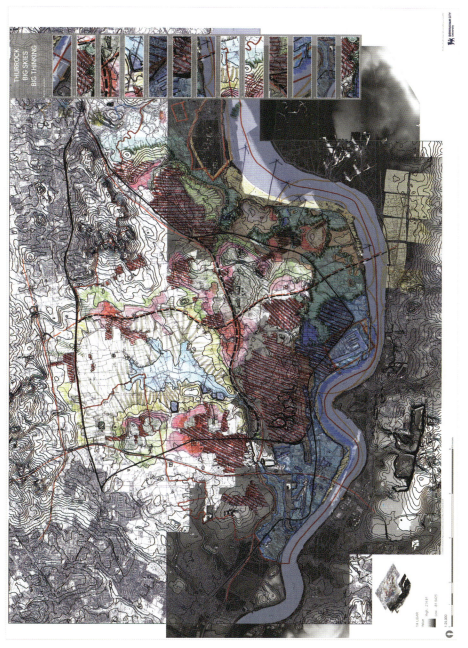

FIGURE 1.5 Kathryn Moore (hand-coloured drawing) and & Paul Cureton (GIS and data), Big Skies, Big Thinking. A new water, land, development and transport strategy for Thurrock 2015–2040, Essex, United Kingdom. Moore's drawn vision juxtaposed and orthorectified with LiDAR data proposes a new kind of urban living based on a holistic approach which connects housing, transport, planning and landscape. Moore views landscape architecture in expansive terms, not its contemporary definition and norms. Such a position is vital, given the fluidity with which the discipline is changing as cross-disciplinary, inter-disciplinary and multi-disciplinary modes of work become the new for the design of cities, towns and landscapes. This holistic vision enables consideration of the structure of the multiple components of spaces – buildings, vegetation, land and sub-surfaces among many others (Doherty and Waldheim, 2015, pp. 285–301).

Why should landscape representation matter? Landscape architecture is at a significant point of development. Within this area, resurging research is emerging, and the representation of landscape significantly extends in other ways through the questioning of reality, reshaping our spatial conceptions or providing expressions of alternatives. New technologies and software, novel approaches, increasing interoperability, open source data as well as the increasing understanding of environmental processes, futures thinking and the Anthropocene are but a few tools and factors creating new design paradigms. Not only does it question and reflect our relationship with human and natural constructs, but it also functions as a device in which we can view our ideas of landscape and map its resonation throughout history. For example, the environmental philosopher Don Gifford notes on photography and landscape that

> separation is urged upon our eyes by the camera lens, the photoframe, and the glance-and-move-on way we have learned to read photographs on a page and have carried over to the way we read paintings on a gallery wall and the way we read the passing landscape.
> (Don Gifford cited in Kemal and Gaskell, 1995, p. 136)

This picturesque framing aspect in landscape experience, is something that pervades and remains in landscape architecture itself post-Brown & Repton (Carlson, 2009; Carlson and Berleant, 2004). The picturesque was an image that paradoxically became an instrument of urbanisation and modernisation (Conan, 2000) – for example the Claude glass acted as a medium to see paintings in the landscape (Andrews, 1990) – and this factor is still under-critiqued. The picturesque is a representational technology that has shaped ways of working with landscape, just as new technologies are currently shaping contemporary approaches to making and meaning in landscape. This does not mean that the photographic medium is limited in landscape architecture; some picturesque tendencies dominate and the desire to shape natural landscape into a synthetic artwork still pervades. However, the photograph in other fields provides essential evidence of landscape conditions in fields such as glaciology, by using repeat photography.

Some representations in landscape architecture, according to Rekittke and Paar, fail to accommodate localised flora and fauna – a specific site is represented using generic global software tools (Rekittke and Paar, 2006). Representations are instrumental towards landscape; they are purposeful towards it, though the resurgence of photo-real 3D models can borrow the aesthetic of game environments, which can be seen generally as an aesthetic of imagination; in other words, it has no relationship and the subject is separated (Boyer, 1996). This in itself is not a negative factor; such ideational work may challenge or enrich design concepts, though the agency of this work should be located within a wider process and development of design work with heterogeneous sources. Such computational worlds also have increasing fidelity to reality making such debates about detachment less relevant.

Given these critiques, how do we practise landscape architecture, present analysis and design which moves away from the static, fixed time, motionless and therefore

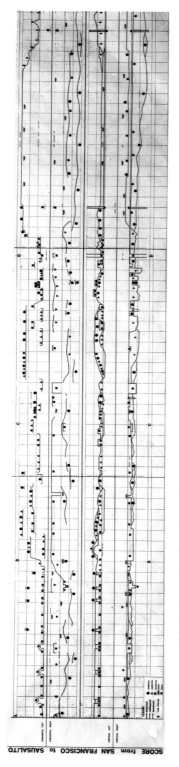

FIGURE 1.6 Lawrence Halprin, Score from Sausalito to San Francisco; Lawrence Halprin Collection, The Architectural Archives, University of Pennsylvania. Halprin viewed a deficit in landscape architecture, for the symbolisation of our ideas. He viewed many representational elements as static. Using movement notation, 'Motation', Halprin devised a system of movement as a basis to generate qualitative and quantitative data to inform design plans (Halprin, 1963, pp. 208–215). See Chapter 2.

non-associative, towards natural systems? How can this character be unpacked through communities' perception of place? These questions are not easily resolved; such questioning and research is an attempt to answer much of the unknown. *Strategies for Landscape Representation* is not novel; it reflects contemporary practice and the changing role of the landscape architect, while also owing much allegiance to the work of Lawrence Halprin, among others, who viewed the city through a time-based lens and championed participatory design and the reflection of natural systems acting as a landscape choreographer (Halprin, 1963, 1965; Halprin and Burns, 1963). Such work has long been called for by Halprin; he states:

> Landscape architects hold a unique role amongst the design professions, that of navigating through the ephemerality of nature and the complexity of communities in order to lay out a process, and finally a design to accommodate and invigorate fluidity, flexibility, and a world in motion.
> (Wasserman, 2012, p.47)

Essentially, *Strategies for Landscape Representation* aims for a revitalisation of landscape representation, which encourages readers to make connections between software, technology and analogue modes, and through a concise chapter workflow to challenge and address these questions. The book is intended as a holistic device in which to incorporate a plurality of visualisation and experimentation, while also providing resources for the reader to identify practice and build upon. The management, choice and combination of such modes can arguably narrow the unknown of landscape character, address the issues of representing time and change in landscape, and engage and represent communities' perceptions and experience of landscape. I mean by this the management of a range of sources which address the representation of time in which landscape form constantly morphs (Jackson, 1994, pp. 3–7). This means not only observing sequences and movements of the site and its inhabitants, but also sequencing the fieldwork and organising this into meaningful landscape assessment, which can thus develop design directions. These issues are ongoing in the field of landscape representation; as Diana Balmori asserts, accepting change in landscape and the living quality of things opens landscape design to a whole host of challenges at the representational level (Balmori, 2014, p. 27; Dee, 2001, 2010; Treib, 2008; Van Dooren, 2012).

The themes of the book cover mapping, fieldwork, notations and diagrams, composites, 3D models and digital fabrication. The book concludes with a discussion on landscape futures. Each chapter is divided between a theoretical discussion, a typology of representational methods and stages and glossary of these methods. Specific step-by-step sources feature in the companion website to allow for updates and new modes of production.

In Chapter 1 I discuss the agency and valence of mapping, common types of data sets, the types of derived data, map outputs and strategies, the principles of map design and the use of unmanned aerial systems (UAS) and unmanned aerial vehicles

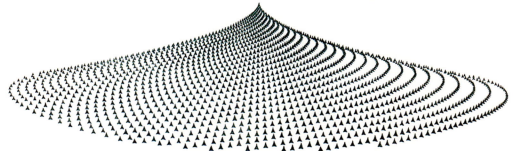

FIGURE I.7 Agnes Denes, Tree Mountain – A Living Time Capsule was realized in full scale at the Pinziö gravel pits, Ylöjärvi, Finland, 1992–1996. Tree Mountain was conceived in 1982 as a collaborative, environmental artwork that touches on global, ecological, social and cultural issues. It is a massive earthwork and land reclamation project that tests our finitude and transcendence, individuality versus teamwork, and measures the value and evolution of a work of art after it has entered the environment. Tree Mountain is designed to unite the human intellect with the majesty of nature (Denes, 2008, pp. 166–169).

(UAVs), popularly termed as drones for mapping the landscape. The use of remote-sensed data is a mode of study that does not come into contact with the subject itself. Remote-sensing provides high-resolution data for use in strategies of representation of landscape or agency and strategies for landscape itself, which is termed valence. Map making remains a point of orientation and functions as a key communicative device, and this representational form is explored. New possibilities of aerial and perspective views enabled through drone use are also discussed. These new possibilities I would term as an emerging paradigm which represent a 'hover space' of landscape, beyond human heights, and possible legal altitude limits (± 400ft). This new hover space means that mapping data can be gathered and provide economic means of site survey.

Chapter 2 develops and discusses fieldwork and notation as an engagement tool in planning and community consultation. Use of augmented reality, eye-tracking devices, mobile applications and other technological forms are discussed in relation to the public's perception and experience of landscape, along with methods to incorporate such work within the representation of landscape. The use of diagrams in landscape architecture is also discussed. Movement notation, which was developed by Lawrence Halprin for American planning in the 1970s, is covered. Its mode was catalytic in embedding community consultation in the planning process. Such work is important, and while there has been a resurgence in interest in Halprin's work, notation systems have remained as a largely historical process in landscape practice (Hirsch, 2014). This discussion is not preferential over other systems of notation, and is intended as a catalyst for notation for landscape representation.

This chapter demonstrates how fieldwork and notation can be interpreted in contemporary landscape practice and related to the mapping and information-gathering activities of Chapter 1. Such work is important and develops a layer for the recording of participant movements and perceptions of sites; as Halprin states:

> Participation and activity are essential factors in a city. One can be a passive spectator in the enjoyment of other arts, but the essential characteristic of the city as an art form is that it demands participation.
>
> (Halprin 1963, p.193)

Halprin developed a scoring process to handle complex layers of design information. The Score was applied as a multi-purpose tool – as a guide to community engagement, an approach to laying out design proposals and as a way to examine specific elements in a project, such as sun angles, fountain noises and movement patterns (Wasserman, 2012, p. 35). From this basis participatory approaches of digital/analogue notation after Lawrence Halprin can be incorporated within the following chapters, strategies and workflow.

Following on from this basis, Chapter 3 discusses time in landscape and the representational issues of time are surveyed with discussion of repeat photography

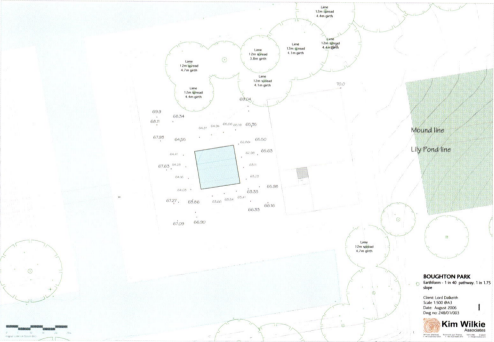

FIGURE I.8 Kim Wilkie, Orpheus, Boughton House, Northamptonshire, United Kingdom, 2007–2009. The inverted grass pyramid descends seven metres below the level of the restored terraces. Walking around the landscape, the new design is invisible, but drawing near to the mount, a gentle grass path spirals down to a square pool of still water deep underground. The water reflects the sky, a little like an inverted James Turrell oculus (Wilkie, 2012).

INTRODUCTION

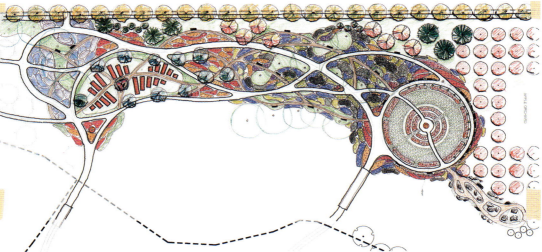

FIGURE I.9 Olin Studio, Geiger Lake Park, Babylon, New York, 2016. Olin Studio redesigned a municipal park and transformed a 24-acre site into a botanical garden and play area. The planting and circulation takes into account the buffers around the existing lake and creates fluid pathways (Olin and Weiler, 2008).

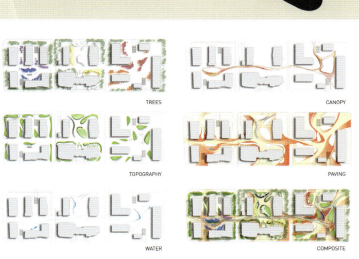

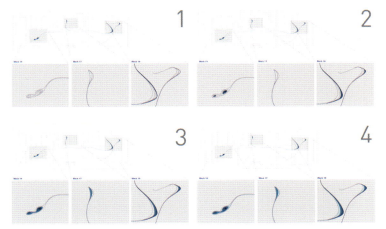

FIGURE I.10
Balmori Associates, Ciudad Empresarial Sarmiento Angulo, Bogota, Columbia, 2016. Project team: Diana Balmori, Javier Gonzalez-Campana, Sara Arteaga, Theodore Hoerr, Linda Joosten, Isabel Lezcano, Reva Meeks, Conor O'Brien, Jessica Roberts and Katie Stranix. The project connects three large blocks of new urban development to make one integrated whole. A public pedestrian spine connects all three blocks with a series of bridges over vehicular cross streets. The centrepiece of this mixed-use development is a public square that contains a new performing-arts centre and hotel. The landscape expresses the diverse ecology found in Colombia, with each block containing a distinct botanical environment and colour palette composed of indigenous Colombian plants. Topographic undulations in the surface of the landscape create depth for large planting areas above the underground parking structure and provide lush enclaves for people to enjoy in an urban setting. Marquette's were created for the undulations and correlated with canopy diagrams, water courses, planting collages and time sequences, tree heights, section sequences and perspectives. A wide range of representational examples were thus employed and this self-supporting range covers a wide variety of landscape elements.

INTRODUCTION 15

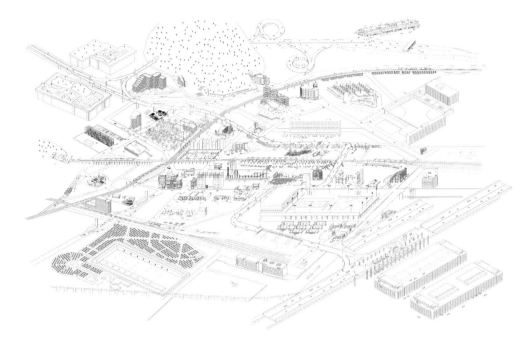

FIGURE I.11 Atelier Bow-Wow, Made in Tokyo Guidebook, 2001. © Atelier Bow-Wow. Atelier Bow-Wow's research focuses on the micro-environments of city spaces, working with high densities and vernacular architecture and their evolution over time (Kuroda and Kaijima, 2001). They examine new hybridised conditions within the city, focusing on utilising small, awkward urban spaces and creating social spaces – 'it is not people who creates space, but social spaces that use people to bring themselves into being' (Bow-Wow Architects, 2010, p. 251).

in the natural sciences, a different form of mapping from the aerial. Though relational, repeat photography captures diverse aspects in the landscape from focal time points, comparing those points and constructing trajectories of the landscapes future – 'the first photographers captured a landscape in the first stages of being rolled over by a wave of change' (White and Hart, 2007, p. 2). Following on from this basis, digital perspective montages or composites are elaborated upon, discussing their time-based distortion through multiple image sources, and a possible design deceit. In contrast to this trajectory, sources are illustrated that represent the changing nature of their sites. The composite is then referred to the principles of perspective and strategies for 2D time-based imagery, developing James Corner's ideas of the positive agency of photomontage through its juxtaposition of disassociated elements which provide new imaginings (Corner, 1999b, pp. 153–154).

Chapter 4 discusses digital 3D modelling and a brief history of computational developments including Paul Cerruzi's four computational future paradigms, the digital paradigm, convergence, solid-state electronics and the human interface (Ceruzzi, 2003). The layering of complexity through big data, parametricism and BIM is also discussed. Two divergent outcomes develop in the form of 3D model generation, script-sculpted mathematical novel architectural imaginary forms and surfaces, and

FIGURE I.12
The SCAPE Team, The Living Breakwaters project, Staten Island, New York, US Department of Housing and Urban Development's Rebuild by Design Initiative, 2015. The Living Breakwaters project reduces risk, revives ecologies and connects educators to the shoreline, inspiring a new generation of harbour stewards and a more resilient region over time. The SCAPE Team designed 'reef street' micro-pockets of habitat complexity to host finfish, shellfish and lobsters, and also modelled the breakwater system at a macro scale to understand how and where they can most effectively protect communities. This living infrastructure will be paired with social resiliency frameworks in adjacent neighbourhoods.

INTRODUCTION   17

FIGURE I.13 Karolis Janulis, Turbine, Elektrenai, Lietuva and Winter Road, Vilnius, Lithuania, 2016. Drone videography and photography provide new outlooks on our surroundings. Janulis photographs the micro-peculiar and super-massive landscape of Lithuania. In addition to this, 'threats of global warming and climate change demand accurate and low-cost techniques for a better modelling and control of the environmental physical processes' (Chao and Chen, 2012, p. 1). Drones are coming to the fore of sensing our impacts and relationship with our landscapes.

prototypes of landscapes and buildings through which visualisations are derived. These two heuristics are reshaping the position of the 3D model in the design process. As Phillip Bernstein states, 'the script represents both a strategy for a solution and its embedded logic of its intent' (Shvartzberg and Poole, 2015, pp. 200–211). Bernstein continues and suggests a new platform in which BIM engulfs design processes and centres itself as a base in which representation is formed. The identification of this trajectory can be evidenced through governmental legislation seeking efficient means of project delivery and the delivery of BIM guidelines by national landscape bodies (Landscape Institute, 2016). Following on from this, practical discussion and mapping of the 3D modelling work stages and strategies is covered. Brian Mcgrath recognises the important role that the 3D model presents in its ability to layer the archive of the city, the integration of 3D and 4D GIS systems and the diagramming of the multiple forces at work in urban settings (McGrath, 2008, p. 192). To work with this conception, the book structure offers a version of this layering concept, linking Chapters 1, 2 and 3 to this modelling process work and linking to the outputs of this in digital fabrication (Chapter 5).

Chapter 5 covers digital fabrication. The chapter works with the landscape data and technology to create an automated process for architectural modelling. Focusing on digital fabrication in particular, this chapter highlights the principles of 3D modelling, solid modelling and the production of large-scale landscape designs and maps. A variety of additional presentation methods are also incorporated, such as using digital projection on the physical model and future manipulation technologies in the collaboration with Space Syntax. Derived model types are also discussed. As Günther Vogt reflects, the model's agency is the reading of the designs and a base on which to form discussion. This agency is difficult to represent in books as the model is formed into a photographic representation (Bornhauser *et al.*, 2015, pp. 196–198). The chapter demonstrates the increasing ability to automate modelling processes, making landscape modelling a more democratic and cost-effective process for student and professional alike. This mode of production is functional only in its relationship to other practices; this chapter is presented as a basis for understanding more complex strategies reliant upon interdependency. This interdependency is termed as the overall strategy of multiple landscape representations.

SUMMARY

Strategies for Landscape Representation offers production techniques, both digital and analogue, for the representation of landscape at multiple scales. The focus of the book on the design of landscape, design sequences and the recording of human and natural movements highlights an important issue in addressing a dominant paradigm in landscape architecture production. The book is intended as a catalyst for both students and landscape practitioners to develop high-quality workflows by utilising emerging technologies, while also being embedded within landscape legislation. The book is intended to incorporate time within landscape architecture. Such a call, while philosophically positioned, is important in practical assessment and landscape production. It is aimed at producing non-static sustainable, participatory and animated natural systems and designs. As Anne Whiston Spirn states,

> For designers, new techniques of notation and representation are required. Conventional techniques are inadequate to the portrayal of time and change, and they encourage the continued focus on visible and static form.
>
> (Spirn, 1998, p. 124)

This principle of strategy locates mapping, modelling and visualisation as part of a cycle of representation of landscape. Landscape is conceptualised and produced, and then represents values or is imaged by its inhabitants, and this cycle continues. Seen in this way, strategy can be indicative of the capacity of the agency of landscape representation, and the resulting valence the evaluation of this agency; both in its ability to decode space and in its ability to collectively find common ground and difference in landscape perception.

NOTES

1. Agency follows Alfred Gell's anthropological study of *Art & Agency*, and looks at how works of art elicit responses. It is one source from which James Corner discusses agency in landscape architecture: 'material entities which motivate inferences, responses or interpretations' (Gell 1998). Ross Bowden critiques Gell's theory, given that '"indexes" (i.e. artworks) "motivate" (i.e. prompt) "patients" (viewers) to make "abductions" (inferences) about "social agency"' (Bowden, 2004, p. 309). An agent to Gell is 'whenever an event is believed to happen because of an "intention" lodged in the person or thing which initiates the causal sequence that is an instance of "agency"' (Gell, 1998, p. 17).
2. For example, see the provocative Iowa State Manifesto for Landscape Architecture: www.public.iastate.edu/~isitdead/dead_f2.pdf.
3. (LH, Oral History Video, Cultural Landscape Foundation) http://72.27.230.88/sites/default/files/pioneers/halprin/videos/index.html.

BIBLIOGRAPHY

Andrews, M., 1990. *The Search for the Picturesque: Landscape, Aesthetics and Tourism in Britain, 1760–1800*, new edition. Scholar Press, London.

Balmori, D., 2014. *Drawing and Reinventing Landscape, AD Primer*. John Wiley & Sons, London.

Balmori, D. and Conan, M., 2010. *A Landscape Manifesto*. Yale University Press, New Haven.

Bornhauser, R., Kissling, T. and Vogt, G., 2015. *Landscape as a Cabinet of Curiosities: In Search of a Position*. Lars Müller, Ennetbaden.

Bowden, R., 2004. A Critique of Alfred Gell on Art and Agency. *Oceania* 74, 309–324. doi: 10.1002/j.1834-4461.2004.tb02857.x.

Bow-Wow, Architects, 2010. *The Architectures of Atelier Bow-Wow: Behaviorology*. Rizzoli International Publications, New York.

Boyer, M.C., 1996. *CyberCities: Visual Perception in the Age of Electronic Communication*. Princeton Architectural Press, New York.

Carlson, A., 2009. *Nature and Landscape: An Introduction to Environmental Aesthetics*. Columbia University Press, New York.

Carlson, A. and Berleant, A., 2004. *The Aesthetics of Natural Environments*. Broadview Press, Peterborough.

Ceruzzi, P.E., 2003. *A History of Modern Computing*, 2nd revised edition. MIT Press, Cambridge, MA.

Chao, H. and Chen, Y., 2012. *Remote Sensing and Actuation Using Unmanned Vehicles*. Wiley-Blackwell, Hoboken.

Conan, M., 2000. *Environmentalism in Landscape Architecture*. Dumbarton Oaks, Washington.

Corner, J., 1999a. *Recovering Landscape Essays in Contemporary Landscape Architecture*. Princeton Architectural Press, New York.

Corner, J., 1999b. *Recovering Landscape: Essays in Contemporary Landscape Theory*. Princeton Architectural Press. New York.

Dee, C., 2001. *Form and Fabric in Landscape Architecture: A Visual Introduction*. Spon Press, London.

Dee, C., 2010. Form, Utility, and the Aesthetics of Thrift in Design Education. *Landscape Journal*, 29: 21–35.

Denes, A., 2008. *The Human Argument: The Writings of Agnes Denes*. Spring Publications, Putnam.

Doherty, G. and Waldheim, C. (eds), 2015. *Is Landscape . . . ? Essays on the Identity of Landscape*. Routledge, Abingdon.

Evans, R., 1996. *Translations from Drawing to Building and Other Essays*. Architectural Association Publications, London.

Gell, A., 1998. *Art and Agency: An Anthropological Theory*. Oxford University Press, Oxford.

Halprin, L., 1963. *Cities*. Reinhold Publishing Co., New York.

Halprin, L., 1965. Motation. *Progressive Architecture*, 46: 126–133.

Halprin, L. and Burns, J., 1963. *Taking Part: A Workshop Approach to Collective Creativity*. MIT Press, Cambridge, MA.

Hirsch, A.B., 2014. *City Choreographer: Lawrence Halprin in Urban Renewal America*. University of Minnesota Press, Minneapolis.

Jackson, J.B., 1994. *A Sense of Place, a Sense of Time*. Yale University Press, New Haven.

Kemal, S. and Gaskell, I. (eds), 1995. *Landscape, Natural Beauty and the Arts*. Cambridge University Press, Cambridge.

Komar, V., 1997. *Painting by Numbers: Komar and Melamid's Scientific Guide to Art*. Farrar, Straus & Giroux Inc., New York.

Kuroda, J. and Kaijima, M., 2001. *Made in Tokyo: Guide Book*. Kajima Institute Publishing, Tokyo.

Landscape Institute, 2016. *BIM for Landscape*. Routledge, London.

McGrath, B., 2008. *Digital Modelling for Urban Design*, new edition. John Wiley & Sons, Chichester.

Moore, K., 2009. *Overlooking the Visual: Demystifying the Art of Design*, new edition. Routledge, London.

Olin, L. and Weiler, S., 2008. *Olin: Placemaking*. Monacelli Press, New York.

Rekittke, J. and Paar, P., 2006. Digital botany. *Journal of Landscape Architecture*, 1: 28–35.

Shvartzberg, M.P. and Poole, M., 2015. *The Politics of Parametricism*. Bloomsbury Academic, London.

Spirn, A.W., 1998. *The Language of Landscape*. Yale University Press, New Haven.

Taylor, N. and Schiller, F., 2011. *William Tell*. Pearson Education, Harlow.

Treib, M. (ed.), 2008. *Drawing/Thinking: Confronting an Electronic Age – drawing in an Electronic Age*. Routledge, London.

Van Dooren, N., 2012. Speaking About Drawing: An Exploration Of Representation in Recent Landscape Architecture. *Topos*, 80: 43.

Walker, D., 1981. *Architecture and Planning of Milton Keynes*. Architectural Press, London.

Wasserman, J., 2012. A World in Motion: The Creative Synergy of Lawrence and Anna Halprin. *Landscape Journal* 31 (1–2): 34.

White, C. and Hart, E.J., 2007. *Lens of Time: A Repeat Photography of Landscape Change in the Canadian Rockies*. University of Calgary Press, Calgary.

Wilkie, K., 2012. *Led by the Land: Landscapes by Kim Wilkie*. Frances Lincoln, London.

1
WORKING WITH DATA (MAPPING)

> In that Empire, the Art of Cartography attained such Perfection that the map of a single Province occupied the entirety of a City, and the map of the Empire, the entirety of a Province. In time, those Unconscionable Maps no longer satisfied, and the Cartographers Guilds struck a Map of the Empire whose size was that of the Empire, and which coincided point for point with it.
>
> (Borges and Hurley, 2004, p. 181)

> The Universe (which others call the library) is composed of an indefinite and perhaps infinite number of hexagonal galleries, with vast air shafts between, surrounded by very low railings. . . . Like all men of the library, I have travelled in my youth; I have wandered in search of a book, perhaps the catalogues of catalogues . . . in the vast library there are no two identical books . . . the library will endure: illuminated, solitary, infinite, perfectly motionless, equipped with precious volumes, useless, incorruptible, secret.
>
> (Borges, 2000, pp. 78–86)

The Borges fable of a map of pure exactitude that covers the world is well known from citation by Baudrillard (1994),[1] the uselessness of such a map even more so. The lesser-discussed Borges fable is the 'Library of Babel'. The Library of Babel fable sets the scene of a dimly lit hexagonal library of knowledge where every book is equitable. This relativism of knowledge is the challenge landscape architects must work with. What is useful? What is relevant? What digital information gives physicality to landscape? Why are certain forms of landscape practice preferable over others? Between these two fables we could correlate the map, the site model and the data sets overlaid upon it. We are mapping, but also selecting from the library of knowledge. In that sense we must find the right ways of working, decoding and editing, but also realise that data (Kitchin and Dodge, 2014) themselves are not a complete solution for understanding landscape. Data are ideological, political, economic, cultural and social (Dodge et al., 2011).

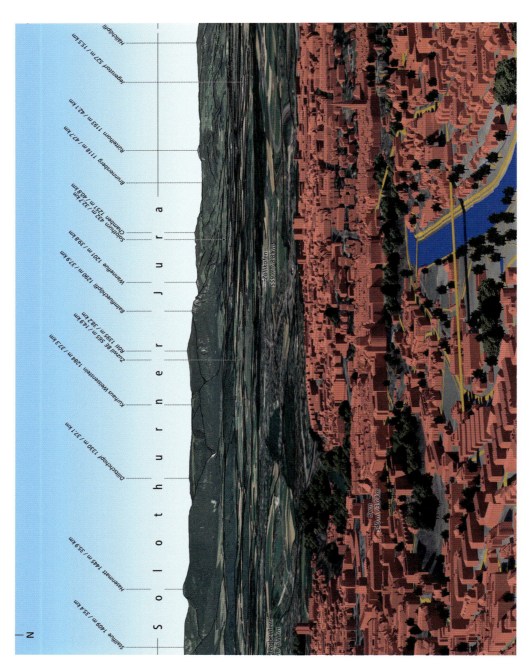

FIGURE 1.1 Swiss Maps, Digirama Deluxe. The landscape of this panorama is indicated from left to right by greyscale hill shading and silhouette lines as well as colour ramps and photo-realistic drapes. The annotation is derived from the 'SwissNames' data set and printed automatically, with a simple subsequent graphic editing.

We need strategies of representation, and the map is a strong source of representation from which to unpack possibilities. Landscape architecture has the potential to meet the challenge of large climate issues and change our environmental outlooks, as well as to create political consensus on the importance of our surrounding. This is not a utopian exercise to note; utopia has no place;[2] the landscape envelops us. One important mapping drive has been the representation of relief on maps, as Florinsky argues (1998). The need to map relief in 3D terms is fundamental for the development of a landscape strategy based on climate, ecology, geology, physiographics and hydrology, as well as anthropogenic influences.[3] Compared to extensive fieldwork, the use of remote-sensed data provides considerably cost-effective means of data collection of large land masses. Remote-sensing provides high-resolution data with which to strategise representation of landscape and strategise landscape itself. Therefore it could be understood that software and data choices in mapping define places, as well as regulate them.

The practical element of this chapter focuses on a number of options for desk-based research and the use of remote-sensing[4] – creating and reading landscape maps with 3D elements. A suitable data strategy means that the representation of landscape data is as much about the thinking and decisions involved in collation as is the actual data sets themselves. This chapter will discuss the rise of large-scale data packets and the use of innovative technologies in the capturing of landscape information. The chapter will also discuss the sharing, management and streamlining of this information, given BIM requirements. Several strategies for gathering landscape data are also discussed and the data sources can be accessed via the *companion website* (www.routledge.com/cw/cureton). Finally, emerging drone technology is discussed and a practical, cost-effective method is provided for mapping using drones and the generation of 3D data. The emphasis on drone use is based on its emerging capability and lack of context in landscape architecture, as well as its cost-effectiveness in data acquisition for students and landscape practices. Drones create new democratised paradigms and mapping practices.

One of the most compelling and representational modes of landscape has been the map. As Michel De Certeau observes,

> The founding gesture is to make a map. It creates a space. It cuts out of the complexity of things a scene on which to draw the operations necessary to remake the world. . . . Born of a withdrawal and designed for a purpose, the map isolates a theatre and offers it up to be transformed. But that working ground also represents the reality from which the map distinguishes itself in order to change it.
>
> (De Certeau, 1985, p. 17)

As data are gathered and a map forms into an image, this image becomes part of a performance; we believe its reality and from this belief we build on its surface, designing, drawing in pencil or polygons, often to change the map to the designed landscape plan, this quite simply is the agency of mapping in landscape architecture: between geography and design. The power of this agency gave rise to James Corner's emancipatory mapping essay on the inauguration of new worlds out of old. There is much work still to be developed in detail and practice since this work (Corner in Cosgrove, 1999, pp. 213–252). For wider audiences, the map is the agent which allows comprehension of the place that is planned to be transformed. The data we and other associated disciplines collect reflect immense science and application in understanding of environments. Such a super-scale datascape means we need to think clearly on what is useful, selectable and applicable to the landscape site. Alongside this need, it is arguable that contemporary information technology seeks fidelity of the landscape it represents. Like the Borges fable, there is a large popular cartographic drive to simulate the world from across disciplines in a live-streamed high-resolution map (Cosgrove, 2012, pp. 1–2). Reality computing has come more to the fore, a digital simulation with near-accuracy of a location which can also be immersive through utilising augmented reality (AR) helmets, virtual reality (VR) booths and many other technologies. The precision that such work brings is welcome, yet the digital agency of landscape architecture mapping may result in furthering the distance with the subject itself. As Richard Muir's book *Approaches to Landscape* evidences, there is a divided historicism of the landscape and its interpretation (Muir, 2000) and this technological drive may further the distance.

The simulation of landscape does not mean that we necessarily gain new knowledge, and this deficiency is often overlooked. In addition, as O'Sullivan and Perry demonstrate, computational simulations are complex, though such models often have a recurring structure (O'Sullivan and Perry, 2013). Thus, we may have a wider vocabulary and toolbox from digital development with which to represent landscape, but must be cautious not to concentrate our efforts purely in learning the tools; the use, thinking and strategy have greater importance. Analogue mapping is just as important; while digital technologies bring an uncontested fidelity, such drawing and mapping remains equally important in strategic terms as in the case of the first development sketch by Richard Buckminster-Fuller for his Dymaxion map.

Digital versus hand-drawn debates are fallacies that ignore the complexity of representation and differing production methods. When Ian McHarg created the 'layer cake' method of data in *Design with Nature* in 1969, geological, hydrological and ecological information layered together to find favourable or unfavourable sites (McHarg, 1995, pp. iv, v), the thinking and strategy was that the comparison of each of the fields made it comprehensible. McHarg wanted ecological understanding, though the book was limited by what it left out and has sometimes been misinterpreted as something that ticks the analytical stage of representation through attractive exploded axonometrics that do not hold under close scrutiny. McHarg wanted strategies for holistic landscape 'the process of becoming' (McHarg, 1995, p. 29). Many subsequent interpretations resulted in spaces and practices that cut up and dissected rather than developed the model. Carl Steniz developed the 'layer cake'

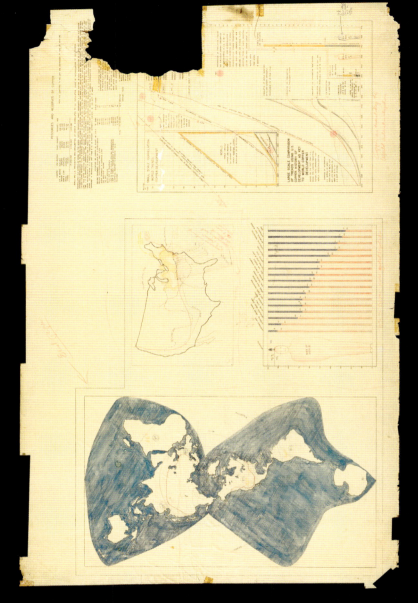

FIGURE 1.2 Richard Buckminster-Fuller, Dymaxion Projection method. Topological transfer of data from the globe onto the two-dimensional surface. Sketches undated, Pencil, *c.*1943. Buckminster-Fuller Archives. This flexible zone of spatial-cultural projection for Fuller, realised through drawing, helped formulate a corrective map projection towards his wider Spaceship Earth project – that is, worldwide collective pooling of resources out of a recognition of environmental and social injustice. This map has undergone several revisions in which various data could be composed, for example extending the 'one continent' idea, demonstrating world energy markets, developing the first comprehensive map showing air traffic patterns and another to show world population statistics (Fuller and Snyder 2009, pp. 171–173). The Dymaxion Map: 'describes the Earth's surface with the minimum total score of distortions from the many well-known geometrical processes inherent in translation of the angle and scale information from a spherical to a flat surface' (Fuller and Snyder, 2009, p. 160).

model of overlays for landscape planning in 1979 to improve the most tested design idea for a site (Steinitz, 1979, 2013). By isolating landscape elements, the comparison can be lost. This is the rich inheritance that McHarg began and many others have built upon for GIS and mapping. GIS history – from Harvard Labs (1964) to Jack and Laura Dangermond forming ESRI (1969), to Geographical Positioning Systems (GPS; 1950s experiments to civilian use in 1996) and many other innovations – demonstrate that contemporary GIS development is far more complex and has greater possibilities. While GIS is much debated in landscape architecture, the importance of mapping from these developments stems from a wide cultural change in the perception of the earth in more holistic terms from space photography, the moon landings and NASA/Soviet Union space exploration. This interest can be evidenced by the reception and influence of the *Whole Earth Catalog* as a counter-cultural publication by Stewart Brand (1968–1972, reprinted in several formats until 1994) (Point Foundation, 1986).

Interoperability for mapping is essential here in practical terms, thinking about the workflow of data sets and how to process parts between software programs. Given the abundance of individual tutorials on specific software features, it is surprising

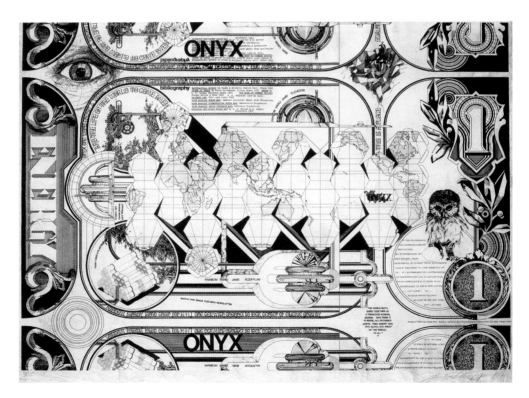

FIGURE 1.3 The World Map, ONYX collective, 1971, © FRAC Centre. Parsec City is a large poster collection for the ONYX collective that, in a similar manner to Ant Farm (Lewallen and Seid, 2004) created free-form architectural visions without constraint, projecting visions dismembered from their present conditions.

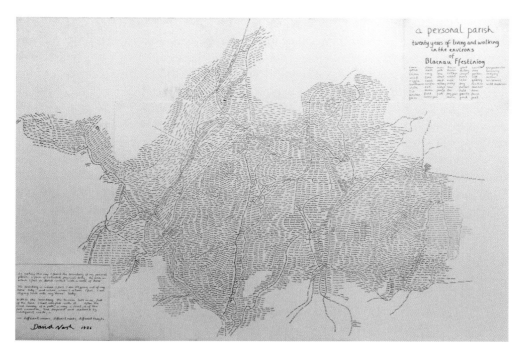

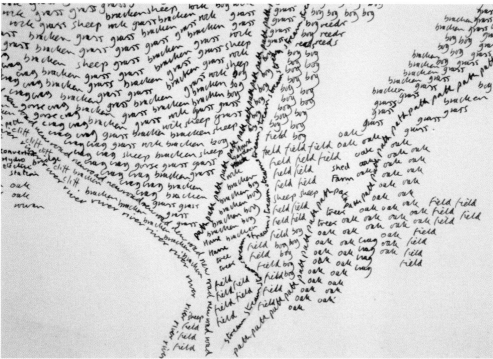

FIGURE 1.4 David Nash, Common Ground, Parish Maps. Common Ground help facilitate the production of community maps as a basis to understand local distinctiveness and places; their natural, social and cultural identities. Founded in 1985, the artists' collective has championed democratic involvement in the environment, and in the Parish Maps project utilise the agency of community mapping as an important data layer over regional and technocratic planning and mapping.

WORKING WITH MAPPING DATA

that so little is discussed on the reasoning and movement between these programs. What is the next step once one set of instructions are complete? How do I achieve the outcome? Pedagogically, digital instruction must be delivered alongside a clear reasoning of why, and for what purpose. This current problematic could be due to the various competing firms seeking to establish all-encompassing platforms for design services, as well as the design of university courses and time pressure for references while working in practice. However, many professionals are now moving to greater interoperability using a number of GIS programs rather than relying on dominant market software, so there are indications of change. As a student or practitioner, the approach to mapping may be restricted to university instructors' or a landscape practice's in-house methods, though a number of publications have displayed the rich variety of approaches possible (Amoroso, 2012). It can be argued that the development

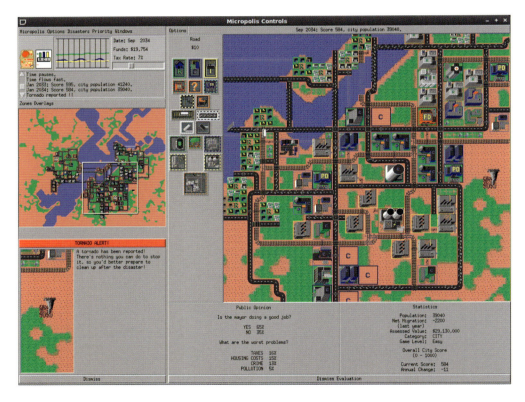

FIGURE 1.5 Will Wright, Don Hopkins, SimCity, Micropolis, 1985, Maxis. © 1989–2007 Electronic Arts Inc. (Open Source). Micropolis, later developed into SimCity, Electronic Arts, was a real-time city-planning game which allowed the design of dream cities or the reconfiguration of real-life cities, such as Tokyo or Rio De Janeiro. Compromising eight city scenarios, Micropolis challenged the user to solve poor city planning practices and fix the 'city' system, managing taxes, immigration, infrastructure and many other factors. Subsequent programs, such as City Planning and Community Consultancy (see Block by Block program, part of the UN-Habitat, Global Public Space Programme 2012: http://blockbyblock.org/about), continue scenario city gaming traditions, and have been adapted to city planning and community consultancy, most notably in the geo-design application City Engine by ESRI.

of mapping and our strategies for future landscape will not rest on existing practices, dominant software or convention; it will emerge from hybrid approaches, hacks and experiments, time to think and reflect. Representation is a more encompassing term; it prevents difficulties in reflecting sociological views, natural changes, histories and future visions. A hybrid approach means working with a plurality of landscape identities, multiple software programmes and wide-ranging data, and bringing these together – in this case into a map.

We miss a critical factor in this agency of mapping its *valence*.[5] The term in this case means the capacity of a map to unite, react or interact with something else. The map is one of the core representational modes in which design work is inscribed and initiated. Our analysis and the representation of these formed maps are essential in the communication process demonstrating professional competence of the landscape architect in understanding the environment. In these processes of mapping we can lose the temporal aspects of landscape, its duration and climate become lost in this agency (see Chapter 3). Mapping may reduce elements, give emphasis or leave out whole tracts of information which in turn affect any subsequent designs or decisions. Thus, we must be careful of the valence that is delivered by the agency of mapping practice. Moreover, remote-sensing technology provides a liberalisation of cartography; the public at large interact, model and recalibrate data sets. To some degree, contemporary mapping is democratised through mobile and tablet interfaces, but mapping valence is often unaccounted for.

The agency of mapping also reflects the technologies available, some of which were developed for military purposes and devolved down to consumer markets. GIS are gaining more currency and developing at speed. The ability of GIS applications to manage data sets and spatial temporal information alongside time-based approaches means that 4D GIS is viewed as a solution for managing complex data sets.[6] However, while fidelity of the earth is the goal, the accounting of errors is also essential. The landscape architect can only bring rigour to the process of mapping by accounting for valence, which includes the omission of limits, voids, gaps and distortions of map data.

Maps remain a fundamental communication tool for landscape architecture; the variety of mapping practices and subjects outside the discipline should always be considered as a mode to enrich landscape practice. Such a wide plurality may upset scholars seeking definitive terms of operation and definition; however, landscape as seen in a holistic way requires the widest sources of data to understand it. This understanding is all we have in the analysis, strategy and planning of future landscapes. The agency of mapping is important to understand; maps act as a surface to communicate ecological, social and cultural information of places. More importantly, map valence and its reception and reaction in design processes and wider communities must be understood. Maps help and assist in the organisation of our thinking and reflect existing technologies and future directions.

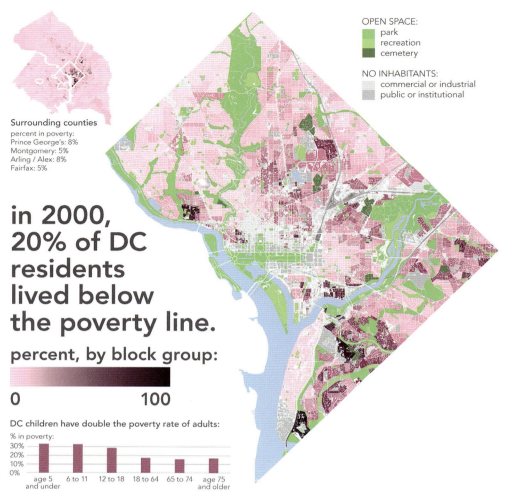

FIGURE 1.6 (*above and facing page*) Bill Rankin, DC Violence, DC Poverty, 2008. www.radical cartography.net. The primary mode of geographic segregation remains racial, particularly in Washington, DC. As Rankin writes, race is often used as a proxy for other social divisions as well – income, crime and education in particular. Rankin's mapping process seeks a mode of representation in symbols that represent more fluidity in the statistics by using colour ramps over colour classes.

COMMON DATA SETS

A brief discussion of common data types demonstrates the incredible cartographic development that has materialised in the last century. Some of these sets may well be known to the reader, but the purpose is to consider their sources and application for landscape architecture. The mentioned sets can be used in the studio or in practice as a basis of gathering and contextualising the landscape. Through using such sets the question develops as to what are the required results, what is to be found out? For example, the Landstat program that was launched in 1972 by the United States

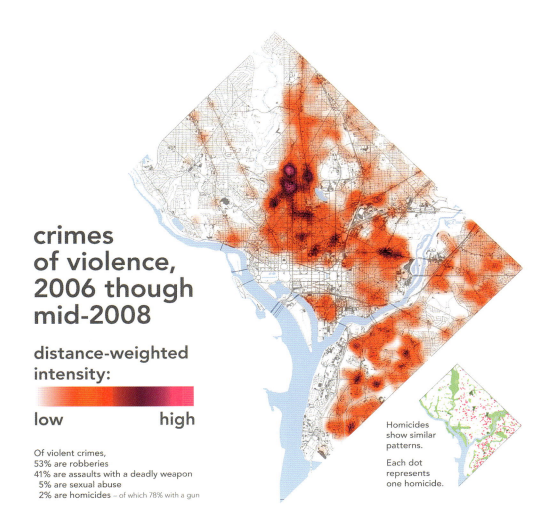

crimes of violence, 2006 though mid-2008

distance-weighted intensity:

low　　　　　　high

Of violent crimes,
53% are robberies
41% are assaults with a deadly weapon
 5% are sexual abuse
 2% are homicides – of which 78% with a gun

Homicides show similar patterns.

Each dot represents one homicide.

Geological Survey (USGS) and NASA provides the most continuous record of the earth, developing satellite technology, processing, archiving and distribution. Historical Landstat data from the USGS can be used for landscape classification and urban development over a set period (Yang, 2011) and there are a multitude of academic works on the subject, as well as works on the coverage and politics (Mack, 1991). Governmental departments may hold vast swathes of information that is accessible to the public; this would be an initial strategy for gathering mapping data, but may require reading of the in-house manuals and processing guides for use in your chosen GIS software package.

While these large-scale bodies host super-massive mapping data packets, there are also options to utilise these sets as base layers for mobile mapping applications such as Mapbox. Such sites allow the mapping and emphasis of any feature in the world, hosting and sharing of this information as well as production of mapping infographics.

WORKING WITH MAPPING DATA

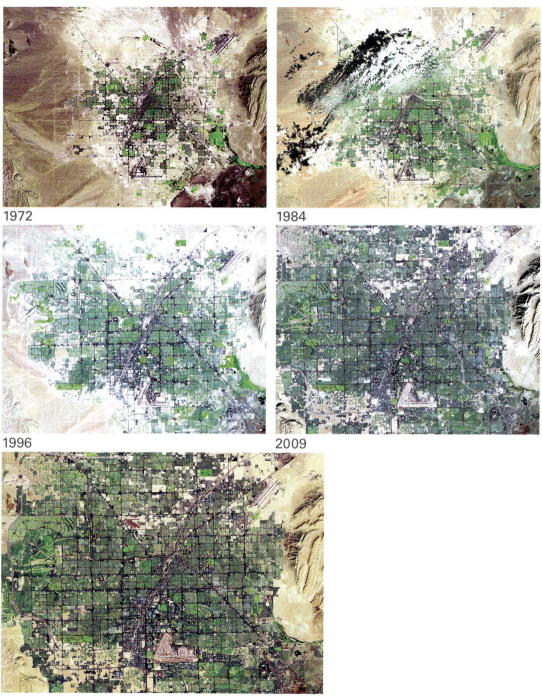

1972
1984
1996
2009
2015

FIGURE 1.8 SIC (Satellite Imaging Corp), upper left, Pleiades – 1A (0.5 m) Satellite of Athens, Greece. Upper right, Pleiades – 1A, valley of the moon, Jordan. Lower left World View 2 (0.5m) Satellite – Rakaia River, New Zealand. Lower right, Ikonons Satellite (1 m) – White Lines, Gobi Desert, China. The high-resolution data sets that can be acquired utilising various named orbiting satellites. The data can be accessed via government agencies or intermediaries which provide processing and acquisition for projects.

FIGURE 1.7 (*facing page*) NASA and the USGS. False colour Landsat of Las Vegas. Stills from time lapse video of the growth of Las Vegas from 1972 to 2015 by Mike Taylor and Marit Jentoft-Nilsen (RSIS): Lead Animator, Matthew R. Radcliff (USRA): Video Editor, Matthew R. Radcliff (USRA): Producer, James R. Irons (NASA/GSFC): Scientist, Aries Keck (ADNET Systems, Inc.): Writer. USGS/NASA Landsat. The red colour band displays vegetation health. The brightest red mainly depicts golf courses. The south-west edge contains a wetland area. Lake Mead is also shown, with declining water levels in the last decade as increasing resource needs deplete environmental conditions. The grey colour depicts man-made structures and infrastructure. The Landsat satellite project has provided accurate land cover since 1972, which has incrementally increased in resolution and coverage, with Landsat 9 due for release in 2023. Landsat is the most critical orbiting asset and is used in many research fields. Its importance lies in the extensive period in which the earth has been observed, allowing super-massive observation of landscape change over time. Such work compares to the theories of Robert Venturi and Denise Scott Brown of the clashing iconography of urban sprawl (Venturi *et al.*, 1977).

WORKING WITH MAPPING DATA

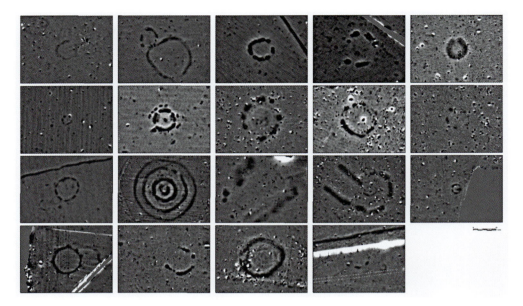

FIGURE 1.9 Stonehenge Hidden Landscape. Ludwig Boltzmann Institute for Archaeological Prospection and Virtual Archaeology. The remains of a major prehistoric stone monument were discovered less than 3 km from Stonehenge. Using cutting-edge, multi-sensor technologies, the Stonehenge Hidden Landscapes Project has revealed evidence for a large stone monument hidden beneath the bank of the later Durrington Walls 'super-henge'.

Thus, the landscape architecture student or practitioner's data acquisition strategy should be to both utilise large national or corporate mapping providers, but also grassroots open-source cartographers (such as those available through GitHub) who are operating in clouds using tablets and smartphones.

TYPES OF DATA CAPTURE

Satellites, aircraft, unmanned aerial vehicles (UAVs), vehicle mounted scanners and handheld devices all provide means to capture landscape in a variety of forms. UAVs and handheld scanners, as well as photogrammetry techniques, have increased affordability and viability for universities and landscape practices. These data sets should be considered as base layers for any design work and would form part of the captured resources for landscape analysis. The data sets listed here are not exhaustive and do not delve into specific methods of collection. Interpretation of images is also difficult; the reading of natural features, and architecture, requires grounding in archaeology, geography and heritage. For example, a sun-shading analysis may reveal landscape earthworks that are not visible at ground level. The features may only reveal themselves in aerial photography or through serendipity. For example, the Stonehenge site was being watered by a groundsman when he noticed brown patches where missing stones may have stood. Following this, the site was surveyed using ground-penetrating radar and other technologies and researchers uncovered extensive new features of Stonehenge. Serendipity and technology completely redefined what was thought to be one of the most comprehensively understood sites to date. The duration and time aspect of landscape is covered in Chapter 3.[7]

Social sets

Social sets of data can be gathered to gauge the anthropogenic influence on landscape if added to data covering the physical environment. These sets are essential for understanding the urban dynamics of cities and can be used at much smaller scales to understand localised communities, pressures and needs. These aspects are increasingly important for multinationals and global trade through big data, and at more local levels enabled through GPS.

Census and ethnicity maps. These geographical works give meaning to statistical data collected by the majority of governments and are useful for gauging the human aspect of the landscape: age, ethnicity, income, education and levels of poverty.

Psychogeographic maps. These are maps derived from individual or group psychological perceptions of the environment. These maps have come more to the fore in the contemporary resurgence of artistic practices of mapping (Harmon, 2003, 2010). These maps develop from the French Situationists and theories of the Derive – or urban drift. See Chapter 2 for further details and exercises.

Walkability studies. These cover the relationship between walking behaviour and the physical environment, with studies claiming health benefits through careful urban and landscape design (Tonkiss, 2013; Edgerton *et al.*, 2014; Schwartz and Rosen, 2015).

Spatial accessibility studies. Spatial access studies use GIS calculations for the evaluation of access to multiple services, often health. Often these studies calculate population–provider ratios, distances to providers and gravitational models based on influence, which provide strategies for pedestrian movements, site locations and spatial design.

Topographical sets

Topographic data sets cover the surface and features of the earth from planetary to plot scales. Space agencies, national map agencies and corporate geographic firms provide vast swathes of data in a variety of formats, resolutions, scales and time periods. These sets are discussed using the following terms.

DSM. Digital surface model; this represents a complete survey of the landscape surface above sea level. Commonly found at different levels of accuracy, for example ±25 cm, ±50 cm, ±1 m, ±2 m resolutions. It will include all the surface objects such as vegetation and architecture. A DSM can be gathered using LiDAR (laser imaging detection and ranging).

MAP DATA TYPES

There are a number of data types, processes and outcomes to map and capture digital landscape form. Understanding these types can help create landscape strategy.

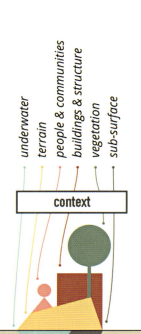

captured data

SATELLITE IMAGERY

- multispectral
  FALSE COLOUR: Infrared, Thermal, Radar
- hyperspectral
  TRUE COLOUR (MAN MADE OBJECTS): Satellite photography
- thermal
- LiDAR
- radar

TOPOGRAPHICAL SETS

- bathymetry
- stereo-satellite imagery
- tri-stereo imagery
- LiDAR
- radar
- hydrological (radar, thermal)
- metrological

SOCIAL SETS

- census and ethnicity maps
- psychogeographic maps
- community & consultation maps

SUB SURFACE

- seismic
- radar
- magnetic
- electro magnetic

process

data is **captured** from the context, and is then used to make maps and models (**derived data**)

FIGURE 1.10 Serena Pollastri, Imagination Lancaster, Lancaster University, mapping data typology, 2016.

derived data

- spot elevation
- contour map
- photogrammetry
- ortho-rectified images
- mosaic composites
- photographic point clouds

- DSM
- DTM
- DEM
- photogrammetry

URBAN DATA

- building heights
- massing study
- BIM object
- aerial photography
- line of sight
- storm water run off
- solar Energy Potential
- flood models
- tree health
- light emissions
- air quality
- fires
- geological
  (hydrogeological, geophysical)
- walkability studies
- accessibilities studies

HOW TO READ THIS DIAGRAM

The range of sensors to capture data is complex, from hand held devices, UAVs to Satellites. Data captures various aspects of the landscape, and the types of processing applied results in a variety of categories which helps strategise design works.

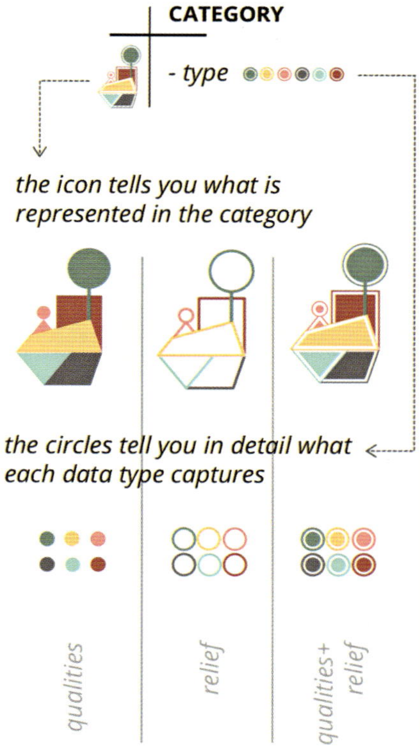

CATEGORY
- type

the icon tells you what is represented in the category

the circles tell you in detail what each data type captures

qualities | relief | qualities + relief

The arrows indicate what data can be **derived** from a **captured** dataset.

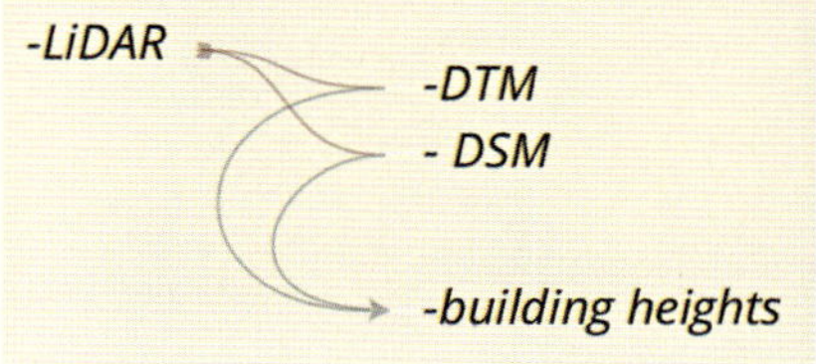

- LiDAR
  - DTM
  - DSM
  - building heights

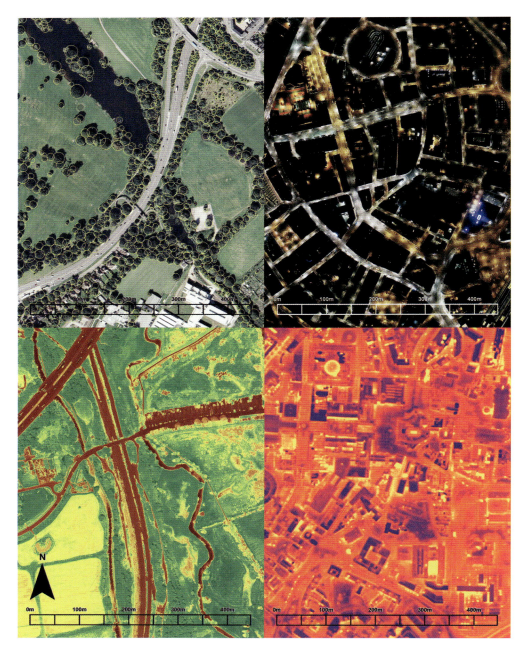

FIGURE 1.11 Bluesky International Limited. Top left: normalised difference vegetation index (NDVI) gives you an instant, detailed insight into the health and maturity of the UK's flora. Top right: This nightsky data records the location of street lights, illuminated road signs and other nighttime sources of light emission. Lower left: national tree map records the location, height and canopy/crown extents for every single tree 3 m and above in height. Lower right: Thermal mapping identifies building heat loss and illegal occupation, as well as pipelines.

DTM. Digital terrain model; this is a topographic image of the bare earth. These data sets can be found in different resolutions, so some sets may not have the details required for small-scale work. A DTM is constructed from a grid or a triangular integrated network (TIN). The sampling of this information can affect the overall quality of the model. DTMs can also be created using LiDAR calibrated to remove surface objects in the scanning process.

DEM. Digital elevation model; this is the elevation data above sea level of a terrain, and is used as a term interchangeably with DTM. The DEM term is preferred by satellite specialists and acquisition teams. DEMs contain elevation points set within a grid which can be constructed into a 3D surface at various resolutions.

Bathymetry. Bathymetry is the equivalent of a DTM; it maps the underwater terrain and can be represented as a raster surface or isobaths (underwater contour). This data type is particularly useful for mapping coastal landscape.

Satellite imagery

Satellites have channels or bands which measure different wavelengths (light). They are multispectral or hyperspectral. Some of these wavelengths are useful for measuring certain landscape features, the range of bands allow the sensing of unseen features and their classification. For example, near-infrared data sets can be used to monitor plant health and vegetation. Short-wave infrared distinguishes mineral deposits and moisture content of soils.[8] Some of the images may be composites which limit cloud cover, or have certain image resolutions which limit scales of enquiry.

Thermal. Thermal data sets can be used to monitor building heat loss, with mitigation through green roofs or passive retrofitting.

Satellite photography. This can be mosaicked or a composite of several studies, combining a number of images to reduce the amount of cloud cover, and can be seen in various image resolutions. This process is called photogrammetry. Aerial imagery must be orthorectified, which means the image is geometrically corrected to be seen from above and remove distortion. The process must change the angle of the sensor recording the information and also react to complex topographies. Satellite photography may not be as up-to-date as needed, and higher resolutions may incur higher costs of acquisition.

Photogrammetry. Photogrammetry is the technique of extracting (derive) geometric information from two-dimensional images or video. This involves mosaicking images, measuring elevations, scaling, angles and distances. One basic application of this process is a cost-effective mode of creating a 3D point cloud from a 2D photograph. For example, an entry-level drone with a GoPro camera can capture a range of photographs which can be processed into a 3D model using freeware or industry-standard software packages (see the companion website). For a basic understanding of photogrammetry, the use of software such as Autodesk 123D Catch, ReCap or ReMake creates 3D mesh models from 2D photographs. These meshes, with some editing, can be 3D printed.

FIGURE 1.12 Scan Labs Bartlett, UCL, Film Still, *Elevated*, Group 2, Ali Zolfaghari, Sarah Firth, Ruben Alonso, 2015. The film *Elevated* explores a perceptual journey in Kielder forest, where nature is an artificial patchwork. Trees are planted over time to ensure a staggered harvest, and the different environments of these various parts of the forest become the raw material of the film. Three scans in three different locations, capturing three different stages of tree growth.

FIGURE 1.13 Cureton, Lidar Model of Birmingham City centre (1 m), Environment Agency. These LiDAR data were captured in the winter months of leaf fall. The data were processed into ASCII format and then converted into a raster surface. The model uses a greyscale colour ramp to indicate heights in metres. The model may have a photographic image draped onto its surface, similar to texturing a 3D design.

FIGURE 1.14 Cureton, spot elevations and contours, North Warwickshire, UK. © Ordinance Survey, terrain-5, 2016. The weight of the contour line is referenced as major or minor. The spot heights are annotated in grey and assembled using OS Terrain-5 contours: a contour data set of 5 m interval standard contour polylines, which includes index contours at 25 m intervals, mean high and low water boundaries and spot heights.

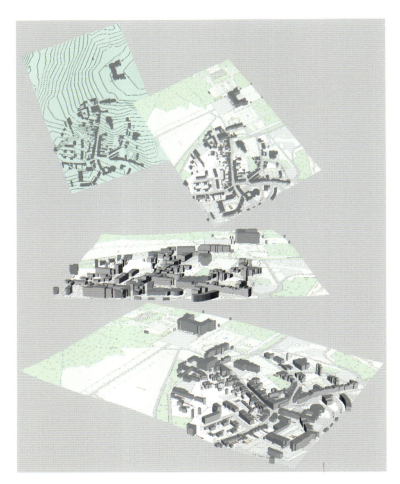

FIGURE 1.15 Cureton, © Ordinance Survey, Master Map, Building Heights (BHA), terrain-5 DTM, 2016. In this case the BHA data allow direct scaled physical modelling (see Chapter 5). The data can be used to simulate sun shading and its effects in between landscape or any vertical landscaping. The DTM can be used to calculate contours at various intervals, the Master Map data in this case is raster tiles draped onto the DTM. The BHA data are also floating on the DTM surface. Once all parts are assembled the model can be used for digital fabrication, further analysis or as a basis to 'design in' at 1:1.

LiDAR. Laser imaging detection and ranging; this is an increasingly used method of capture that revolves around laser returns, or point clouds of the surface of the earth. The data can be collected from satellite, light aircraft or drones. These can be rasterised to create a DSM – a complete 3D surface. Most LiDAR surveys are land-based. Infrared beams used in the survey tend to be absorbed by water and show very little or no return when they hit it; they are referred to as data voids. These can be filled by collating LiDAR data with a DTM or manually adjusting the mesh. LiDAR data can be highly accurate, though the frequency of the laser scan can give higher-quality returns of a surface, and thus high accuracies in mapping. Some lasers can fire multiple points and signal returns, allowing the measurement of a tree canopy and the forest floor at the same time, for example. A contour map can be derived from the LiDAR data once processed.[9]

Spot elevation. Also known as spot heights, these are single elevation values at specific points and interludes in relation to sea level. Spot elevations are used in construction alongside contour sets; the choice of use is down to the reading of the plan. The point as a convention will have a unique point number, elevation or z-value, description and a marker. Spot heights can be used to triangulate a contour. TIN surfaces can also be created from spot heights.

Contour map. A contour map is used to represent relief on a 2D plan. A contour line (equal height line) never splits into two lines – they always run parallel, they are always closed and join. Contours only cross when a new grading is proposed or there is an overhang. Contour lines may have a lower line weight if they are less significant. Peter Petschek's text on landscape grading principles is useful when the mapping process is being developed into a designed plan (Petschek, 2008).

Urban data

Architectural data sets may be provided by space agencies, national agencies or more directly through collaboration on projects. These data sets have important implications for mapping and for the development of landscape plans. ESRI City Engine, City GML and many other sites host city and landscape models of various qualities and resolutions. The derived data discussed here are not exhaustive; many possibilities exist, from building height visibility studies, stormwater runoff calculations, solar energy potentials, flood models, tree health surveys, light emissions and air-quality studies.

Building heights. Building heights can be derived from a shadow analysis of buildings or derived from DTM and DSM data. The principle is that the height is gauged from absolute surface to absolute height of roof type. One strategy of using the data is the comparison of urban and architectural development and control, sun shading and impact on the surrounding landscape. Building height data can be easily and directly translated into a physical block model.

Massing studies. These are shapes that are used to conceptualise a building. They are used to explore spaces in relation to the building envelope (zoning envelope), conduct energy analysis and other forms. Building elements such as walls and floors can be added once the massing is developed. The massing studies are useful information sources prior to any further developed design decisions. One strategy of using massing studies could be the consideration of interior gardens and/or green walls and roofs in relation to the overall building energy performance.

BIM objects. These are various objects or parameters used in construction. The object or parameter may have been provided from the manufacturer and contains specific standards of construction. In landscape architecture, BIM objects are hosted online and can be incorporated into design works integrating visualisation and building specification. The advantage is that specific elements used refer to national building specifications and give detailed specification, including LEED or BREEM scoring. The BIM objects allow specification in 3D models; team working and project management bring new project workflows to the fore.

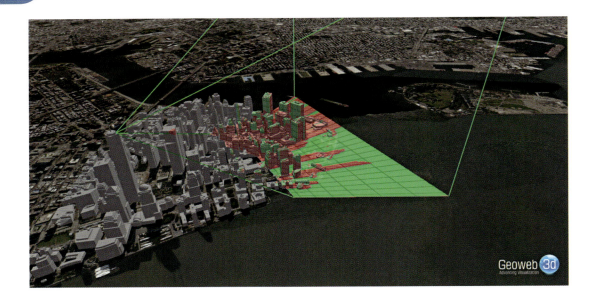

FIGURE 1.16 (*above and facing page*) CyberCity 3D, Inc. 2016, 3D studies: New York City, NY line-of-site study, Cambridge, MA water pressure calculations, Honolulu, HI neighbourhood and occupancy calculations, Honolulu, HI solar potential. With multiple city data sets, Los Angeles-based CyberCity 3D (CC3D) is advancing GIS and visualisation tools, creating 3D cities from multiple applications and supplying models to major built environment software companies. Relevant roof points are measured and coded; the company's patented CC-Modeler automatically converts these codes (point clouds) into 3D roof structures. From there, the walls are generated by

intersecting the drawn-down roof polygons with the DTM. Quality control and editing are then done using CC-Edit. CC3D models can then be exported to a host of software file formats including Collada, Geodatabase, Shapefile, .dxf, .kml, .fbx, .skp, and .obj. The completed BIM 'smart' models contain useful attribute information. These datasets are interoperable with most commercial software platforms, and can also be streamed to form the basis of sustainable analysis tools.

WORKING WITH MAPPING DATA   47

MAP DATA OUTPUTS, DESIGN AND STRATEGIES

From these data sets a myriad of possibilities can arise and the agency of mapping can begin. With large volumes of data, careful information design is required; for all maps a legend, scale and direction symbol are necessary elements; the output source must also be considered, whether print, tablet, mobile or web device. Map data and projection choices are needed (Iliffe and Lott, 2008). Neat lines are also useful to provide a boundary of the map data. Consider any symbol placements, any obscurities and most importantly the legibility of the work. For example, using a hill shade may obscure reliefs in sections. Data periods of capture should also be considered; the date of capture in relation to the type of application needed. For example, aerial photography that does not show the latest contemporary urban development.

Computer-aided design (CAD) and GIS software are currently quite distinct. Assembling maps should preferably be completed in a GIS package that provides control of the type of geographic projection system, scale, annotation and layers, such as ESRI Arc GIS, QGIS or Map Info, among others. This assembly can include hand-drawn elements and historic data. Any landscape plans can be added either in a vector package or in the GIS software overlaid against the map base layers. These maps and plans can then be exported and graphically edited in Adobe Illustrator or Photoshop. Photoshop has 3D capability from CS5.5 onwards and is capable of handling 3D maps as long as the available hardware is also capable. Additional 3D modelling can also be developed by exporting 3D attributes from the GIS package. This clear principle of interoperability between GIS and CAD ensures that current market software can be used to its full potential.

Principles of map design for landscape architecture

While the software choices are important, the overarching principles of map representation should remain paramount. Edward R. Tufte, in *Envisioning Information* (Tufte, 1990), quotes the principle of Ockham's razor, which rests on the idea of parsimony or simplicity of representation over complexity. While the use of medieval philosophy as an argument for information design is questionable, such ideas are nonetheless important, as Catherine Dee writes following this logic, arguing for an 'aesthetics of thrift' in landscape (Dee, 2012). The following principles apply.

Colour and hue. Using large classes (symbol classifications) in legends means that colours could situate themselves too closely to each other, therefore effecting readability. If you use a colour ramp, indicate the unit of measurement and ensure the map is produced to match the printer specifications so colour is not distorted (e.g. CMYK) (Brewer, 2015). The Color Brewer is a long-standing tool that provides useful colour-band designs (http://colorbrewer2.org)

Symbol system. Ensure legibility of any symbol system. Use existing symbols if it refers to its equivalent. Shape choices are equally important; their scale may obscure or be hidden. Use transparencies for each symbol if the underlying layer still needs to be visible.

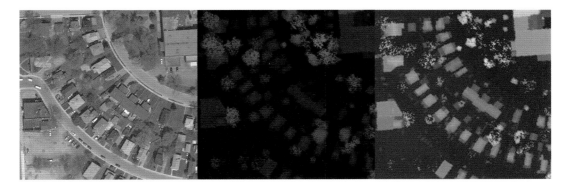

FIGURE 1.17 Jonathan Li, University of Waterloo and Haiyan Guan, Nanjing University of Information Science & Technology, 3D building reconstruction from LiDAR point clouds fused with aerial imagery, 2011. Li and Guan present a data-driven workflow for accurate 3D models fused with aerial imagery, connecting processes for refined definitions. Following on from this vehicle-borne mobile LiDAR capture and ground photography provides the skins required for building facades (Yang, 2011, pp. 75–91).

Layout. Fonts, labels, and explanations; in-house layouts may include company information, author, checking author, dates, scales, referring drawings and sheet numbers. Map grids and graticules may be necessary to understand the coordinate systems and area being mapped, as well as providing quick-reference areas for correlation with other data and maps. Multiple views (data frames) may be used to emphasise particular areas, and this allows improved reading through the use of different scales (Lewis, 2015).

Emphasis. There has been comment on the line, its weights and endings which give emphasis. For example, access points to sites conventionally involve arrows; however, the arrow head may be too harsh a symbol – an unnecessarily strong element in map production (Brewer, 2008).

Generalisation. The map may generalise statistical data. Ensure important nuances are accounted for. For example, a small use of data fields (classes) may generalise a geographic area (Lima, 2011).

Engagement. The map product must be engaging to the reader; it may not necessarily be a 2D product but an interactive map, animation or video. Thus the map in other mediums creates engagement through its 3D (and or immersive) quality. It also can visualise the passing of time in landscape of both histories and futures, making the map a compelling medium. Consider flyby speeds, pauses, iterations, callouts and annotations to develop the narrative.

Data outputs and strategies

While these mapping principles should be considered throughout construction, landscape strategies should also be in place. What data are to be selected and what output are to emerge? A number of possibilities can be generated from these common data types once they have been processed and assembled in a GIS package. Please refer to the companion website for each tutorial and the files required. These tutorials can be executed individually or connected.

Data sharing. Set up a teamworking mode in Esri, QGIS, Revit or Vectorworks amongst others. A number of software packages allow teamworking and administration. This provides control of the elements that are to be worked on by individuals, but also the pooling of resources to create a 3D model from across disciplines, which holds phasing, specification and drawings necessary for contractual operation.

Geo-referencing. This applies real-world coordinates to an image. These coordinates could be collected in the field using a GPS unit or applied by matching features (Letham and Letham, 2008). Feature matching to create a geo-reference must be carefully executed as the image may differ in the time collected and many features may since be transformed.

Orthorectification. Any hand-drawn or historical maps can be orthorectified, meaning any tilts or perspectives of an image can be made into a true planometric view. Maps and images will need control points – specific *x,y,z* coordinates that allow different images to correlate. You can also use control points as a method in repeat photography (Webb *et al.*, 2010). You are essentially providing a spatial reference point. These points can be created using different methods; the type of method used would be determined by the image being processed. Selecting consistent features in all the images being processed ensures accurate registration.

Urban sections. Using BHA data and a base topographic map, an urban section can be derived (Mantho, 2014). This can be transferred to a CAD package such as Revit or Vectorworks and digitally fabricated.

Massing study. Using the BHA set and building footprint, massing can be calculated *in situ* or exported to other software.

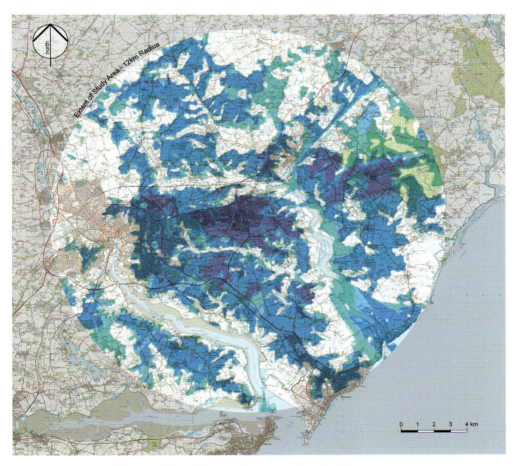

FIGURE 1.18 David Watson CMLI, ZTV study, This is a multi-point ZTV analysis using five study points to represent the mass of a proposed hotel building. The coloured areas on the map represent the degree of potential visibility, with darker colours indicating higher visibility. The study uses a composite radial-line type of analysis and is based on a bare-earth digital terrain model.

WORKING WITH MAPPING DATA

Viewshed, zone of theoretical visibility (ZTV) or zone of visual influence. This is a process in which the visibility of an object, architectural work or development can be measured using DTM or LiDAR, and a map created. It is an indicator of the position and line of sight, though requires site surveys to correlate for complete accuracy as local elements may affect results. For example, a wind farm development would seek to conduct a ZTV to measure its impact on the surrounding landscape for planning purposes.

Hill shading or sun shading. Sun-shading analysis is used to simulate climate conditions on a proposed building and figure passive design strategies. This analysis can help figure suitable landscape strategies in relation to the overall works, considering sun-path movement, solar heat gain, daylighting and solar generation. Sun shading can also be used on natural features to uncover hidden objects or landscape features. Moving sun positions may reveal hidden fortifications, artefacts or historical practices, which moves this data into the realm of landscape history studies and archaeology.

Windflow. Windflow analysis helps situate and orient buildings, and helps with massing and planning openings to minimise channelled windflow, and to devise appropriate screening and landscaping choices.

UNMANNED AERIAL SYSTEMS AND UNMANNED AERIAL VEHICLES

UAS can capture data and offer landscape architecture a unique cost-effective mode of surveying sites across a set period (Cheng, 2015). Other methods of mapping and capture are also possible using light aircraft, balloons and dirigibles. The uses of drones (UAVs) to create a DEM and aerial photography are the main drivers for increasing use. Commercial drones are being used, though increasingly enterprise drones are emerging to create new workflows for site survey and 3D mapping.

William Gibson's novel *Peripheral* (Gibson, 2015) talks of a future of drone abundance and causality. Drones are being used for the film and game industry, science, military and many other disciplines. The multiple applications of drones enable a new representational field between mapping that is aerial and aerial perspectival. With GPS control and way-marking the drone moves towards a mapping desire that has existed since the Renaissance: the total vision and representation of topographic relief. Just as Lucia Nuti describes, the Renaissance developed new representational paradigms in the perspective plan (Nuti, 1994) and what De Certeau calls a celestial eye (De Certeau, 2011, p. 92). Drone racing using VR helmets further increases new navigational possibilities to see landscape anew and embedded vision with technology. Drone use not only provides data on environmental conditions, but can be used archeologically and futurologically, flying in a particular aerial/perspective space that creates new mapping narratives from its flight position which offer both map and perspective. These new visual possibilities I would term as an emerging paradigm which represent a 'hover space' of landscape, beyond human heights, and possible legal altitude limits (± 400ft) between plan and aerial perspective. This new hover space means that mapping data can be gathered and provide economic means of site survey.

FIGURE 1.19 Thomas Lennon, Delaware river watershed, 2015. Photo courtesy of Thomas Lennon. Lennon is an award-winning film maker, using cameras to see again new possibilities in landscape through motion and flight, particularly for artists and environmentalists, much as the work of Ansel Adams changed the conception of American landscape and the creation of American National Parks.

WORKING WITH MAPPING DATA 53

FIGURE 1.20 Drone Air, Reykjavik, Iceland, 2015. © Aerial Photography by Drone Air. Drone Air provide aerial surveying and cinematic filming solutions, here shooting Reykjavik at dawn and dusk. Drone flight provides aerial views, sweeps and flybys which are not otherwise possible, animating the urban condition of Reykjavik, its weather systems, public spaces and light emissions.

A UAS describes the entirety of the tool: the controller, camera or sensor and vehicle. UAV refers to the vehicle itself and is a preferred term for fixed-wing aircraft rather than quadcopters. Practically drones may be fitted with HD cameras, LIDAR sensors, radar, contact sensors (e.g. humidity) or spray systems (e.g. fire retardants or pesticide). Drones can have the majority of parts 3D-printed, or have 3D-printed replaceable parts. To note, the term drone is generic and inaccurate; UAVs are fixed-wing aircraft with the same array of sensors or UAS. Remotely piloted craft (RPA) refers to the degree of pilot control; autonomous flight (AF) refers to computer control of the system, though in civil applications there is a mixture of the two with less AF. By and large, most drones actually refer to remote control quadcopters which have gimbals that provide a stable platform for a HD camera.

A drone can take different distances of flight and be programmable using way-markers (paths and follow me markers). It uses GPS to navigate or can be fully automated and pilotless – an example of flight control can be seen in the eMotion software. The drone may be regulated to maintain heights, fixed positions or to execute certain aerial manoeuvres. It may have programmable return to its take-off point. Degrees of autonomy generally increase the cost (Chao and Chen, 2012). If the reader wishes to take up the use of a drone for landscape purposes, national legislation will need to be referred to; in some countries the device may require registration. Commercial activity using drones may also require training and a licence to operate. If operating for the first time, a low-cost hobby quadcopter should be purchased as a training device to mitigate loss of expensive equipment, such as a Syma X8.

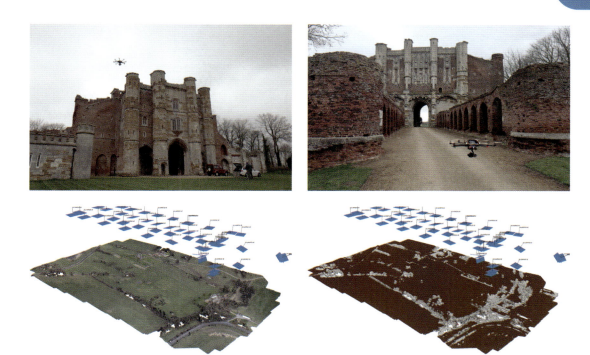

FIGURE 1.21 Remote Sensing Team (Jon Bedford and Dave Went), Historic England, Thornton Abbey, survey mapping and GIS interface screenshot. Images taken by cameras mounted on small unmanned aircraft may now be photogrammetrically processed without requiring access to expensive software and specialised hardware. Such techniques have enormous potential for the visualisation of landscapes, sites and monuments and are being applied in a number of ways by Historic England's Imaging and Visualisation Team.

Check with aviation authorities before any flight.

Competence, control, safety and legality are essential factors in drone use. A licence may be required to pilot any drone. A landscape practice may have to apply for a licence for commercial application. A customised drone with additional weight or sensors may have to meet a weight restriction for use. Drone operation may be difficult in certain weather conditions such as high winds and extreme temperatures. Drone use is not permitted in any large-scale urban setting or critical infrastructure, power plants, airports, etc. Unlicensed mapping and surveillance also raises privacy and security issues, as well as larger discussions of the relationship of drones and big data. Please refer to national guidance and the International Civil Aviation Organization (ICAO). Airspace may be regulated or controlled and guidelines issued on minimum and maximum heights; in addition, drones can have pilot control taken over or can be shot from the skies depending on the activity type and intended surveillance and survey target (Li et al., 2009). Anti drone devices are also on the rise from complex gun net systems to trained eagles seeing drones as prey.

Sample UAS flight plan suitable for generating a photogrammetric point cloud (emotion software).

UAS photogrammetric point cloud with stream cross section overlay (generated in Quick Terrain Modeler).

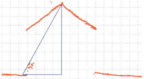

Measuring building height from LiDAR point cloud: 8.01 Meters.

Measuring building height from a UAS photogrammetric point cloud: 8.02 Meters.

FIGURE 1.22 Jarlath O'Neil-Dunne, using photogrammetric point clouds: a substitute for LiDAR, UVM Spatial Analysis Laboratory, Vermont, 2015. Originally published in *LiDAR Magazine*, 5(5), 2015. O'Neil-Dunne explores photogrammetric point clouds in comparison to LiDAR survey, using a drone to evaluate the accuracy limitations and benefits between the two modes.

Photogrammetric point clouds and LiDAR point clouds

Another technique that is highly cost-effective derives from photogrammetry. It basically means that a 2D photograph and its colours are interpreted to measure distance from the camera to create a 3D point cloud model. This method is used in archaeology, among other disciplines. Thus, a simple HD camera, smartphone or tablet can be used to create a 3D model if the photography is taken correctly. Purchasing a low cost drone with a mounted camera means that locales can be flown and 3D models created. More importantly, it allows updates to any urban development and existing data to be surveyed and collated to form an accurate 3D model of a city. Of course, the quality of return is dependent on the budget and investment in products.

Two possible strategies for mapping are possible, depending on the UAS choice.

Strategy 1: budget drone or fixed wing or professional quadcopter and GoPro camera, flight, 1080 px photography, software processing, 3D map, aerial photography draped onto the 3D model. Using a budget drone with a mounted camera, a flight can take place and still images and/or video can be collected. These data are then processed into a 3D model, which provides geo-referenced orthomosaics and DEMs. Alternatively, the still photography can be draped over an alternative DEM in a GIS package.

Strategy 2: aircraft or drone LiDAR sensor, software processing, LIDAR; raster surface, drape satellite image on LIDAR surface – 3D map model. In this case an intermediate cost of survey is used in which aircraft commissions or higher-end drones are used to capture a place using a LiDAR scanner. These data are processed to produce a geo-referenced DSM model. LiDAR scanners are falling in cost and weight, making this strategy a viable option for landscape practices. LiDAR processing will still need to be undertaken and seasonality can affect the quality of data return.

LiDAR's benefit is its vegetation penetration to create DTMs as well as its ability to capture canopies. Ortho-photos and clouds can also provide a number of benefits including cost effectiveness, quicker data processing times and higher resolutions from quality lenses.

SUMMARY

The range of data types and the development of a landscape strategy from these types is complex, as is the choice of representational tools for these activities. Understanding the principles of the various processes of data capture allows an understanding of appropriate tools to deliver outcomes. As well as this, the practitioner should have in mind the finish and layout and intended audience of these outcomes. The rich variety of data must be considered and utilised, from community-based maps to national government data sets. McHarg began a process of bringing the complexity of landscape together; the humanistic aspect and technological innovations add to this project. The idea of this chapter has been to document the rich variety of tools and strategies that could be used and to begin connections between them. The democratisation of GIS through open-source and mobile mapping software adds an additional positivity to mapping. Some data types may provide a higher degree of quality and fidelity of places, but the social and political aspects should also be mapped in developing strategies. Agency and valence are fascinating aspects of mapping and their influence in design processes and evaluation of environments is critical. These terms are not abstract when applied to the data types discussed and there is a clear pragmatic basis for landscape architecture. The next chapter discusses landscape, participation, notation and fieldwork as a means of humanistic data collection, developing mapping possibilities through discussion of notation and the diagramming of localised conditions. This develops landscape strategies utilising mapping.

NOTES

1. Baudrillard suggests simulacra and simulation – simulacra are copies without an original; a simulation is the mimicking of reality. In this case the map precedes the territory; in simpler terms we visualise geographic image of the place prior to ever visiting it.
2. After Thomas Moore's *Utopia*, 1516.
3. Geology refers to solid rocks, glacial and river deposits and slope processes. Physiographics identifies the evolution of land forms and how they have formed over time. Climate refers to wind, temperature, solar radiation and precipitation. Hydrology refers to the movement of water on and in the earth's surface. Ecology refers to biological nature and its interrelationships of flora (vegetation) and fauna (animals). Anthropogenic covers the influence of human beings on the physical landscape. Refer to Peter Smithson, Ken Addison and Ken Atkinson's coverage of the fundamentals of the physical environment for a comprehensive introduction to these environmental elements (Smithson *et al.*, 2008).
4. Any observation that does not come from direct contact with the place.
5. Used as a term in chemistry and psychology, valence descends, unites or reacts. The term is borrowed here as a measurement of affect in mapping. Agency defines an action; valence is the relative effect or reaction.
6. See MapScholar (Edelson and Ferster, 2013)
7. Historic England has an engaging interactive learning tool for decoding landscape features (http://ehhelm.articulate-online.com/p/2877919950/DocumentViewRouter.ashx?Cust=28779&DocumentID=745379b2–4659–417b-a03f-c552973907b6&Popped=True&v=2&InitialPage=story.html).
8. The USGS has a useful guide to selecting appropriate bands to emphasise certain features, as well as a spectral characteristics viewer (http://landsat.usgs.gov/best_spectral_bands_to_use.php)
9. See NOAA for an excellent introduction http://coast.noaa.gov/digitalcoast/_/pdf/lidar101.pdf.

BIBLIOGRAPHY

Amoroso, N. (ed.), 2012. *Representing Landscapes: A Visual Collection of Landscape Architectural Drawings*. Routledge, London.

Baudrillard, J., 1994. *Simulacra and Simulation*. University of Michigan Press, Ann Arbor.

Borges, J.L., 2000. *Labyrinths: Selected Stories and Other Writings*, new edition, Penguin Classics, London.

Borges, J.L. and Hurley, A., 2004. *The Aleph and Other Stories*, reprint. Penguin Books, New York.

Brewer, C., 2008. *Designed Maps: A Sourcebook for GIS Users*. ESRI Press, Redlands.

Brewer, C., 2015. *Designing Better Maps: A Guide for GIS Users*, 2nd edition. ESRI Press, Redlands.

Chao, H. and Chen, Y., 2012. *Remote Sensing and Actuation Using Unmanned Vehicles*. Wiley-Blackwell, Hoboken.

Cheng, E., 2015. *Aerial Photography and Videography Using Drones*. Peachpit Press, San Francisco.

Cosgrove, D., 1999. *Mappings*. Reaktion Books, London.

Cosgrove, D.E., 2012. *Geography and Vision*. I.B. Tauris, London.

De Certeau, M., 1985. Pay Attention: To Make Art, trans. Di Piero, T., in Harrison, H. and Harrison, N. (eds) *The Lagoon Cycle*. Herbert F. Johnson Museum of Art, Ithaca, NY.

De Certeau, M., 2011. *The Practice of Everyday Life*, 3rd revised edition. University of California Press, Berkeley.

Dee, C., 2012. *To Design Landscape: Art, Nature & Utility*. Routledge, London.

Dodge, M., Perkins, C. and Kitchin, R. (eds), 2011. *The Map Reader: Theories of Mapping Practice and Cartographic Representation*. Wiley-Blackwell, Chichester.

Edelson, S.M. and Ferster, B., 2013. MapScholar: A Web Tool for Publishing Interactive Cartographic Collections. *Journal of Map & Geography Libraries*, 9: 81–107. doi: 10.1080/15420353.2012.747463

Edgerton, E., Romice, O. and Thwaites, K. (eds), 2014. *Bridging the Boundaries: Human Experience in the Natural and Built Environment and Implications for Research, Policy, and Practice*. Hogrefe Publishing, Toronto.

Florinsky, I., 1998. Accuracy of Local Topographic Variables Derived from Digital Elevation Models. *International Journal of Geographical Information Science*, 12 (1): 47–61.

Fuller, R.B. and Snyder, J., 2009. *Ideas and Integrities: A Spontaneous Autobiographical Disclosure*, new edition. Lars Muller Publishers, Baden.

Gibson, W., 2015. *The Peripheral*. Penguin, New York.

Harmon, K., 2010. *The Map as Art: Contemporary Artists Explore Cartography*. Princeton Architectural Press, New York.

Harmon, K., 2003. *You are Here: Personal Geographies and Other Maps of the Imagination*. Princeton Architectural Press, New York.

Iliffe, J. and Lott, R. (eds), 2008. *Datums and Map Projections: For Remote Sensing, GIS and Surveying*, 2nd edition. Whittles Publishing, Boca Raton, FL.

Kitchin, R. and Dodge, M., 2014. *Code/Space: Software and Everyday Life*. MIT Press, Cambridge, MA.

Letham, L. and Letham, A., 2008. *GPS Made Easy: Using Global Positioning Systems in the Outdoors*, 5th edition. Mountaineers Books, Seattle.

Lewallen, C.M. and Seid, S., 2004. *Ant Farm 1968–1978: Timeline by Ant Farm*. University of California Press, Berkeley.

Lewis, K., 2015. *Graphic Design for Architects: A Manual for Visual Communication*. Routledge, New York.

Li, D., Shan, J. and Gong, J. (eds), 2009. *Geospatial Technology for Earth Observation*. Springer, New York.

Lima, M., 2011. *Visual Complexity: Mapping Patterns of Information*. Princeton Architectural Press, New York.

Mack, P., 1991. *Viewing the Earth: Social Construction of the Landsat Satellite System*. MIT Press, Cambridge, MA.

Mantho, R., 2014. *The Urban Section: An Analytical Tool for Cities and Streets*. Routledge, London.

McHarg, I.L., 1995. *Design with Nature*, 25th anniversary edition. John Wiley & Sons, Chichester.

Muir, R., 2000. *The New Reading the Landscape: Fieldwork in Landscape History*. University of Exeter Press, Exeter.

Nuti, L., 1994. The Perspective Plan in the Sixteenth Century: The Invention of a Representational Language. *The Art Bulletin*, 76: 105–128. doi: 10.2307/3046005.

O'Sullivan, D. and Perry, G.L.W., 2013. *Spatial Simulation: Exploring Pattern and Process*. Wiley-Blackwell, Chichester.

Petschek, P., 2008. *Grading for Landscape: Architects and Architects*. Birkhäuser GmbH, Basel.

Point Foundation, 1986. *Essential Whole Earth Catalog*. Doubleday, Garden City.

Schwartz, Rosen, 2015. *Street Smart*. Public Affairs, New York.

Smithson, P., Addison, K. and Atkinson, K., 2008. *Fundamentals of the Physical Environment*, 4th edition. Routledge, London.

Steinitz, C., 2013. *A Framework for Geodesign: Changing Geography by Design*. ESRI Press, Redlands.

Steinitz, C., 1979. *Defensible Processes for Regional Landscape Design*. American Society for Landscape Architects, Washington.

Tonkiss, F., 2013. *Cities by Design: The Social Life of Urban Form*. Polity Press, Cambridge.

Tufte, E.R., 1990. *Envisioning Information* . Graphics Press, Cheshire, CT.

Venturi, R., Brown, D.S. and Izenour, S., 1977. *Learning from Las Vegas: The Forgotten Symbolism of Architectural Form*, 2nd revised edition. MIT Press, Cambridge, MA.

Webb, R., Boyer, D. and Turner, R., 2010. *Repeat Photography: Methods and Applications in the Natural Sciences*. Island Press, Washington.

Yang, X. (ed.), 2011. *Urban Remote Sensing: Monitoring, Synthesis and Modeling in the Urban Environment*. Wiley-Blackwell, Chichester.

2
LANDSCAPE, PARTICIPATION, NOTATION AND FIELDWORK (NOTATION AND DIAGRAMS)

> We build our image of the world with data from our senses. By presenting these data in novel patterns, artistic inventions alter our sensibilities – change what we see and therefore how we conceive the world and again how we look at it.
>
> (Lynch, 1976, p. 163)

We may converse about directions, or scrawl and inscribe a line on paper with loose symbols to aid a traveller. The paper may be passed to the traveller; the traveller navigates by reading a line and symbols. The traveller relies on a roughly delineated 2D surface to navigate a physical space. This process records the larger agency and valence of visual representation. As Kevin Lynch observes, the representation of data from our senses changes our vision of it. This humanistic environmental quality is important in the gathering of source information from communities in the design of the built environment. Social time and movement are vital to understanding landscape relationships. The recording of these perceptions can be achieved through a variety of means. In Henry Dreyfuss' *Symbol Sourcebook* (Dreyfuss, 1972), symbols on surfaces are found in the act of walking and collected into an extensive typology, giving meaning to places via maps but also by being physically inscribed. Likewise, the plan derived from a map visually communicates in such a fashion; thus cartography and anthropology share a vast commonality (Ingold, 2007; Ingold and Vergunst, 2008). This chapter discusses the use of analogue and digital methods for capturing community perception and participation in landscape design and surveys a number of modes in which this can be captured. Notation, fieldwork and diagramming are important aspects for landscape design, providing human sense perceptions and observations of landscape and site through walking (Schultz, 2014). Fieldwork can be defined both in scientific terms, for example as part of strict phase-one ecological habitat survey,[1] geological survey or in more experimental modes such as psychogeography. PDA (personal digital/data assistant) collection and GIS fieldwork are not covered in this chapter as there is already a wide availability of instruction resources for these areas. The emphasis on fieldwork covers the human aspect in relation to landscape and the development of design diagrams from this environmental experience.

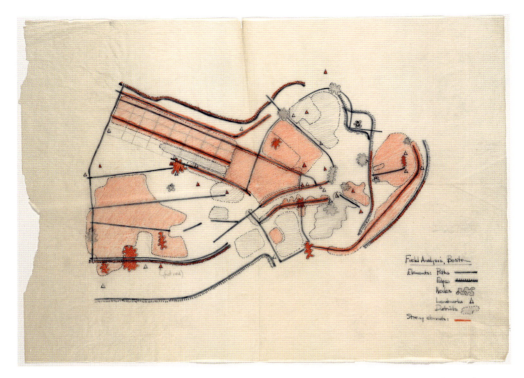

FIGURE 2.1 Kevin Lynch, extract from The Perceptual Form of the City, Boston, Massachusetts, 1954–1959. Image courtesy of the MIT Archives. © Copyright 2014. Lynch's hand-drawn map results from extensive survey of participants' perceptions of the city, interviews, photographs and field trips, resulting in Lynch famously classifying nodes, paths, edges, districts and landmarks as shared and common perceptual city forms (Lynch, 1960).

Fieldwork involves understanding landscape and urban features as well as the human aspects of its habitation. Strategies for fieldwork involve the robust collection of data and the consideration of how this will be interpreted; how will it be used to inform design approaches? What strategies are appropriate? Approaches to landscape architecture fieldwork have varied greatly and contain a rich history of representational practice from visual, oral and haptic collections. Validity of approaches and competing schemes still intensify the range of responses available to landscape. Perspective composites, video work, augmented reality, sound recordings and oral histories are just a small example of these approaches.

In design works generally there are works stages in developing a project.[2] In the UK they are referred to as Landscape Workstages. Once the brief and client relationship are established, working drawings are developed; the work stages progress and involve community and stakeholder participation in most cases. When working around this point in the project, notation, fieldwork and diagrams are valuable tools in engaging stakeholders and refining designs.

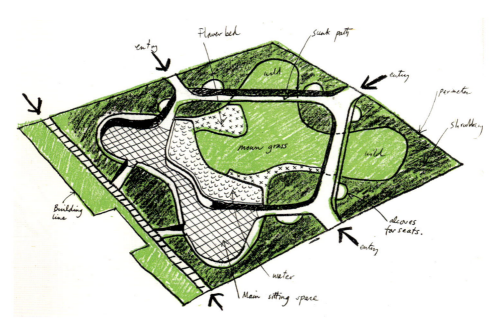

FIGURE 2.2 Gordon Cullen, *Architectural Review*, 112, 1952, p. 167. Ebury Square, London. Cullen draws a proposed design for an ornamental square in London using sunken paths, meandering entry points and a seating area and water feature for congregation, which do not immediately present themselves, but emerge from sequential movement.

An example of fieldwork can be found in the work of Gordon Cullen, whose work pervades landscape and urban design curricula. Cullen devised an urban design method called 'serial vision', which has proven influential in the design of areas that provide 'emotional impact'. The method involves a walked route mapped to a plan with referenced perspective drawings showing the walk progression or seriality (Cullen, 1961, p. 17). This impact is created by designing transitory routes which provide existing and emerging views that create stimulating mixtures. The book *The Concise Townscape* contains many static images in the text mixed with studied perspectives relating to a plan (Cullen, 1961). *The Concise Townscape* provided a humanistic method of survey of urban conditions and dynamics. The text has picturesque tendencies for urban planning, as Colin Rowe has argued:

> In other words, townscape could readily be interpreted as a derivative of the late eighteenth century Picturesque. And, as it is implicated all that love of disorder, cultivation of the individual, distaste for the rational, passion for the various, pleasure in the idiosyncratic and suspicion of the generalized which may, sometimes be supposed to distinguish the architectural tradition of the United Kingdom.
> (Rowe and Koetter, 1978, p. 34)

Such a picturesque label stems from the idea that the design of spaces should, as a result of the serial reading of its form, be framed by experiential visual tendencies to objectively survey, focus and spectate a panorama as well as the framing of a vista or picture. The method held that the eye acts as a dominant force which thus creates an urban ensemble of things which improve the quality of the space. Moreover, here the idea of a visual ensemble resurfaces from eighteenth-century aesthetics, particularly ideas of natural and personal improvement and cultivation (Brewer, 2013). By extension, Townscape theory was a conservatism of preservation which Colin Rowe alludes to in his critique. Essentially, Cullen's method is an intuitive experiential activity of a designer with a visually reductive output. Other representational forms are left out and edited in the resulting process. Such work is important for the development of visual site analysis and the understanding of many complex forms. Townscape principles were attacked by Brutalists and many others. However, while the system and preference for the visual seems naive, its success lies in its ability to enable and communicate designers' responses to areas and to be descriptive of a site, and more importantly to retain a humanistic scale. Form in this case is separated from content. Cullen's approach to solve more holistic urban issues is to be commended, though the fundamental approach fails to deal with issues discussed here, in the re-orientation of representational practices for landscape architecture and urban design and the development of multiple strategies.

Alternative perceptual models were also propagated. The serial narration of space by Cullen was akin to the landscape prospect/refuge theories of Jay Appleton in *The Experience of Landscape* (Appleton, 1987). Appleton postulates that within a landscape

FIGURE 2.3 Underground, from the Other Spaces series, 1997–1998, 4 × 5 original black and white Polaroid, scanned in high resolution and printed in variable dimensions, performed and photographed by Alex Villar. The performance artist has notably subverted awkward non-spaces, gaps, voids and urban peculiars throughout the city, using his presence and movement to highlight the jarring chaos out of supposedly rational spaces, temporarily occupying these dead spaces and timeless quarters.

there are preferred locations that are prospect dominant or areas that are refuge dominant. Thus, a visual prospect of a wooded landscape is more 'attractive' as it provides areas of 'escape' and 'protection'; the visual therefore provides various psychological states. Prospect allows the viewing of prey; hiding is the refuge, essentially a human biological theory – the visual thus becomes a psychological driver for feelings of safety.

Appleton's suggestion is in line with Kantian readings of disinterested viewing (Kant, 1987); removed from the experience, viewing 'magnificence' through a safe lens. In *The Experience of Nature: A Psychological Perspective*, Rachel Kaplan suggests there are modern environmental preferences based on a similar view of biological preference found in Appleton, that environments are preferred when containing complexity, mystery, coherence, texture, identity, ability and spaciousness (Kaplan, 1989). In Appleton, Kaplan and Cullen, a correlate is found in the preference for certain environmental experiences and designs. Further work on experiential landscape appears in the work of Kevin Thwaites, Ian Simkins and Ombretta Romice (Thwaites

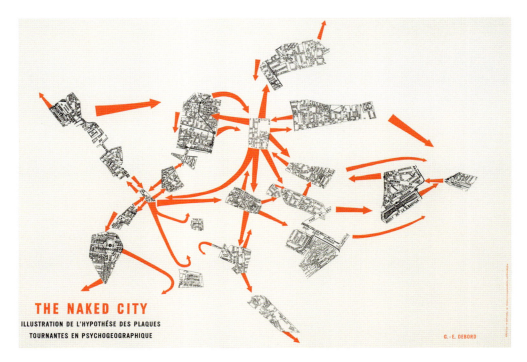

FIGURE 2.4 Guy Debord and Asger Jorn, *The Naked City*, 1957. This highly reproduced psycho-geography captures movements and interactions between various isolated zones and quarters of Paris, the emphasis of line weight signifying a greater level of 'play', pleasure, forgetting, drift and displacement. *The Naked City*, referencing the name of a film noir from the previous decade, presents a truer cartography; not everything can be seen. Conventional maps deceive us with a complete totality. The Situationist map is a representation that shows traces of actions; it is temporal.

and Simkins, 2006; Thwaites *et al.*, 2013; Edgerton *et al.*, 2014). Landscape thus becomes a product of mind and the experience of landscape alludes to certain preferences; certain urban features come to *mean*. Much has been written on Townscape; however, the source of 'emotional response' in these urban designs as Clement Orillard comments on Cullen's drawing notes[3] was based on a Freudian understanding. Cullen, like Appleton and the Kaplan, utilised psychology to justify personal subjectivities through drawing (diagramming in Appleton's case), presenting and reforming these subjectivities into an apparent visual objectivity.

The different languages of decoding landscape and urban settings were a larger problematic for the avant-garde. In the case of French Lettrism, the movement sought a new form of communication which blended various arts – poetry, cinematography, print and painting – essentially aiming and reacting to bring poetry to an everyday setting. Predominantly Lettrism's outputs focused on notational styles; they invented a graphic form called Hypergraphics which was a synergy of poetry, text, cinema, typography and hand graphics. Maurice Lemaître also described Hypergraphics as an ensemble of signs capable of transmitting the reality served by the consciousness more exactly than all the former fragmentary and partial practices (phonetic alphabets, algebra, geometry, painting, music, and so forth).

(Ford, 2005, p. 20; see also Seamon, 1993)

Lettrism continued its experimental activity in the form of psychogeography through a breakout group, the Situationists. As a member of the group, Guy Debord terms psycho-geography as 'the study of the precise laws and specific effects of the geographical environment, consciously organised or not, on the emotions and behaviour of individuals' (Debord, 1955, cited in Knabb 2007, pp. 8–12). Here, Situationists opened a new graphic communication and critique of capitalist society architecture and urbanism out of a distinction of a particular undertow of psychological–geographical relief of urban centres, which apparently discourage or enable certain movements and activities (Mcdonough, 2004, pp. 55–87). Psychogeography developed from earlier theories of the flâneur.[4] Lettrism and the Situationists are thus firm markers in the history of landscape representation with graphic experimentation and radical mapping practice.

Exploring maps as constructions and perceptions of space, the work (notably in the Naked City 1957) conveyed maps figured as narratives of isolation rather than as tools of 'universal knowledge' (Mcdonough, 2004, p. 62). As Debord states, 'the production of psycho-geographical maps may help to clarify certain movements of a sort that, while surely not gratuitous, are wholly insubordinate to the usual directives' (Knabb, 2007, pp. 5–8). The most constructive example from the Situationist International group was the notation of the 'derive' or drift, in which atmospheric points or locales connect with others at unrecognised scales, forming a composite map of fragmentation states[5] and drifts between and around obstacles while referencing other zones through the various line weights of arrows. This work created at a representational level an abstract reduction of the Parisian space to social relations, but this in itself was more 'truthful' than the presented fidelity of a 'whole' Parisian map seeking a totalising impossible eye or 'voyeur' (Foucault, 1991; De Certeau, 1984) in which the terrain is laid bare. Thus, psychogeography as fieldwork in principle may provide a more true report to banal, fragmented landscape. The visuals produced from this activity act as artefacts from actions; the resulting fieldwork cannot be isolated or mistaken as an aesthetic form itself (Sadler, 1999). The work of Henri Lefebvre is his last and uncompleted book *Rhythmanalysis*, which, while differing to the goal of Debord, sought a similar analysis of understanding the rhythm of a place:

> Rhythm is always linked to such and such a place, to its place, be that the heart, the fluttering of the eyelids, the movement of a street or the tempo of a waltz. This does not prevent it from being a time, which is to say an aspect of a movement or of a becoming.
>
> (Lefebvre, 2013, p. 89)

FIGURE 2.5 Mark Boyle, Holland Park Study, 1967. Earth on resin and fibreglass. Dimensions: object: 2388 × 2388 × 114 mm. Courtesy of Tate Images & DACS. Boyle used fibreglass to record the urban terrain in three dimensions. The deliberate abstraction of the work can appear as a late modernist work, though in reality it is a study of the everyday and a square section of our urban fabric.

FIGURE 2.6 (*facing page*) Ray Lucas, Meiji Shrine, from *The Sensory Notation Handbook* (Lucas, 2014). The Meiji Shrine is the main Shinto shrine in Tokyo. Lucas asks what alternative modes are possible for sensing spaces and their temporal qualities. Senses are not isolated; they overlap feedback responses to the environment. Lucas develops a system of notation that records this environmental navigation using a radar map to which a number of priorities can be marked. The notation progresses from location, priority, corroboration, descriptor and temporality. The temporality indicates movement through spaces, whether singular, constant, situated, ambient, directional, repetitive, switching or varying. Using descriptors of visual, aural, tactile, kinetic, thermal and chemical located on the radar, to which experiences are mapped, in this case the visual spectacle of trees corroborates both the chemical simulation of the foliage and the aural spectacle of the wind. Crunching gravel paths corroborates movement.

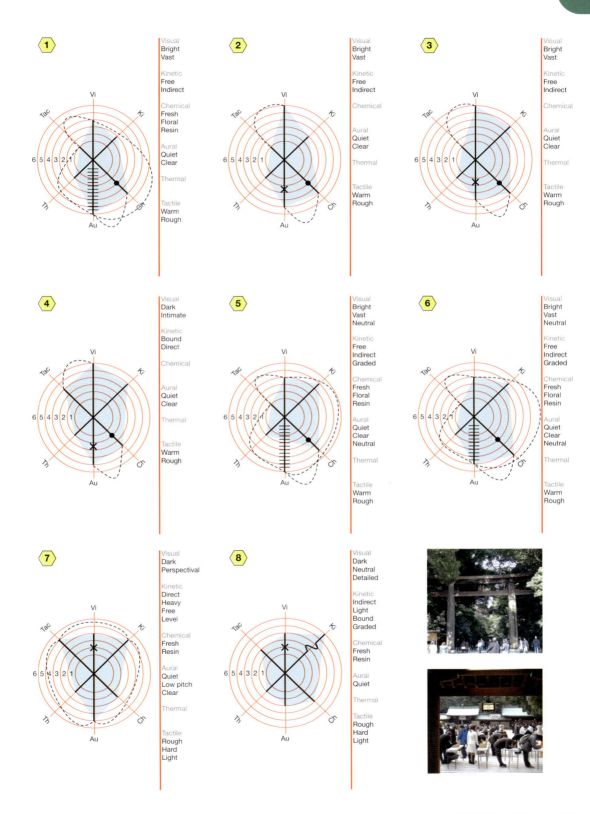

NOTATION AND DIAGRAMS 69

FIGURE 2.7 Nigel Coates, *Gamma Tokyo*, 1985, Crayon graphite, collage, photomontage et pastel sur calque contrecollé sur papier, 42 × 59.4 cm, Photography: François Lauginie, Collection FRAC Centre, Orléans. Coates' interest is in the representation of wider scales of narrative and living in built environments which morphs into digital collage, reflecting the complexity of competing information and experiential navigation of cities (Coates, 2012). Gamma Tokyo is a composite vision of the metropolis merging Tokyo, Cairo, London, New York, Rome, Mumbai and Rio de Janeiro (Coates *et al.*, 2003). His Ecstacity oeuvre is an imaginary city collaged from multiple spaces, like Calvino's (1974) *Invisible Cities*.

The understanding of rhythms to Lefebvre was vital to our gauging the radical changes affecting everyday life. The grasping of rhythms were vital for societal change and move towards the right to the city – changing ourselves to change our city (Lefebvre, 2010; Harvey, 2013).

Such *avant garde* work was not produced in isolation, but built upon a rich history of commentary on urban experience and walking. For example, the Swiss sociologist Lucius Burckhardt developed a method called strollology which examined sequences in which a person perceives his surroundings. Burckhardt sees strollology and the perception of environment as a unique filter through which to discard our cultural baggage. Strollology is a method of walking to raise environmental perception which can inform planning and design. The walk synthesises a range of impressions in the mind; there is no single image (Burckhardt, 2015, pp. 288–294). Burckhardt emphasised the totality of landscape; it has no beginning, it is not a single entity:

> For landscape is to be found not in the nature of things but in our mind's eye; it is a construct that serves as a means of perception for any society that no longer lives directly from the land.
>
> (Burckhardt, 2015, p. 19)

In some cases Burckhardt is correct. Certain picturesque views or way-marks repeat themselves in tourism, and careful framing of these views is undertaken by the tourist armed with a camera; even if the 'picturesque spot' is laden with artificial waste, those imperfections are often edited out to retain this idealised landscape experience. These aesthetic issues are heavily discussed in the field of environmental aesthetics (Berleant, 1995; Porteous, 1996; Carlson, 2002). Strollogy creates a sequential movement that shows through the act of walking the incoherence of places, their landscapes and architecture. The process demonstrated the cacophony of design voices, the incoherence of places and, more importantly, the main question: what is the experience of landscape?

Like Burckhardt, the American landscape architect Lawrence Halprin conducted practical community exercises to gather the participant's perceptions of space. Halprin sought to integrate these movements through the use of notation, and these results featured in a wider framework for design development and landscape practice – the RSVP cycles. Halprin developed a series of symbols that convey bodily movement in space with reference to a map, as well as developing a way to record the perception of the individual making the drawing. Halprin's research of dance and musical scores as a symbol of process, of activity – developed with his wife, the choreographer Anna Halprin – analysed the non-static. This mode of working allowed participants to explore their environmental perceptions and to evaluate as a group common elements, whether human, natural or man-made. The system was called 'motation' – movement notation was a small practical exercise in a wider programme of involving community, editing results and developing design proposals. Motation was not a flawless method and there were many issues in delivery, as Alison Hirsh has discussed (Hirsch, 2014). The ability to curate views as the workshop leader can damage what can be a democratic process. This view stems from the author's experience of delivering Motation workshops. Burckhardt and Halprin viewed walking as a unique tool for spatial understanding, just as the Situationists – Cullen, Lynch and many others – have incorporated in their design works.

For Randolph Hester, the landscape architect and sociologist, drawing is but part of a process of 'representational acts of representation'. Hester uses drawing and scores for an ecological democracy, 'representative representation',[6] which is termed 'government by people', emphasising direct, hands-on involvement. Drawing and scores are used by Hester towards creating actions guided by understanding of natural systems and social relations locally, as well as wider structures (Hester 1984, 2010, 2012).

FIGURE 2.8 (*above and facing page*) SWA, Jeffrey Open Space Trail. Schematic landscape diagram of the trail, illustrating the 'woodsy' aspect of the park design, and ground plane diagram illustrating trail layout, land form, planting and drainage. This diagram was part of the results of a series of consultation workshops with residents to arrive at the identification of key elements which then led to a consensus plan.

When Hester was asked to become a community designer for Manteo, North Carolina, Manteo faced deep issues with a freeway that bypassed the community (Seamon, 1993). Hester worked with the community through workshops and walking tours to identify what he calls 'sacred spaces', which is the identification of important social patterns and areas. The results were collated into the drawing. There are those places which are protected by law and those places which the public hold as important in their everyday lives; these places are termed 'sacred'. These areas were not just monuments, but more localised places such as post offices, grocery stores or libraries. To address unconscious feeling of place by the residents, Hester conducted behavioural mappings and collated the sketches, giving a cultural mosaic. Hester notes that 'daily ritual was place specific, and the cultural dependence on places seemed more widespread than people had reported' (Seamon, 1993, p. 273). These results were then advertised in newspapers to residents and the residents were asked to rank the more important or sacred and return the survey. Thus, the information could be used to feed planning and design responses for the re-invigoration and metamorphosis of the community. What Hester develops through the 'sacred spaces' process is a phenomenological and ecological process for landscape. In comparison to Halprin, Hester's work develops design activities conducive to wider goals of ecological democracy, and interactive with societies at large, and fits with the general

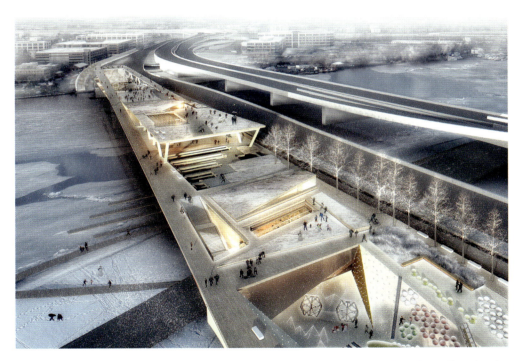

FIGURE 2.9 Olin Studio, the 11th Street Bridge Park Equitable Development Task Force. Ensuring the new 11th Street Bridge Park will be a driver of inclusive development, OLIN & OMA have established an Equitable Development Task Force to provide opportunities for all residents in neighbourhoods surrounding the Bridge Park regardless of income and demography.

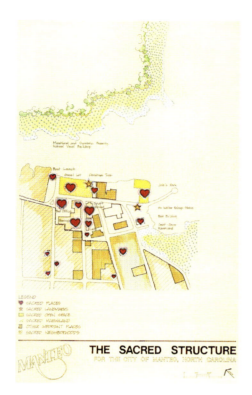

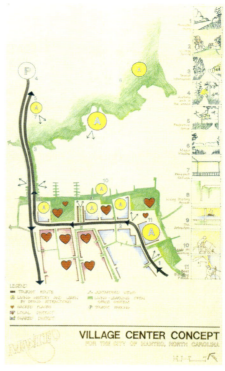

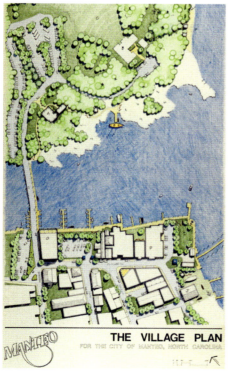

FIGURE 2.10 Randolph Hester, Manteo, North Carolina, Sacred Structure, Concept Plan and Village Plan, 1981–1982; courtesy of Randolph Hester. Manteo faced several urban challenges and Hester articulated the cherished aspects of community life through interviews and behaviour mapping. Within this consultation, areas that were to be protected and areas to be changed were mapped; some of these areas were 'sacred spaces' – landscapes and spaces of everyday life and rituals. These sacred spaces were mapped to a concept plan, of areas in which development would take place resulting in a village plan with open shopfronts, enhancement of fishing industries and support of craft industries (Hester, 2010, pp. 116–135).

NOTATION AND DIAGRAMS

theory of Henri Lefebvre of creating a 'right to the city' (Lefebvre, 1991), of inclusive democratic shaping of urban centres and the research of everyday life. The possibilities for urban scoring have real applicability in addressing landscape architectural representation interested in multiplicity, embodiment and agency.

Landscape fieldwork does not reduce down to perceptive elements. However, the importance of the perceptual experience, as well as decoding of social meanings of landscape, cannot be understated. This area of work has defined the practice of landscape architecture more than any other avenue. Juhani Pallasmaa suggests that there is hegemony of the image which has led to a displacement with other senses, resulting in a loss of realness. Searching for the sense of the real, Pallasmaa cites haptics as an important resource for architecture, given this hegemony (Pallasmaa, 2009, 2011). These perceptive studies derive from competing philosophies such as Maurice Merleau-Ponty, who was a phenomenologist[7] who wrote about perceptions and experiences of places, their materiality and their atmosphere, influencing Dalibor Vesely (2006), Christian Norberg-Schulz (1980) and Alberto Pérez-Gómez (2000), among others, who all seek to understand uniqueness of places and experience as well as their revulsion.

While the practitioner may find this chapter slightly fragmented and highly theoretical, more simply the landscape architect in community consultation must reflect on the social meaning of the landscape. This social meaning is explored by Halprin and Burckhardt in different modes, as well as by Cullen, Appleton, the Kaplans and the Situationists, along with many others. Some landscape architects continue to pay lip service to this work stage, to the detriment of the design. The different searches and research for meaning of landscape and urban settings from all of the mentioned practitioner devolved from an urgent recognition of changes in city development, each with different political goals and with specific geographical challenges. Nonetheless, understanding of human experience of landscape remains a compelling area of work for landscape architecture with an appetite for new strategies to enable this.

Two new technological drivers continue this area of enquiry; inventions such as eye-tracking devices, which can be used to map environmental perceptions, with heat maps showing high and lower areas of interest. With increasing availability and lower costs, the technology provides a novel solution to students and landscape architects. However, the tracking technology requires a rigorous survey approach to gain useful insights. Quality of photographs, sample study size, ethnicities and backgrounds can make these exercises difficult to execute and coordinate. Eye tracking may also be used to draw challenging relationships between the analogue and digital dichotomy. It may simply function as a tool for field sketching and annotation.

In addition to eye-tracking technology, augmented reality (AR) systems allow a decoding of site features but are used also as a tool to create composites of proposed designs with ever-increasing fidelity and ease of use. AR systems allow several other

FIGURE 2.11 Magic Leap, Augmented Weather System, 2015. Magic Leap develops AR and VR technology as a natural function of human biology, physiology, creativity and community. Inventing hardware and software for a visceral experience.

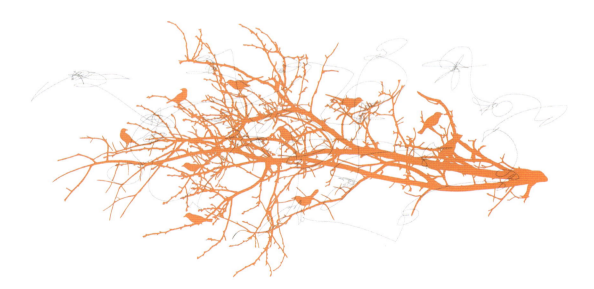

FIGURE 2.12 Michel Paysant, *Eye Drawing*. Paysant writes with his eyes at more or less the same speed as his hand. Jean Lorenceau, CNRS researcher at the Centre de Recherche de l'Institut du Cerveau et de la Moelle Epinière (CNRS/UPMC/Inserm), developed the eye drawing device to record smooth transitions to enable people with limb paralysis to write (Lorenceau, 2012).

FIGURE 2.13 Lien Dupont, eye tracking in landscape perception research. Recently, eye tracking has been demonstrated to be a very useful technology for conducting landscape perception research. It is a technique that can measure eye movements and fixations made by an observer and thus can reveal how people observe landscapes. 'The results indicate that the observation pattern appears to be affected by the way the landscape is represented (photograph type), the background of the observer (landscape experts vs. novices) and the features of the landscape itself (degree of openness, complexity, urbanisation of the landscape). Derived products, like saliency maps (image-based predictions of the viewing pattern), can be used for visual impact assessments of new buildings and constructions' (Dupont *et al.*, 2013).

data layers to be viewed. They also allow a first-person viewpoint of unmanned aerial vehicles (UAVs) and drone piloting, allowing a visually immersive experience when completing a map survey (Chapter 1). However, many AR systems have exaggerated their abilities to retain prominent positions as a technological driver in professions within the built environment. Various AR helmets are in development and some commercial releases have taken place, with an emphasis on gaming systems. Some AR systems have integrated eye tracking and these devices are starting to gel with other developments such as 4D GIS and interactive systems of cities, architecture and landscape. In practice terms a simple cardboard device, Google Cardboard, with an eye frame on which to mount a smartphone, runs AR applications for less than $10, making a basic AR system deliverable in community consultation and fieldwork. This technological driver has been in place for a number of years, meaning students and practitioners do not necessarily have to develop applications from scratch. These two drivers, eye tracking and AR, both continue the investigations of our relationship with perceiving places as well the creation of meanings from them.

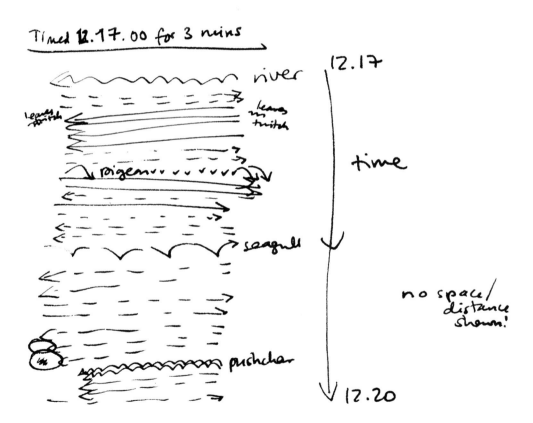

FIGURE 2.14 Isabel Griffiths, Representation of Movement on a Site Over Time. The sketch attempts to note the different forms and speeds of movement observed in a specific location in Bahnhofstrasse, Lucerne, Switzerland. They illustrate the difficulties of recording both the temporal sequence and spatial character of those forms of movement in one drawing.

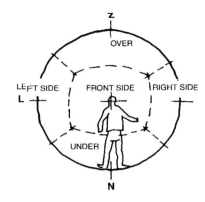

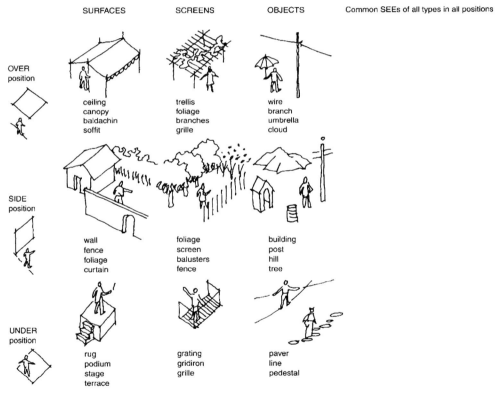

FIGURE 2.15 Phillip Thiel, People, Paths, Purposes (Thiel, 1981, 1996). Focusing on eye-level perceptions and movements of users. Thiel developed a system of notation to describe the environment which in turn would be used in the design process to reshape that space.

DIAGRAMS OF LANDSCAPE

The diagram is an abstracted and edited result of a thought process presented in visual form; the role of the diagram in fieldwork and participation cannot be overestimated. The diagram is an image of a visual agency at work influencing a design outcome. Often the diagram remains part of an internal development process, hidden in student sketchbooks or coffee-stained practice notebooks. The diagram may change after revision and testing to a presentation stage. The limits of diagrams in recording landscape are clear, given a landscape's rich phenomenological experience, as Bowring and Swaffield (2010) have commented. In representational terms the landscape diagram is democratic; it is advantageous over complex maps and high-fidelity data (Chapter 1) or composite perspectives that are often simulacra (Chapter 3).

Representation goes beyond graphic thinking (visualisation), though graphic thinking is as much mixed in the agency of representation as a vehicle for the representation of psychological, social and political meanings and ideas of things. The vitality of the diagram is not its graphic seduction, but its humbleness to carry and transmit a simple selection of ideas. This economy (Ockham's razor) of information design can potentially work for wider audiences. As Phillip Thiel states on visual communication: 'it is broadcast and received and in that it uses a code or language which has to be intelligible to the reader' (Thiel, 1981, p. 11).

DIAGRAM TYPES

The following diagram types involve a number of fieldwork strategies. These strategies can be derived from a base map or plan, or formed without scale. Information diagrams may be layered digitally or drawn on layout/trace paper. The diagrams may not necessarily be highly detailed; the more immediate the diagram, the quicker it is to overlay the diagram with another thought or development. The use of diagrams allows the refinement and organisation of a design across a period of time, which is known as phasing. The diagram can also go beyond the period of phasing.

Commonly, diagrams in their most basic application are used to record the following, among other things.

- **Site access**: entry routes for contractors during construction, and public paths and entry points.
- **Edges**: site boundaries, zone edges, hardscape edging etc.
- **Grades**: elevation changes and the increment between, as well as new, grading proposals.
- **Circulation**: the intended movement of the users in the space.
- **Configuration**: the position and sizing of soft and hard elements such as trees and urban furniture.

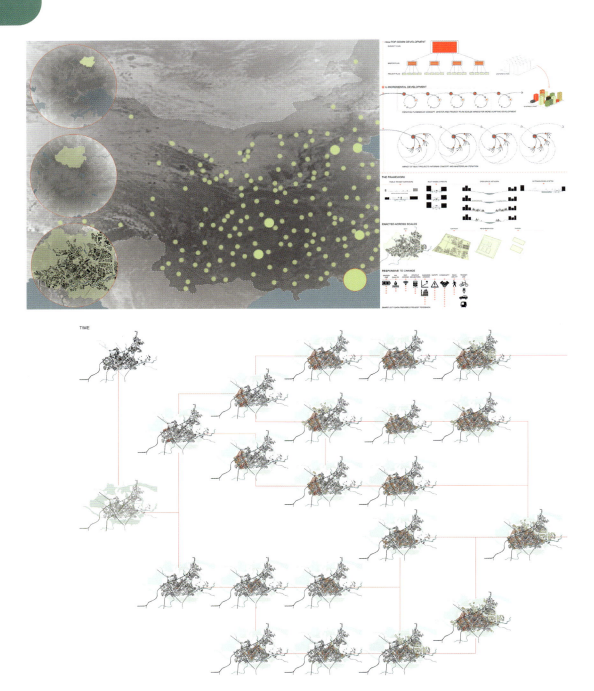

FIGURE 2.16 Johanna Hoffman and Karl Kullmann, Incremental Development, UC Berkeley, 2015. A planning and design framework that pushes for large-scale change with small-scale steps, incremental development has the potential to make the creative and spontaneous a key foundation of modern new town urban growth. Devised through literature reviews and precedent analysis of existing urban examples, the concept eschews the current new town focus on building entire cities from scratch in favour of enacting large-scale change with small-scale steps.

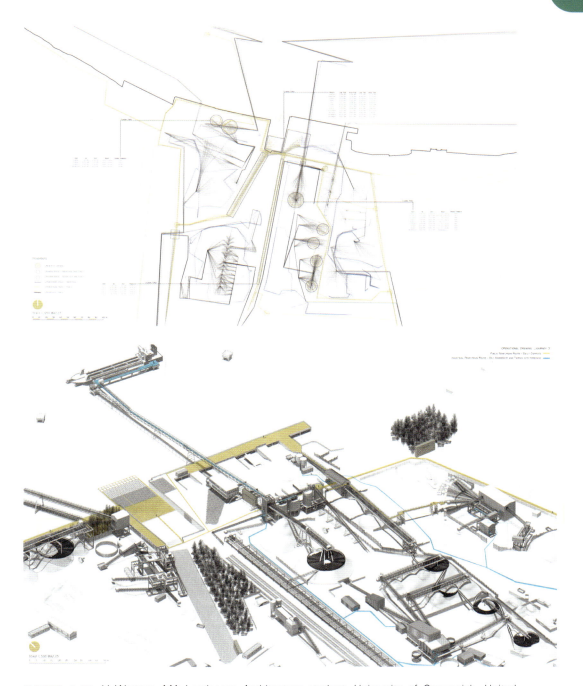

FIGURE 2.17 JJ Watters, MA Landscape Architecture student, University of Greenwich, United Kingdom, 2015. JJ Watters maps movement conditions integrating public space and an active industrial processing plant.

NOTATION AND DIAGRAMS

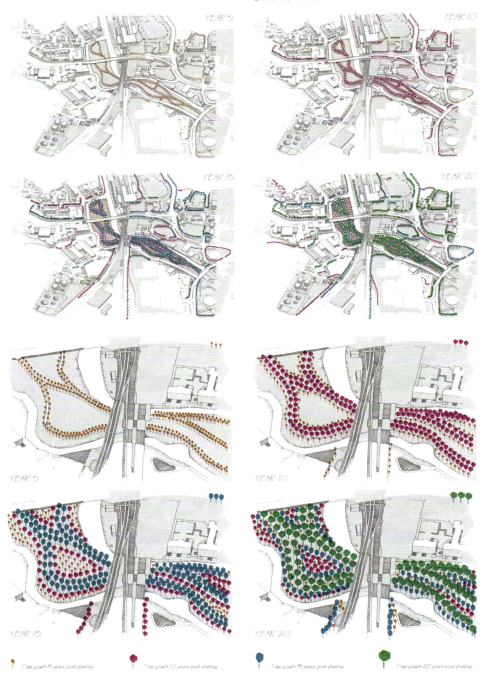

FIGURE 2.18 Sophie Parker-Loftus, Footmeadow Urban Island Park Tree Strategy, Northampton, United Kingdom, 2016. Parker-Loftus utilises traditional landscape architecture diagrams, with inventory modes of working, creating a bird's eye view line base to which tree growth is projected at site and wider planning scale.

However, these diagramming types can also limit the dialogue that the drawing of diagrams provides. Creating a focal point diagram, for example, can disrupt the evolution of a design; they may lock ideas into place and create a static picturesque sequence in which certain views are experienced. The diagram may provide a false sense of satisfaction that sufficient analysis has been undertaken, that locks the conceptual base and structure of thought. Likewise, circulation diagrams are often the most disingenuous of all diagramming types, assuming paths of the users. More often than not, the desire line/path shows the true path used after production, with users often cutting through areas or creating their own urban paths. Diagrams have the potential to abstract and represent perceptions from fieldwork as well as democratise the design process, but can also entrench a singular mode of working. To mitigate this entrenchment, diagrams should be considered as fleeting ideas that are fluid, editable and act as artefacts in the recording of time in the landscape, and signpost future landscape design. It may be an uncomfortable term, but diagrams are metaphors of ideas, actions and places. The diagram infers an idea, and it does so to a high degree. Thus, diagramming in landscape architecture if fundamental for abstract thought and describing landscape complexity through a simple set of symbols. They are signals of a deeper evolving complexity, as the draughtsman Oliver Regan states (pre-empting the contemporary resurgence and interest in haptics) in *Pencil Points: Journal of the Draughting Room*, it is desirable to acquire 'an acute sense of the feel of his pen or pencil on the paper, a delicacy of touch that is not unlike that of the skilled surgeon who is said to be able to almost "see" with his fingertips' (Hartman and Cigliano, 2004, pp. 6–7). Regan, here, views the drawing as metaphorical, being the same as its unrelated thing, the landscape. As long as this suggested metaphorical aim is considered and the drawing maintains a connection with the phenomenology of our environment, diagramming can become a rich source of landscape representation and strategy.

Pragmatically diagramming should be considered to include a number of interrelated layers. Some of these layer types are listed below, though the list is not exhaustive. Please refer to the companion website for instruction and tutorials for diagramming.

Figure ground. Actually derived from a map, a figure ground diagram separates into black and white the built and unbuilt form. It is a diagrammatic abstraction of space. It was invented by Giambattista Nolli when mapping Rome in 1748. It is used in planning terms primarily; the diagram can be reversed, which can give emphasis to the surrounding space (Gibberd, 1955).

Site inventory diagram. This diagramming type is more conventional and rests on the recording of existing layout and existing elements; however, the diagram contains personal design assumptions such as what can be repurposed, what is restricting or what gives identity.

Response diagrams. These are diagrams that result from a continuing thought process in relation to a site visit. They may be created in isolation or be linked to maps or other representational types.

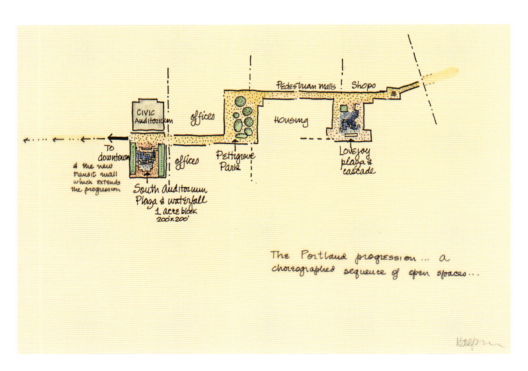

The Portland progression... a choreographed sequence of open spaces...

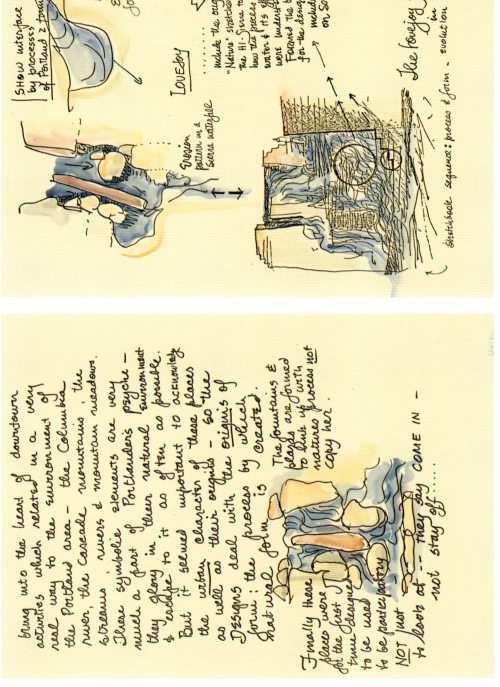

FIGURE 2.19 Lawrence Halprin, Portland Open Sequence, c.1960s. Published in the Sketchbooks of Lawrence Halprin, 62 (Halprin, 1986). Lawrence Halprin Collection, The Architectural Archives, University of Pennsylvania. The Portland sequence was intended to be a transition between spaces on foot through a long block sequence, and the journey between each area of retail, of park space, was intended to be punctured, a sort of rhythm was scored for Halprin's design.

Pattern diagrams. These were developed by Christopher Alexander; this diagram seeks patterns in our environment in the assemblage of a complex typology which can be used to evaluate appropriate design responses (Alexander, 1978, 1980).

Movement diagrams. These diagrams rely on a symbol system to convey movement. This could be a gradient map, line weight or a mixture of each. Philip Thiel's notation is one approach to understanding people's movement in space (Thiel, 1996).

Visual field diagram. This diagram abstracts the visual perception of a place in order to create a material typology of the environs. Similar to a perspective drawing, the view is reduced to summaries of the site's sets of materials.

Phase diagram. A phase diagram can signify the stages of production of a design and the order in which work will commence, and relates to a setting out drawing, which provides specific coordinates on the site with major works.

Planting diagrams. The planting diagram is the most temporal of the diagramming types and can be developed beyond a design, build, maintenance and deficit period of a landscape design. Planting diagrams may see the landscape over a much longer timeline, as continual succession, attempting to perceive the process of change in the species and structure of an ecological community over much longer periods (Wöhrle, 2008). Moreover, the diagram may describe existing planting and be used as a mode of understanding site conditions such as drainage, soils and sun paths.

The creative and practical aspects of diagramming and their vital role in visual communication is especially useful in relation to fieldwork; they provide an immediacy that very few other forms of visual representation provide.

MOVEMENT NOTATION

Movement notation as devised by Lawrence Halprin has been reinterpreted into digital form. Motation consist of a score sheet influenced by Laban notation and work produced by Lawrence's wife, the dancer and choreographer Anna Halprin. Motation is an activity that would form one resource as part of the RSVP cycles (see below; Halprin, 1982). You may access the score sheet and symbol sheet used in this exercise on the companion website.

> Since movement and the complex interrelations which it generates are an essential part of the life of a city, urban design should have the choice of starting from movement as the core – the essential element of the plan. Only after programming the movement and graphically expressing it, should the environment, an envelope within which movement takes place – be designed. The environment exists for the purpose of movement.
>
> (Halprin, 1963, pp. 208–209)

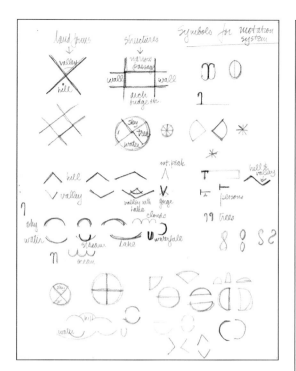

FIGURE 2.20A Notes on a Notation System, University of California, Berkeley, graduate seminar, November – December 1964. Courtesy of the Lawrence Halprin Collection, The Architectural Archives, University of Pennsylvania. See also Halprin (1965).

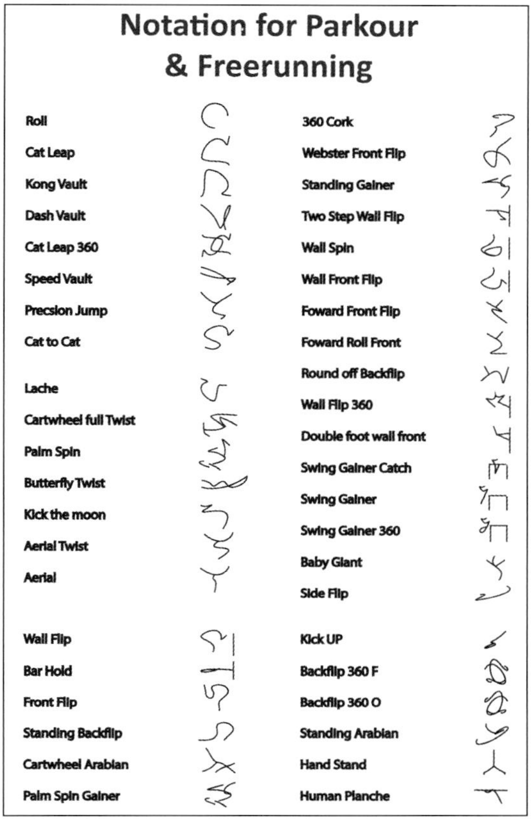

FIGURE 2.20B Paul Cureton, Parkour Symbol System, 2014. An investigation of parkour and freerunning to establish direct paths (Lines) first involved the creation of a symbol system to describe the various movements of free-runners tracing direct routes and a typology of moves.

Motation records the user's perception of a space through a movement sequence and is recorded using a pre-established symbol system. While remaining a largely historical mode, scores still have value in that participants' perceptions of the places are heightened through the process. The value in Motation is that as each user conducts a study the results can be compared and evaluated to find significant and perceived landscape and urban form.

> His scores choreographed the body to respond to the 'sensuous environment' with heightened perceptual awareness.
>
> (Hirsch, 2014, p. 139).

Movism, AR, eye tracking and other systems all aim to highlight landscape, sequence it and decode its significant finds. Motation is just as cognitive, though must be executed carefully. As Hirsh asserts, there is significant possibility and evidence of manipulation of the results.

NOTATION AND DIAGRAMS   89

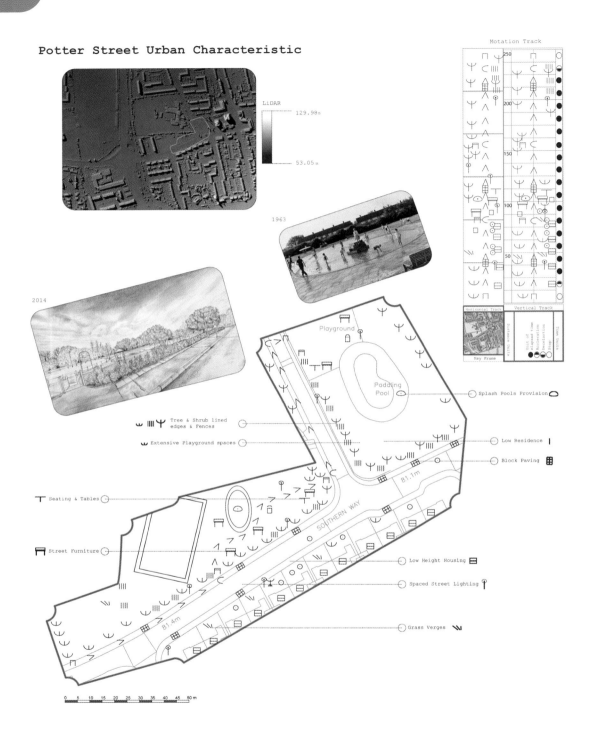

FIGURE 2.21 Paul Cureton, Motation Score Sheet after Lawrence Halprin, 2014. Here a prescribed Motation sequence has been completed and mapped in CAD plan, and the overriding and repetitive features extracted to provide an overall urban perceptual form.

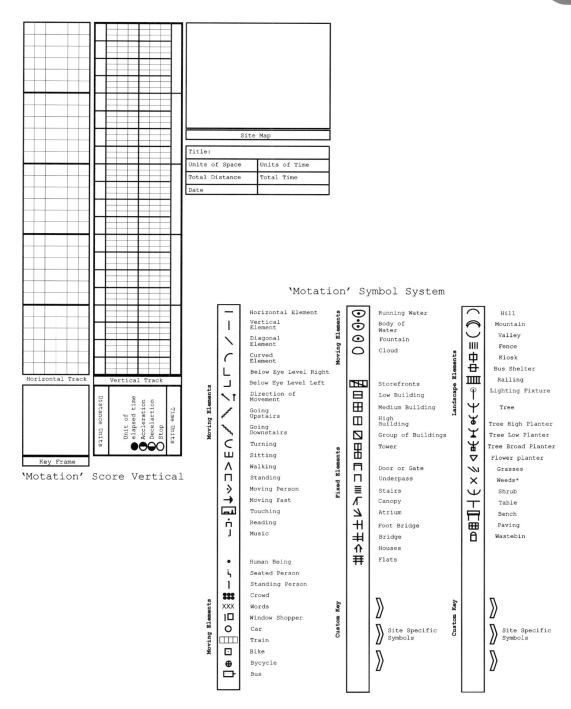

FIGURE 2.22 Paul Cureton, Motation Score Sheet after Lawrence Halprin, Details, 2014. See also Premjit Talwar (1972), *Notation in Architecture*, for a student interpretation of notation systems.

NOTATION AND DIAGRAMS

Users have a score sheet (a blank music sheet) and a symbol system is provided. The briefing of participants must be carefully led, giving some indicator of the purpose of the workshop (**R**). The symbol system used to record environmental perception requires some learning, though participants may also input their own symbols. The score sheet also requires some instruction, given that the horizontal and vertical movements are divided and run concurrently. A test exercise is useful, providing a test walk and prescribed route. The route design can be open or closed and the route may also incorporate a number of set nodes, questions and activities, as Halprin often did with set times and the final meeting place.

UNDERSTANDING MOTATION

A horizontal track on the left side records the horizontal plane of movement and changes of direction and records other mobile elements in a number of large frames. The process starts at the bottom of the page, moving upwards as the arrow shows (**S**). The score sheet can also be created in landscape format.

This relates to a track on the right side that records the vertical plane, composed of smaller frames; it records the visual horizon 'which we see ahead as we ride or walk' (Halprin, 1972, p. 130). Here, a walk is recorded at each frame and railings, shrubs and trees are seen to the right and apartments to the left as the walk progresses. This track is divided into two, to record the left and right experiences respectively; the line between the boxes symbolises your movement.

Two additional strips are located either side of this vertical track. One indicates distances and one indicates time. In these strips other climatic elements and sounds are also recorded. The closer the dot symbols used in the time strip, the slower the movement. Breaks in dots indicate a change in movement, irregularity indicates change of pace. To the side of the score sheet are a block indicating title, total distance, time and date. The symbols used in the score sheet consist of various moving (fountain, bike, car) and still objects (building or tree) and directional notations (above/below eye level). For example, in the vertical track the use of a diagonal symbol and its angle indicates a slope and its degree. Additional symbols such as landscape features can of course be added and customised. Motation thus provides scoring processes of the 3D-ness of a body moving in space and raises perceptual experience. It provides a layer of data of the perceptive and visceral observations of the participants moving through space (**V**). The evaluation of these results relies on the participants comparing results and evaluating the significant elements of the place, similar to Kevin Lynch (1960). Thus, what are the repeating symbol elements from each participant? What are the differences? What are the significant findings? How did they find the exercise and how does this reflect their own values? Often, participants notice how insulated their normal mode of movement is. This evaluative and performative stage defines further action, provides a pluralism and openness and communicates rhythm, time, spaces and people (**P**).

SUMMARY

Social time and movement are vital to understanding the nature of the landscape. The emphasis is not on environmental preference or establishment of hierarchy, but because these areas of enquiry are often 'soft' data. However, the nature of the perception of landscape is fraught with issues, modes and methods. Landscape architectural representation, if seen in a timeline, evidences the continual struggle for the creation of individual and social meanings of places. It is all the profession has as its main aim. The technological drivers from other disciplines, which have been incorporated, are useful in the continual development of achieving this aim. Fieldwork requires a personal response, but also one conducted using established methodologies and by reference to legislation. The diagram has a unique relationship with site visits as it has an unrivalled immediacy and can function as a transparent tool of design thinking. Diagrams can also be used to continually monitor change in the landscape; the time-based possibilities alongside maps and photographs cannot be underestimated. Time, duration and rhythm in landscape are difficult notions to grasp and represent. Moreover, this difficulty is most evident in landscape composites where free collaging from a variety of sources, image banks and archives create some of the most static and least descriptive representations of landscapes. Chapter 3 seeks to explore time in landscape with reference to composites and explore a number of strategies to change this dominant paradigm.

NOTES

1. A system of recording semi-natural vegetation and wildlife habitats in the UK. The system uses specific names, numeric codes and unique mapping colours and symbols. See JNCC (2010).
2. Landscape Workstages in the UK: A/B: inception and feasibility; C: outline; D: sketch; E: detailed; F/G: production/tender action; H/J: contract preparation; K: site operations; L: completion. There are also separate services and lists for specialist functions. These stages are very similar to the Royal Institute of British Architects Plan of Work, which goes through the following stages: 0: strategic definition; 1: preparation and brief; 2: concept design; 3: developed design; 4: technical design; 5: construction; 6: handover and close out; 7: in use. See www.ribaplanofwork.com/Default.aspx
3. It shows how a stimulus is activated through images and references, the 'emotion pool', which then activates emotional symptoms ('tears', 'rapid heart' [beat], 'sweat') through the nervous system. This drawing is associated with a text in which he wrote about the 'school of thought which identifies aesthetic emotion with [an] echo of sex life', about 'inhibitions' and about 'the energy [that] was sublimated' (Orillard, 2012, p. 722)
4. Playful constructive behaviour and awareness of psychogeographical effects or an unplanned journey through a landscape.
5. This fragmented urban nature condition was further explored by Tschumi and Virilio, among others (Virilio, 2000).
6. By 'representative representation' I refer to the way drawing engages the public through grass-roots democracy for designing open space, neighbourhoods, cities and regions. This requires representing both the public and the landscape. Face-to-face collaborative drawing provides the political representation. Graphic depictions provide what we professionally call 'representing the landscape'. The complex combination gives us a special way of drawing: representative representation (Hester in Treib, 2007, p. 97).
7. The study of experiences of being in the world and our consciousness.

BIBLIOGRAPHY

Alexander, C., 1978. *A Pattern Language: Towns, Buildings, Construction*. Oxford University Press, New York.

Alexander, C., 1980. *The Timeless Way of Building*. Oxford University Press, New York.

Appleton, J., 1987. *Experience of Landscape*, new edition. Hull University Press, Hull.

Berleant, A., 1995. *The Aesthetics of Environment*. Temple University Press, Philadelphia.

Bowring, J. and Swaffield, S., 2010. Diagrams in Landscape Architecture. In M. Garcia (ed.), *The Diagrams of Architecture: AD Reader*. John Wiley & Sons, Chichester, pp. 142–151.

Brewer, J., 2013. *The Pleasures of the Imagination: English Culture in the Eighteenth Century*. Routledge, London.

Burckhardt, L., 2015. *Why is Landscape Beautiful? The Science of Strollology*. Birkhauser, Basel, Switzerland.

Calder, B., 2014. Brutal Enemies? Townscape and the "Hard" Moderns. In J. Pendlebury, E. Ertem and L. Peter (eds), *Alternative Visions of Post-War Reconstruction: Creating the Modern Townscape*. Routledge, London.

Carlson, A., 2002. *Aesthetics and the Environment: The Appreciation of Nature, Art and Architecture*, new edition. Routledge, London.

Coates, N., 2012. *Narrative Architecture*. John Wiley & Sons, Chichester.

Coates, N., Field, M. and Hallon, B., 2003. *A Guide to Ecstacity*. Princeton Architectural Press, New York.

Cullen, G., 1961. *Concise Townscape*, new edition. Routledge, London.

De Certeau, M., 1984. *The Practice of Everyday Life*. University of California Press, Berkeley, CA.

Dreyfuss, H., 1972. *Symbol Sourcebook*. McGraw Hill Higher Education, New York.

Dupont, L., Antrop, M. and van Eetvelde, V., 2013. Eye-Tracking Analysis in Landscape Perception Research: Influence of Photograph Properties and Landscape Characteristics. *Landscape Research*, 39(4): 417–432.

Edgerton, E., Romice, O. and Thwaites, K. (eds), 2014. *Bridging the Boundaries: Human Experience in the Natural and Built Environment and Implications for Research, Policy, and Practice*. Hogrefe Publishing, Toronto.

Foucault, M., 1991. *Discipline and Punish: The Birth of the Prison*. Penguin, London.

Garcia, M., 2010. *The Diagrams of Architecture: AD Reader*. John Wiley & Sons, Chichester.

Gibberd, F., 1955. *Town Design*, 2nd revised edition. Architectural Press, London.

Halprin, L., 1963. *Cities*. Reinhold Publishing Co., New York.

Halprin, L., 1965. Motation. *Progressive Architecture*, 46 (July): pp. 126–33.

Halprin, L., 1972. *Lawrence Halprin Notebooks 1959–1971*. MIT Press, Cambridge, MA.

Halprin, L., 1982. *R.S.V.P. Cycles: Creative Processes in the Human Environment*. George Braziller Inc., New York.

Halprin, L., 1986. *Sketchbooks of Lawrence Halprin*. Intl Specialized Book Service Inc.

Hartman, G. and Cigliano, J., 2004. *Pencil Points Reader: Selected Readings from a Journal for the Drafting Room, 1920–1943*. Princeton Architectural Press, New York.

Harvey, D., 2013. *Rebel Cities: From the Right to the City to the Urban Revolution*, 2nd edition. Verso Books, New York

Hester, R., 1984, *Planning Neighborhood Space with People*. Van Nostrand Reinhold Company, New York.

Hester, R.T., 2010. *Design for Ecological Democracy*. MIT Press, Cambridge, MA.

Hester, R., 2012. Scoring Collective Creativity and Legitimizing Participatory Design. *Landscape Journal*, 31 (1–2): 135–143.

Hirsch, A.B., 2014. *City Choreographer: Lawrence Halprin in Urban Renewal America*. University of Minnesota Press, Minneapolis.

Ingold, P.T. and Vergunst, J.L. (eds), 2008. *Ways of Walking: Ethnography and Practice on Foot*, new edition. Ashgate, Aldershot.

Ingold, T., 2007. *Lines: A Brief History*, new edition. Routledge, London.

JNCC, 2010. *Handbook for Phase 1 Habitat Survey: A Technique for Environmental Audit*. Nature Conservancy Council, Peterborough.

Kaplan, R., 1989. *The Experience of Nature. A Psychological Perspective*. Cambridge University Press, Cambridge.

Kant, I., 1987. *Critique of Judgement*, trans. Pluhar, W.S. Hackett Publishing, Indianapolis, IN.

Knabb, K. (ed.), 2007. *Situationist International Anthology*, revised and expanded edition. Bureau of Public Secrets, Berkeley.

Lefebvre, H., 1991. *The Production of Space*. Wiley-Blackwell, Cambridge, MA.

Lefebvre, H., 2010. *Writings on Cities*. Wiley-Blackwell, Cambridge, MA.

Lefebvre, H., 2013. *Rhythmanalysis: Space, Time and Everyday Life*. Bloomsbury Academic, New York.

Lorenceau, J., 2012. Cursive Writing with Smooth Pursuit Eye Movements. *Current Biology*, 22: 1506–1509. doi: 10.1016/j.cub.2012.06.026.

Lucas, R., 2008. Taking a Line for a Walk: Flânerie, Drifts, and the Artistic Potential of Urban Wandering. In Ingold, T. and Lee Vergunst, J. (eds), *Ways of Walking: Ethnography and Practice on Foot*. Ashgate, Aldershot.

Lucas, R., 2009. Designing a Notation for the Senses. *Architectural Theory Review Special Issue: Sensory Urbanism*, 14 (2): 173.

Lucas, R. and Romice, O. 2008. Representing Sensory Experience in Urban Design. *Design Principles and Practices: An International Journal*, 2 (4): 83–94.

Lynch, K., 1960. *The Image of the City*. MIT Press, Cambridge, MA.

Lynch, K. 1976, *What Time is This Place?* MIT Press, Cambridge, MA.

Mcdonough, T., 2004. *Guy Debord and the Situationist International: Texts and Documents*, new edition. MIT Press, Cambridge, MA.

Norberg-Schulz, C., 1980. *Genius Loci: Towards a Phenomenology of Architecture*, new edition. Rizzoli International Publications, New York.

Pallasmaa, J., 2009. *The Thinking Hand*. John Wiley & Sons, Chichester.

Pallasmaa, J., 2011. *The Embodied Image: Imagination and Imagery in Architecture*. John Wiley & Sons, Chichester.

Pérez-Gómez, A., 2000. *Architectural Representation and the Perspective Hinge*, new edition. MIT Press, Cambridge, MA.

Porteous, J.D., 1996. *Environmental Aesthetics: Ideas, Politics and Planning*. Routledge, London.

Rowe, C. and Koetter, F., 1978. *Collage City*, new edition. MIT Press, Cambridge, MA.

Sadler, S., 1999. *The Situationist City*, new edition. MIT Press, Cambridge, MA.

Schultz, H., 2014. Designing Large-Scale Landscapes Through Walking. *Journal of Landscape and Architecture*, 9: 6–15. doi: 10.1080/18626033.2014.931694

Seamon, D. (ed.), 1993. *Dwelling, Seeing, and Designing: Toward a Phenomenological Ecology*. State University of New York Press, Albany.

Thiel, P., 1981. *Visual Awareness and Design*. University of Washington Press, Seattle.

Thiel, P., 1996. *People, Paths, and Purposes: Notations for a Participatory Envirotecture*. University of Washington Press, Seattle.

Thwaites, K. and Simkins, I.M., 2006. *Experiential Landscape: An Approach to People, Place and Space*. Routledge, London.

Thwaites, K., Mathers, A. and Simkins, I., 2013. *Socially Restorative Urbanism: The Theory, Process and Practice of Experiemics*. Routledge, London.

Vesely, D., 2006. *Architecture in the Age of Divided Representation: The Question of Creativity in the Shadow of Production*, new edition. MIT Press, Cambridge, MA.

Virilio, P., 2000. *A Landscape of Events*. MIT Press, Cambridge, MA.

Wöhrle, R.E., 2008. *Basics Designing with Plants*. Birkhäuser GmbH, Basel.

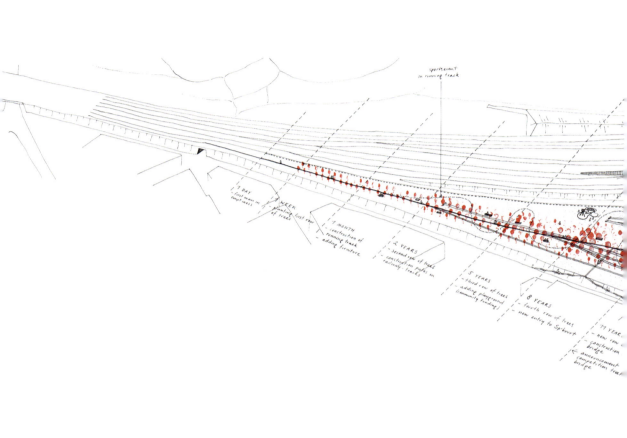

FIGURE 3.1 Valentina Chimento, Hannah Schubert, Astrid Bennik, Time Drawing of Westerpark, Drawing Time Now; Workshop, co-ordinator Noël van Dooren, David Kloet, 2013. Time-drawing of Westerpark in which every section resembles a development phase. In Westerpark, the park grows not only spatially but also in richness and dynamics through plant succession.

3
TIME IN LANDSCAPE (COMPOSITES)

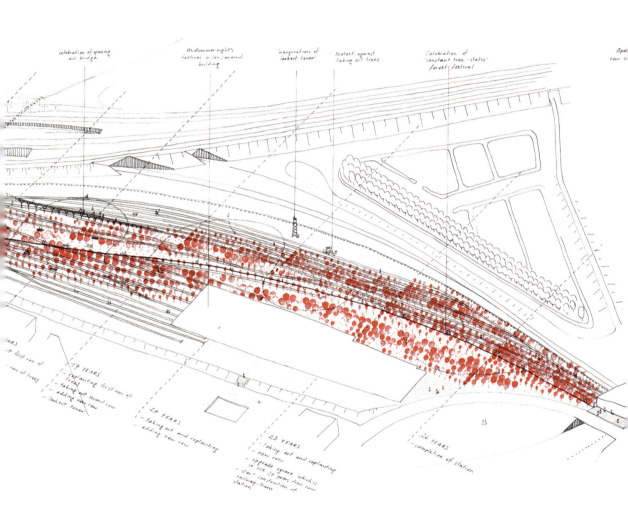

> A sense of place is something that we ourselves create in the course of time. It is the result of habit or custom.
>
> (Jackson, 1994, p. 151)

The relationship between landscape design representation and the everyday experience of spaces is sometimes located on two completely different vectors, and we have seen some of the difficulties in organising fieldwork in response to this in the previous chapter. This poses the question about methods from design professionals where this 'experience' can be incorporated within the scope of landscape architectural representation and environmental assessment. J.B. Jackson's numerous works are important in the observation of the vernacular, but moreover should be read as time-based studies of landscape complexity.

Such an interest in mapping time in landscape reflects the paradoxical processes in which the landscape architect's role is to define space and thus identify cultural sensibilities at play in that moment of commission, in initial design and at an appraisal or evaluative stage. Another part of this paradox is that there is no permanence to landscape; the human relationship with landscape is testimony to this effect. Such problems of scoping the landscape and the lived, and the repetitive experience of inhabitants utilising landscape, can be understood working from ideas of Michel De Certeau, who discusses heterogeneous spaces. For De Certeau places are deemed as fixed locales and spaces are constituted of polyvalent (sometimes conflictual) practices of its inhabitants (De Certeau, 1984). Thus, the relationship between designed place and representation and spatial uses is a highly complex research enquiry involving heritage and history.

FIGURE 3.2 Taktyk, Meirama Mine Trypitch, Phasing 2010, 2030, 2050. Taktyk propose radical phasing for a brown lignite mine in north-west Spain. Part of the restoration involves flooding the mine pit and extensive restoration (Jarvie-Eggart, 2015, pp. 497–498).

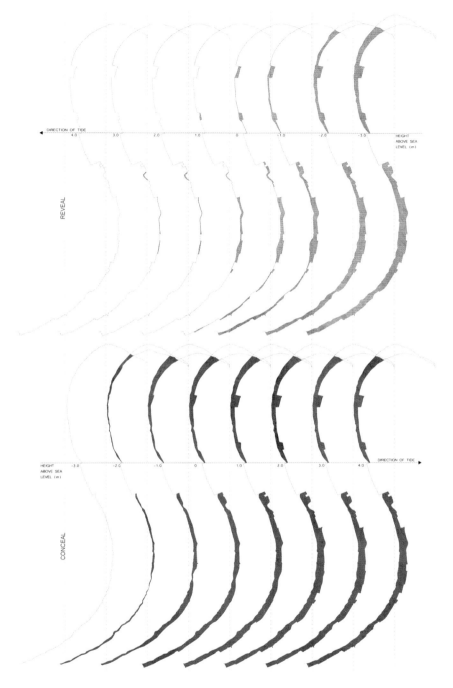

PROCESS DRAWING

FIGURE 3.3 Iona Meldrum, MA Landscape Architecture Student, University of Greenwich. Process Drawing of Tidal Movements, Greenwich Peninsula. Meldrum creates tidal studies of water movements to inform a masterplan utilising the forms and levels for the shorefront of the Greenwich Peninsula.

TIME IN LANDSCAPE

We create abstract concepts of time of duration measured and monitored through mechanical means of clocks; this abstract time concept is mapped to landscape in an attempt to gauge landscape change. Change in landscape may occur beyond a lifetime, or it may be immediate; the ecological principle of succession and climax is a prime example of a natural period of change beyond a human life. These two time-based problems are intertwined. Agnes Denes sees time as intangible, a 'continuous, measurable duration in which events take place whose succession is unidirectional and seem to be pointing to the future' (Denes, 2008, p. 58). This reflects Sonja Duempelmann and Susan Herrington's observation that landscape is measured in what they call 'divided' time in terms of season, a sort of chunked time, and also a seamless continuum (Duempelmann and Herrington, 2014, p. 1). This position arises from our cultures and the interaction with the land form itself. Some may argue that this time is not present in the wilderness, where divided time is less prevalent and more difficult to observe, though there is little wilderness left in the world. Geographers thus cite cultural landscapes as the actual type of place in discussion (Muir, 2000; Cosgrove, 2012). Then perhaps landscape reflects our ideas and our working with it. This could be understood through the most primary form of landscape design, the earthwork (Muir, 1999, pp. 51–60). The earthwork as a design form is particularly telling of cultural and religious societal beliefs. The unending research question, then, is what are the subtly complex stories of everyday spatial practices in landscape and the landscape form sculpted by such action?

FIGURE 3.4 Mark Klett and Byron Wolfe, Panorama from Point Sublime, 2007. Digital inkjet print. Dimensions: 24" × 96". Details from the view at Point Sublime on the north rim of the Grand Canyon, based on the panoramic drawing by William Henry Holmes, 1882. Sheets XV, XVI, XVII. Panorama of Point Sublime. From Clarence Dutton, Atlas to Accompany the Monograph on the Tertiary History of the Grand Cañon District (courtesy of the Library of Congress). Utilising a triptych drawing of a panorama of

Interactions between people and the physical environment are complex, some having anthropocentric, biocentric and egocentric preferences. Landscape design may create an immediate space within its time zone; its site management contracts are thus of critical importance in retaining the design ideas implemented. Time in landscape is fundamentally at odds with capital transactions; it has no immediate tangible economic value. However, recent changes in economic theory and urban governance attach economics and places in the idea of systems of cities, and this may change the relationship of landscape, design and time. Stewart Pickett (2012) suggests an ecological landscape and metaphoric mode, a metaphor, an implied comparison that ecology has a significant and comparable role to play with urban design. Landscape architecture utilising a time-based approach may be metaphorical in practice. Without that metaphorical approach, there is not an implied comparison, there is only landscape design that is clinical, singular and isolated from its surrounds. Heterogeneity is then an important concept for designers to consider the diverse character of place and diversity of spatial practices.

Working with such complexity and the representation of time in landscape has generated a number of approaches. However, repeat photography, first used as a method of recording glacial movement and retreat, is a cost-effective mode of recording land dynamics and shifts (Webb *et al.*, 2010, pp. 60–76). The process involves multiple shoots from the same vantage point. Such a process feeds future photography

the Grand Canyon by Holmes, Kleet and Wolfe use photographs to remap the canyon space inside the drawing frame, mapping fixed and transient feature details from the photographers' own experiences of surveying the site. Kleet and Wolfe term this 'historic mashup' using a consistent geographic space to connect things at different periods of time (Senf, 2012, pp. 29–30).

FIGURE 3.5 Denali National Park and Preserve Museum Collection, 2001–2010: Alpine Flood Plains and Terraces and Fans near Savage River, Alaska Range Mountains, DENA 21089, Photography (1925–1950); Layne Adams (2001), Tamás Szerényi (2010). These photo pairs shows what is known as 'Marmot Rock' or 'Savage Rock' near where the park road crosses the Savage River. The earlier photo shows the first Savage River Bridge, completed in 1925. In the latter two photos, the bridge is not visible as it was rebuilt in 1983 south of its previous location. Thus the current bridge is off the right edge of the frame. Shrub growth can be seen on the high mountain along with balsam poplars to the right of the rock face.

work with specific locations. The Landscape Change Program in Vermont, for example, also calls for participatory modes and community assistance in the creation of repeat photographs. The photos are often executed at a human level and perspective, providing tangible evidence of a variety of climatic effects and changes (White and Hart, 2007). These works are fundamentally different from photomontage and digital realism. Repeat photography reinforces place, the reoccurrence increases the observation of historical changes as a basis to enact future practices. Repeat photography can be displayed as a single photograph of different time points, to which a narrative is constructed (Senf, 2012, p. 31). Repeat photography is an inexpensive mode of representation that can complement mapping systems, as discussed in Chapter 1. Repeat photography is a visual medium of small durational points in time which are referential. The use of drones for repeat photography is a very new advance; drones can rotate around fixed coordinates or shoot at fixed positions, so the use of drones in repeat photography can only come more to the fore, given their unique position between perspectival and aerial mapping, and lack of expense. The photograph here is evidence to the natural scientist of succession, habitat change and climate change. The use of repeat photography in landscape architecture is much understated; while landscape and urban archives are utilised in precedence studies, the use of comparative GIS techniques could be improved. This mode of research would thus provide evidence supportive of design schemes that may incur more costs or face hostility.

In comparison, photomontages in which a design is proposed often make use of conventional pictorial perspectives and add new realities to an (often) existing place. This design work distorts the representation of a time; the relationship is markedly different. It may make use of precedence and/or current spatial practices, though in the same pictorial frame it may add fictional possibilities and digital media derived from plural or imaginative sources. The photomontage predominately asks questions in a future tense without much reference, while repeat photography uses historical time points to form future projections.

COLLAGE/COMPOSITES

The digital perspective photomontage has emerged as a prerequisite for design competitions, public engagement and portfolios. The composite is a combination of images moving elements to create a single image or scene. The composite can be viewed both as an element that has emancipatory possibilities juxtaposing unforeseen elements – virtual combinations in the generation of new realities (Corner, 2000) – and also as a visual medium which distorts time and functions as a fundamental tool of deceit, with political and ethical concerns. This dichotomy has arisen from the vital agency the perspective has for explanation of projects for lay persons, and the ability of the perspective to elaborate on structural elements proposed. The production of perspectives has also changed, given 3D modelling and informatics capability. A study of our approaches to perspective composites is by extension a study of landscape

FIGURE 3.6 Mark Tansey, Action Painting II, 1984 oil on canvas, 193 × 279.4 cm. © Mark Tansey, image courtesy of Gagosian Gallery, New York. In the painting a group of afternoon painters employ a method of representation that is completely at odds to a space shuttle launch. The amateur painter's realism is believable, though the process and event duration are jarringly contradictory. However, the group seem to have been successful in their depiction. The painters position their bodies in the cliché of realist painters while also making the amateur error of blocking the view with their own easels. Paradoxically, the painting itself captures such an event in a photographic cyan filter. The humour is apparent, the complexity of its construction even more enjoyable. Tansey's careful composition stages questions that relate to the problem of digital and analogue landscape perspectives which are static images of spaces in constant change (Taylor, 1999).

FIGURE 3.7 Edwin Church, Twilight in the Wilderness, 1860. Frederic Edwin Church (American, 1826–1900). Oil on canvas; 101.6 × 162.6 cm. © The Cleveland Museum of Art. The magnitude of the autumnal sunset of Church's work captures a very transitional time period, perhaps derived from a small sketch titled Twilight, originally depicting sunset in spring/summer. Church's work may reflect his increasing concern about the despoliation of the wilderness (Wilton and Barringer, 2002, pp. 129–130).

FIGURE 3.8 Georges Méliès, A Trip to the Moon, 1902. A Trip to the Moon is a satire in which the innate conservatism of the scientific community is overcome by the convictions of a lone charismatic figure (played by the film maker himself). In the film, astronauts prepare for a rocket-launch; they take off and land on the moon (hitting it in the eye), and finally splash down back on earth. Méliès was the first film maker to apply effects such as time-lapse photography, hand colouring and layered exposures.

FIGURE 3.9 Max Ernst, Europe After the Rain, 1940–1942, oil on canvas, 54.8 × 147.8 cm. Wadsworth Atheneum Museum of Art/Art Resource, NY/Ernst, Max (1891–1976) © ARS, NY. Ernst presents a post-war apocalyptic landscape, with reference to coral and acid rain, promoting the use of collage; 'is the noble conquest of the irrational, the coupling of two realities, irreconcilable in appearance, upon a plane which apparently does not suit them' (Rosemont and Warlick, 2001).

106   TIME IN LANDSCAPE

FIGURE 3.10 Helmut Jacoby, Water Carpet & Cone Area Campbell Park, Milton Keynes; photograph by John Donat, 1976. Image copyright of the Homes & Communities Agency, courtesy of Milton Keynes City Discovery Centre. Jacoby was much sought after as an architectural illustrator, and as Deyan Sudjic discusses, when Jacoby was drawing for Norman Foster his drawings acted as endorsements of the quality of architectural subjects (Sudjic, 2012, p. 76). Jacoby's drawings were also measured as the accuracy of construction to original design intent. As Jacoby states, 'As an architectural renderer one comes into extremely close contact with the author, as does the translator of a poem or a literary text. Drawing like translation, is a very intimate process' (Jacoby in Bofinger *et al.*, 2001, p. 202).

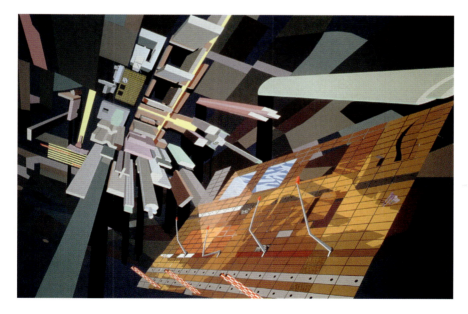

FIGURE 3.11 West 8, Adriaan Geuze, Schouwburgplein, Rotterdam (Redesign), 1990 (reworked 1993), edited by the SLA Foundation Rotterdam. Raising the surface of the square for a variety of performances with crane lights operated by the public, the design reflects Rotterdam's port. Notably, Geuze experimented with montage techniques and a later edition reworked the visualisation with the Ar-Key program, allowing two different ground planes to be juxtaposed. This highly worked collage presented a radical abstracted perspective and is significant in the history of landscape architectural representation.

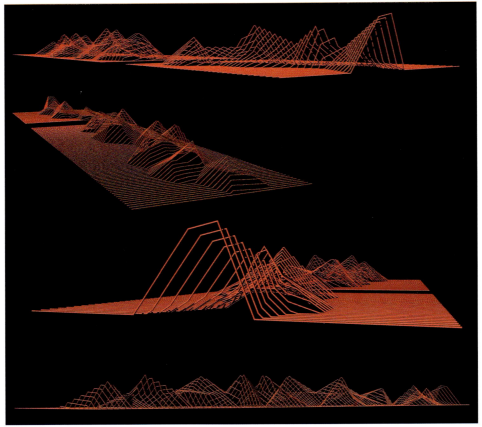

FIGURE 3.12 Gross Max, Beijing Central Park, 2013. Founded by Elco Hooftman and Bridget Baines, the firm notably developed a calligraphic visual language and photomontage technique that allows a clear distinction between elements. The distinguishing of elements alters perceptions and presents open juxtapositions and possibilities of a space to become a metaphoric mode of digital perspective.

architecture's visual language. These perspective representations have impact in the production of space and are fundamental to our imaginative capacity.

The composite can also in a practical sense be seen as a communications marketing tool for securing firms' and individuals' work, suggesting the landscape to come. This matter is under-discussed in academic circles, given that it has a unique representational agency in capital exchange. There is no issue with this position per se, though it is the promotion of perspective montages as unique artworks created in the spirit of artistic genius, rather than illustrative documents for a larger design package, that is disingenuous – the use of perspective montages as screening devices for less attractive elements of a project. The perspective could be better seen as a fundamental tool of landscape branding – the design process and promotion of landscape (Porter, 2015). Thus, designing unique places is important, though maintaining a business has equal footing. Some firms offer specific skillsets and 3D visualisation artists for landscape practices who are able to develop work from simple sketches and concepts. In these cases, practices should thoroughly engage with the artist in order for the artist to understand their concepts and intended outcome.

The composite role is to suggest things to come, a unique futurological insight into a project. Of the representational techniques discussed so far, mapping and modelling, notation and diagramming, the digital perspective photomontage represents time, as does each, in a unique manner.

The American Sublime painters or Hudson River School[1] of the eighteenth century are a useful source to trace perspective developments and articulate time distortions and notions of deceit in the composite dichotomy. One of the painters in particular, Fredric Edwin Church, was as much a surveyor and prolific traveller, constantly sketching and engaged in the natural sciences following Alexander von Humboldt (1759–1869). The landscape as subject developed from Sublime aesthetics in England (Burke, 2015), among others,[2] and en plein air painting.[3] The works are magnificent and highly acclaimed and the reasoning here is not to detract from their importance in landscape painting history; however the process of construction is worth discussion.

These landscape representations were often peopled in the foregrounds; they are the locators to propel landscapes of infinite and magnificent scale between the local and the emerging American national identity found in its lands and reflected back to its urban audience (Grusin, 2009). The fully worked paintings are often rendered with enhanced atmospherics and shadow. However, these worked up images are often composites of sketches and observations made during travels. These composites could not have been produced in any other manner, given the medium of oil paint. Thus, the cohesive vision masks its fragmentary construction from samples from various geographic regions executed at various time periods. The large-scale works of Church, in particular, were often displayed in special conditions with curated interiors and lighting. Church was not alone in exploring the boundaries of painting as a medium for spectacle. For the American Sublime these paintings idealised the American landscape:

> Adjustments in topography spoke of social rifts smoothed over, and formal harmonies blunted the sharp edge of technology. Such aesthetic accommodations offered an ideal mirror of a longed-for social condition.
>
> (Miller, 1969, p. 209)

The American Sublime painters are analogous to a large number of contemporary digital landscape perspectives constructed in the same manner in digital form; site photographs, merged with personal image libraries, image stock, custom brushes and atmospheric filters and effects, among other things. For contemporary perspective composites, new idealisms continue in the tradition of these painters, often without awareness to this longer tradition. Fundamentally, the issue of visual representation, and particularly perspective photomontages, is that they fail to address specific periods of time. Often these works present a distorted time space of various fragments on a ground plane. This dichotomy must be carefully considered. As Kingery-Page and Hahn state, such aesthetics can result in a kitsch that is unhelpful:

> When ultra-realistic renderings are accepted as the ultimate design graphic, the result can be kitsch; designers have an ethical obligation to avoid the pitfalls of such easily-accepted landscape kitsch.
>
> (Kingery-Page and Hahn, 2012, p. 58)

Similarly Karl Kullmann suggests that there is a paradoxical skills gap, but penchant desire for hyper-reality and a different rubric should be employed in which to represent landscape complexity (Kullmann, 2014).

A collage of time uses various layers and visual accumulation and overlap (Lynch, 1976, p. 171). Kevin Lynch refers to a temporal collage of past and future traces and the insertion of new imagable activities. Humphry Repton pioneered a similar technique with flap overlays. For Repton, the device was for improvement and the 'cultivation' of landscape; for Lynch, the temporal collage is useful for demonstrating reoccurrence: 'The future is here with us because it will be like something we knew in the past' (Lynch, 1976, pp. 173–174).

This emulsion of time-based assets is arguably more favourable than composites that seek to gel and resurface the perspective into apparent coherence. Composites, however, have a particular role in environmental planning; where the impact of a proposal can be 3D modelled, this proposal can then be referenced to single line-of-sight points. Thus, the photomontage juxtaposes still photography, drone capture or 3D model points with the design proposal. This allows an evaluation on the level of intrusion that any development will have on the existing field of view. In the UK, for example, these processes are called visual impact studies which are part of an overall Environmental Impact Assessment (EIA).[4] In this process the objective of a photomontage 'is to simulate the likely visual changes that would result from a proposed development and to produce printed images of a size and resolution sufficient to match the perspective in the same view in the field' (Landscape Institute 2011). When

VIEW FROM THE FORT, NEAR BRISTOL.

VIEW FROM THE FORT, NEAR BRISTOL.

FIGURE 3.13 Humphry Repton, 1805, Observations on the Theory and Practice of Landscape Gardening, 1805. By permission of the Master and Fellows of St John's College, Cambridge. Including some remarks on Grecian and Gothic architecture, collected from various manuscripts, in the possession of the different noblemen and gentlemen, for whose use they were originally written; the whole tending to establish fixed principles in the respective arts.

FIGURE 3.14 (*facing page and above*) Caravan Images, Remote Ecological Power Station on Alluvial Plain with Access Drone, 2016. Rendered seasonal perspectives from a 3D model generated from the author's hand-drawn sketch.

TIME IN LANDSCAPE

composites are used as part of a legislative requirement, their geographic position can be evidenced; the field of view is defined through set lenses and makes photographic reference to current surrounds, similar to the idea of reoccurrence proposed by Lynch. However, the superimposed asset can be manipulated to an extent through seasonal preferences, and perspectives of course are radically different from the user experience and vision of the site. This cannot be easily overcome, and should be recognised as the limit of perspective views and perspective representation in design communication.

It is important to describe the limits of the medium for it to remain as a valid design tool. Perspectives have long promised a new pictorial freedom, but confined the designer within a perspectival cage (Evans, 2000, p. 43). This cage to an extent holds the emulsified range of time-based assets, derived from multiple digital sources. These sources are often images of images, pictures of pictures, and this is deliberate in the work of the artist Mark Tansey (Taylor, 1999, p. 29). Tansey, however, does not hide the sources or the juxtaposition. Often in landscape architecture perspective, composites, repeating elements, texture packs, stock packs and brushes appear in different proposals on different continents, and a digital monoculture has materialised. In addition to the repetition of materials, the idea of perspectives needs to be opened up:

> The Definitions of perspective in landscape restricted to linear perspective, as representative of the persistence of Cartesian subject/object duality, or to picturesque views, are therefore unable adequately to engage an exploration of potential complex landscape space.
>
> (Clarke, 2005, p. 50)

A number of possibilities exist, however, to mitigate the deceit implicit in perspective visualisation and utilise perspectives as a mode of exploring complexity and the imaginative agency proposed by Corner. The first strategy is the showing of succession and climatic effects. As a minimum this evidences the consideration of landscape design and season. Working with government weather system data can provide an overview of average rainfall and precipitation, ultraviolet (UV) radiation, temperature, humidity, daylight hours and many other data sets, to give an indication of climatic conditions for the perspective montage. This gives some sense of a truer site condition than consistent perspectives of Mediterranean climates, and the range of digital assets that can be prepared by visually reflecting these conditions. The second strategy follows the first in that horticulture knowledge is applied in the perspective over generic or blurred infilling, reflecting and referencing planting plans and localised flora.

FIGURE 3.15 (*facing page*) Stoss Landscape, Minneapolis Riverfront, 2,200 acres, Minnesota, 2011. The project re-imagines 5.5 miles of Mississippi riverfront in Minneapolis, from the cultural riverfront in downtown north to the city limit. Stoss' proposal is titled Streamlines; it's about sheer, unfiltered experiences of direct contact with the river and river life, in many ways and at multiple moments. Stoss weaves these experiences back into the everyday city. The entry makes clever use of seasonal perspectives and a related video to explore phasing and change.

FIGURE 3.16 (*above and facing page*) Turenscape, Zaryadye Park, The Blue Circle of Moscow, 2013. In June 2013 the Turenscape Consortium was selected from a shortlist to prepare a design proposal for Zaryadye Park, Moscow. The park concept revolved around the creation of a living puzzle that locks together the city's memory, culture, ecology and people, which reveals the memory of the past and makes a prophecy for the future. In this case the Turenscape sequential images address both seasonal time and usability, but refer back to the base concept.

The third strategy involves truer census and density of the spaces to be designed. Often, people are added to perspective composites for scale reference. These assets are too often generic in addition, creating a kitsch perspective of elated people positioned in the most leisurely poses garbed in high fashion. The positioning of these digital persons is often highly spaced, indicating a low-density inhabitation even in the largest metropolis. Ethnicities are also often under-represented and these factors all contribute to a composite far different from the place itself. The lighting on figures is also telling of the generic nature of the composite, often sharper than the surrounds,

and the shadows cast by figures often look like those cast by a photographic studio rather than natural daylight conditions.

Finally, a sequential strategy may offer the most benefit in breaking perspectival limits and indicating a time-based approach. Sequences of perspective 2D composites highlight the multiple uses of a site, but can also be used to evidence seasonal change to a fuller degree. This option is more time intensive, but offers clients a more considered use in the design proposal. The perspective thus provides static snapshots

TIME IN LANDSCAPE 117

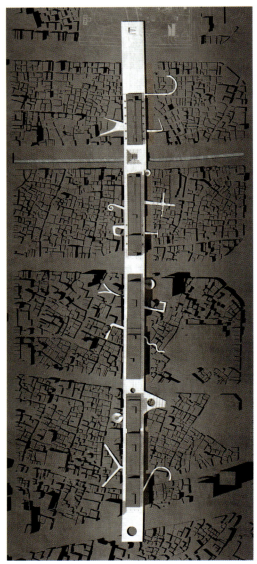

FIGURE 3.17
Hassell, Seunsangga Citywalk Design Competition, Jon Hazelwood, Ben Duckworth, Richard Mullane, David Tickle, Sharon Wright, Georgia Darling, Jianshan Dou, Jessica Lock, Ed Mitchell, Antoine Pascal; 1 km scale, Seoul, Korea, 2015. Reimagining the Seunsangga Citywalk, a dilapidated 1 km mall running through the heart of Seoul in Korea, meant reconnecting with ideas of the past, exploring new ideas and at times turning traditional ideas upside down. The perspective in this project is fundamental in the communication of scale and spatial layering as it is intertwined with existing conditions.

FIGURE 3.18
Sasaki Associates, Midtown Detroit TechTown District, Detroit, Michigan, 149 acres, 2013. TechTown – an emerging knowledge district in Midtown Detroit – is currently characterized by surface parking, vacant properties and inward-facing siloed hubs of activity. The TechTown District Plan articulates an inspiring vision for the revitalization of the district. Developed by Sasaki Associates in collaboration with Midtown Detroit Inc. and U3 Ventures, the plan accelerates innovation, promotes entrepreneurship and builds community around the generation of ideas in a vibrant, mixed-use setting. The plan repurposes the historic building stock with uses that support innovation and create vibrancy, and also strengthens connections within Midtown Detroit and to surrounding neighbourhoods. The series of perspectives addresses the complex and dense spatial use of the site and addresses the wide demographics and ethnicities featured.

TIME IN LANDSCAPE   119

FIGURE 3.19 Groundlab, Conceptual Framework for the Development of the Sokolniki Park Territory, Wowhaus (Architecture), Groundlab (Landscape Urbanism), Moscow, Russia, 2015. Embassy of Nature seeks to identify Sokolniki as the main gateway to nature in Moscow by linking the park with its surroundings and the Elk's Island natural reserve. Working with three complex site factors of a natural reserve, forested zones and urban park, the perspective point of view seeks to elaborate all three conditions through an aerial view. The perspective leads directly to a rendered plan and analysis for a conceptual framework with further localised perspectives in different time zones. These sources have an essential weighted reliance on each other for the communication of this strategy.

FIGURE 3.20 MAUD, Tainan Main Station – Tainan, Taiwan, Max Yang, Samya Kako, David Miller, Design Area: 54 Acres, 2012. The proposal aims to optimise connections from Tainan Main Station area with the surrounding districts, while reconciling the gap between the different districts, acting as a device that will transfer programme diversity to the site and surrounding areas. Furthermore, the development responds to the cultural and ecological urban fabric of the surrounding west and east side of the area. The guiding principle of the proposed masterplan is to inspire a meaningful sense of community and a shared commitment to social and environmental responsibility. The aerial view helps to elaborate the main scheme, which is supported by additional sequential perspectives executed at different times. Each perspective then elaborates the details of the districts and their relationship with the main structural element – the super tree.

TIME IN LANDSCAPE   121

FIGURE 3.21 Giona Andreani, Arch-viz & Photography, Double Negative, Reinterpretation of the Sol LeWitt installation at Europos Parkas, Lithuania, 2015.

of a design responding to different sensitivities of time. Depending on the nature of construction, these still images could be derived from 3D models and videography. These strategies do not limit the perspective medium, but give a degree of fidelity to landscape representation. This fidelity does not mean that the creative, explorative and emancipatory potential of composites is limited or curtailed. This means the instigation of specific recognisable elements, with clearer design intention and, most importantly, the liberation of the perspective as a purely illustrative agent. Figures 3.11–3.21 have used similar strategies in their design communication, seeking alternative composites and compositions to elaborate complex designs. These works are fundamental exemplars seeking engaging sources that have an agency.

PRINCIPLES OF PERSPECTIVE

A number of highly accurate survey modes mean that landscapes, cities and territories across scales can be accurately mapped and compared. Historical records can also be accessed to measure change. Chapter 1 discussed mapping data types and these sources can be integrated here in the generation of perspectives. Given these possibilities and availability of this mode, this section discusses working and creating such models, its use in survey and in developing design work alongside modes discussed previously.

Most common perspectives are created using artistic perspective, which are eye measurements of the relative scale and position of assets within a composition. Two-point perspective or three-point perspective gives a rigidity which is unhelpful. The perspective does not have to be a wholly artistic output; the perspective can make real reference to existing conditions and situations.

To create a perspective two strategies are possible. The perspective may be created from scratch or with reference to a 2D site photograph or sketch. The second option derives from a perspective view of a 3D CAD/GIS model. The 3D model may also be referenced to a site photograph, CAD work or sketch using perspective-matching tools.

Digital advances mean these two different strategies have become blended. You may use 3D elements in a 2D image. You can convert 2D images into a 3D object. You can also use 2D or 3D images to create a time-lapse motion perspectives. These options can mean efficiency in production; however, often the biggest hurdle in landscape perspectives is the choice and location of view. These three elements should be considered in the planning of your perspective in whichever strategy is used.

Framing. The choice of frame should be carefully considered. The extent of view of the site should focus on the key elements to be communicated.

Aperture. This is the opening of the lens. While this should be considered in the gathering of site photography, it may also be used in image editing and in the construction of the perspective as a way of blurring or focusing objects, and the depth of field in your digital perspective. For example, a smaller aperture lets in less light and gives a longer depth of field, ensuring the foreground and background are in focus in landscape shots. A wide-angle lens and ensuring the subject is at a distance to the camera ensures sharpness and depth. A larger aperture creates *bokeh* or out-of-focus points of light for foreground and background parts and this can be used if certain aesthetic effects are required (Mackie *et al.*, 2008).

Personal viewpoint. The personal viewpoint is the viewer's position in the perspective. It may be advantageous for off-centre low or high viewpoints for the perspective to give emphasis and disrupt the standard composition. It may also be necessary to shoot at specific heights and distances if this is part of a legislative requirement. The aerial perspective for example is preferred when wishing to represent whole schemes.

Source. Using climate data, a diverse image stock, personal sources, sketches and site images to create the perspective will mitigate the danger of creating 'images of images' and a generic composition.

STRATEGIES FOR TIME-BASED 2D IMAGERY

Once an initial plan and viewpoint are chosen, the perspective can be progressed. If creating a perspective from a 2D image, the following stages will be utilised. The companion website provides tutorials and strategies for this area. Chapter 4 provides strategies and workstages for using 3D models to develop perspectives. This includes working with reality-capture software, GIS and parametric models. Perspective still remains a highly valuable visualisation technique for describing the effects of a project, and two different modes of working should be recognised here, whether the perspective composite is generational or ideational or is part of a planning application and landscape analysis for the project. As Andrea Hansen and Charles Waldheim reflect, 'strategies of photomontage were understood not simply as representations of a future reality, but rather instruments of imagination in their own right, occasioning new relationships, and new landscapes' (Comer *et al.*, 2014, p. 21). While Hansen and Waldheim are reflecting on wider practices beyond digital perspective composites, the dual operative dimension is still in effect. As mentioned previously, however, the media provides static points of a landscape time axis, and through the composition of elements distorts the temporal aspect of the landscape and the time space which they purport to represent. These issues can be mitigated to an extent, though should at least be recognised as the limit of the medium. In some cases the distortion of the time aspect in the landscape affords a new understanding to the design process for laypersons. The workflow below follows to an extent both strategies of perspective composites and further discusses the type of agency and valence that the media embodies.

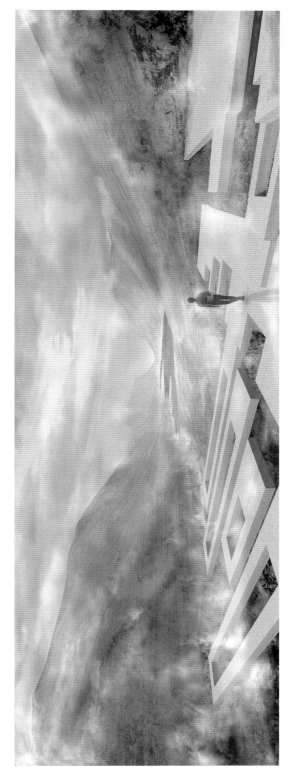

FIGURE 3.22 Paul Cureton, Capitalism & Sublimity in National Parks, Coire Etchachan Burn, Cairngorns National Park, Aberdeenshire, Scotland, 2016. Verified topographical view. See book companion website to follow the tutorials for this model. Produced with Dynamo, Autodesk Revit and Adobe Photoshop.

TIME IN LANDSCAPE 125

FIGURE 3.23 Paul Cureton, Trees in Time, 2016. A detail of a fictional staggered berm with two terraces and tree pits has been visualised to attempt to display the growth of trees and root systems across time. See book companion website to follow the tutorials for this model. Produced with Trimble Sketchup Pro and Adobe Photoshop.

Generational perspective composites

Generational perspective composites will make use of a variety and plurality of references, applied effects and motion graphics. The generational perspective composite strategy may be to create a project vignette, to relate to fieldwork and diagramming that has been undertaken (Chapter 2); it may also seek to blend other representational modes, such as maps and 3D models, in a sort of 'emulsion' of many forms and also relate to any initial maquettes and early project mock-ups that explore the 3D spatial form. As singular objects they create a static pictorial, though as sequential items they allow a series of snapshots, storyboard and sequence of space. As James Corner suggests, the media of execution could be varied for the demonstration of ideas (Corner, 1992). If generational work uses purely photographic elements, sources can be diverse though must be carefully gathered. The emphasis is the quality of materials to be juxtaposed rather than the recycling of popular culture, unless it is cultural critique such as Richard Hamilton's, famously seen in the 1956 work 'Just What is it that Makes Today's Homes so Different, so Appealing?'. This aspect of landscape critique as the assemblage of the landscape material as a sort of junk space and visual report of the scope of contemporary thinking is less prevalent. The agency is different here;

the perspective composite assembles photographic environmental aspects as a reflection of landscape values and ideas – a reflective device as a forward-moving development. Its future aspect is its agency and valence, by a function of two interrelated components. These components are the material assembly and digital craft, as well as the response of what that landscape will come to mean.

Visual impact

The perspective composite can also demonstrate in planning terms the visual effects of a design proposal. The agency at work here is similar to future aspects, though the valence adheres to reflect the legislation and policy of the landscape and its character areas. The illustration of effects of a project can make reference to each particular country's landscape architecture chartered body and their guidance and legislation, if applicable. For example, UK guidance on landscape and visual impact assessment (LVIA) (Landscape Institute, 2013, pp. 113–134), which is part of an EIA,[5] provides advice on the creation of perspective composites as part of a necessary study. The study's remit is decided in the scoping process. The EIA presents the landscape effects of any works and the LVIA deals with the effects of change and development on available views. Visual effects may also be recorded through ZTVs or viewsheds as well as photo-montaged perspectives. There are also cumulative effects of both EIA and LVIA, or the totality of proposed development and its impact. The LVIA perspective composite would then be illustrated in a visual impact report which forms part of the overall EIA document, and aid communication. It aims to describe landscape character and associated values from the viewpoints, similar to repeat photography methods. The perspective composite would have reference points from the point of shoot and GPS coordinates, and be referenced to a map as part of the overall report and referred to a ZTV (zone of theoretical visibility) study (see Chapter 1). In essence a landscape visual impact study is the future-facing counter-medium of repeat photography, which is a methodology to measure historical change. Thus, the sources represent historical and futurological time axes and situate themselves in the present. From this presentism they then re-project the values in landscape, for example creating future simulative models of receding glaciers or a sort of reverse visual impact, in which studies can be read backwards in order to understand the position from which the work is undertaken.

The following strategy can be adopted in order to create generational perspective composites and visual impact studies. Visual impact studies must adhere to national and landscape bodies' guidelines that refer to the parameters of their construction.

- **References**: photographs, hand drawings, mapping data. It is always worth starting your composition with the furthest background element. This provides a source on the depth of the image.
- **Layering**: photo-editing packages are essentially grown-up collage; the importance of layering sources will help to build-up middle-ground and foreground elements. The layers may be carefully distinguished, showing proposed elements, or seamless in that the layers are carefully blended and merged. If creating a time-lapse image, the layers can be useful to control and connate movement.

- **Clipping**: this places one image inside the shape of another and is particularly useful in layering textures and detailing planting.
- **Filters and effects**: the editor has many pre-built filters and effects to apply to brushes, shapes or images and can be used to block out areas, mask or apply atmospheres to the perspective.
- **3D elements on a 2D plane**: Photoshop allows the use of 3D elements on a 2D plane, or it can create 3D images from a 2D image. These can be set in a timeline and animated as necessary.
- **Textures**: textures can be applied in the layering and clipping phase; a strong texture library is extremely useful and a number of packages can be purchased.
- **Lighting**: programs such as Photoshop have rendered lighting options, and these can be applied to individual elements. The use of filters and effects can also suggest certain light conditions.
- **Final production**: this involves the editing of video work using a video editor such as Final Cut Pro, or motion graphics editor such as AfterEffects. These programmes are designed for multi-platform use so they can incorporate the perspective assets; annotation and callouts can be added and transitions can be controlled to provide a practice branding or portfolio identity.

SUMMARY

The representation of time in landscape remains a complex issue. Suitable methods of representation to depict both natural and artificial process remain difficult. The digital perspective montage has a unique position in its imaginative speculation, but also as an unhelpful tool in the propagation of picturesque aesthetics and distorted depictions. Repeat photography may offer additional tools to perspectival designs in the production of succession evidence. Likewise, drone use may also provide novel or unexplored bases from which to derive a base image for composites. The perspective composite may also be used in planning terms to evaluate the visual effects of a project coupled with an environmental assessment of landscape character, creating a cumulative evaluation of any design proposals and development. The perspective composite may also be assessed in value terms to place association or eye-tracking evaluation.

The expanding nature and variety of sources to which these perspectives can be executed mean that the production of these works will be less averse to digital kitsch, and will function as a key agent in visual explanation of complexity to the public if there is suitable investment in their production. The existing dichotomy between imaginative agency and deceit must be understood, particularly given the changing role of digital 3D models and the derived and layered information that is attached to them.

Following Lynch's idea of 'reoccurrence', the perspective also provides an explicit reassurance with base elements such as site photographs or recognisable assets, and juxtaposes a future tense next to them. This may be unsettling, mis-represented or a delivered emulsion, though this unique agency is important to recognise. The digital perspective excels in the explanation of proposed structural elements, though faces difficulty in visualising temporal elements and time in particular; new strategies of time-lapse and sequential packaging can limit these issues to an extent.

NOTES

1. Asher B. Durand, Thomas Cole, Albert Bierstadt, Frederic Edwin Church *et al.*
2. The *Critique of Judgement* (Kant and Gregor, 1987), *Introductory Lectures on Aesthetics* (Hegel and Inwood, 1993); see also (Morley, 2010).
3. Barbizon school, Hudson River School, and Newlyn School.
4. Information is gathered and structured for a planning authority to form judgements on proposals and whether they are successful.
5. National Planning Policy Framework, United Kingdom, Town and Country Planning (EIA) Regulations 2011.

BIBLIOGRAPHY

Bofinger, H., Jacoby, H., Voigt, W., *et al.*, 2001. *Helmut Jacoby: Meister der Architekturzeichnung: Master of Architectural Drawing*. Wasmuth, Tu_bingen.

Burke, E., 2015. *A Philosophical Enquiry into the Origin of our Ideas of the Sublime and the Beautiful*, 2nd edition. Oxford University Press, Oxford.

Clarke, H.G., 2005. Land-scopic Regimes: Exploring Perspectival Representation Beyond the 'Pictorial' Project. *Landscape Journal*, 24 (1): 50–68.

Comer, D.J., Freytag, A. and Hansen, A., 2014. *Composite Landscapes: Photomontage and Landscape Architecture*. Hatje Cantz, Ostfildern.

Corner, J., 1992. Representation and Landscape: Drawing and Making in the Landscape Medium. *Word & Image*, 8: 243–275. doi: 10.1080/02666286.1992.10435840.

Corner, J., 2000. *Taking Measures Across the American Landscape*, new edition. Yale University Press, New Haven.

Cosgrove, D.E., 2012. *Geography and Vision*. I.B. Tauris, London.

De Certeau, M., 1984. *The Practice of Everyday Life*. University of California Press, Berkeley, CA.

Denes, A., 2008. *The Human Argument: The Writings of Agnes Denes*. Spring Publications, Putnam.

Duempelmann, S. and Herrington, S., 2014. Plotting Time in Landscape Architecture. *Studies in the History of Gardens & Designed Landscapes*, 34: 1–14. doi: 10.1080/14601176.2013.850240.

Evans, R., 2000. *The Projective Cast: Architecture and Its Three Geometries*, new edition. MIT Press, Cambridge, MA.

Grusin, R., 2009. *Culture, Technology, and the Creation of America's National Parks*. Cambridge University Press, Cambridge.

Hegel, G.W.F. and Inwood, M., 1993. *Introductory Lectures on Aesthetics*, reprint. Penguin Classics, London.

Jackson, J.B., 1994. *A Sense of Place, a Sense of Time*. Yale University Press, London.

Jarvie-Eggart, M. E., 2015. *Responsible Mining: Case Studies in Managing Social & Environmental Risks in the Developed World*. SME.

Kant, I. and Gregor, M.J., 1987. *Critique of Judgement*. Hackett Publishing, Indianapolis.

Kingery-Page, K. and Hahn, H.,H., 2012. The aesthetics of digital representation: Realism, abstraction and kitsch. *Journal of Landscape Architecture*, 7(2): 68–75.

Kullmann, K., 2014. Hyper-Realism and Loose-Reality: The Limitations of Digital Realism and Alternative Principles in Landscape Design Visualization. *Journal of Landscape Architecture*, 9: 20–31. doi: 10.1080/18626033.2014.968412.

Landscape Institute, 2011. Photography and Photomontage in Landscape and Visual Assessment. Advice Note 01/11.

Landscape Institute, 2013. *Guidelines for Landscape and Visual Impact Assessment*, 3rd edition. Routledge, London.

Lynch, K. 1976, *What Time is This Place?* MIT Press, Cambridge, MA.

Mackie, T., Neill, W., Noton, D. and Wiggett, D., 2008. *The Digital SLR Expert Landscapes.* David & Charles, Cincinnati.

Miller, J., 1969. *Drawings of the Hudson River School, 1825–1875.* Brooklyn Museum, New York.

Morley, S. (ed.), 2010. *The Sublime*. Whitechapel Art Gallery, London.

Muir, R., 1999. *Approaches to Landscape*. Palgrave Macmillan, Basingstoke.

Muir, R., 2000. *The New Reading the Landscape: Fieldwork in Landscape History*. University of Exeter Press, Exeter.

Pickett, S.T.A., 2012. Ecology of the City: A Perspective from Science, in McGrath, B.P. (ed.), *Urban Design Ecologies*. Wiley, Chichester.

Porter, N., 2015. *Landscape and Branding: The Promotion and Production of Place*. Routledge, Abingdon.

Rosemont, F. and Warlick, M.E., 2001. *Max Ernst and Alchemy: A Magician in Search of Myth*. University of Texas Press, Austin.

Senf, R., 2012. *Reconstructing the View: The Grand Canyon Photographs of Mark Klett and Byron Wolfe*. University of California Press, Berkeley.

Sudjic, D., 2012. *Norman Foster: A Life in Architecture*. Phoenix, London.

Taylor, M.C., 1999. *The Picture in Question: Mark Tansey and the Ends of Representation*, 2nd edition. University of Chicago Press, Chicago.

Webb, R., Boyer, D. and Turner, R., 2010. *Repeat Photography: Methods and Applications in the Natural Sciences*. Island Press, Washington.

White, C. and Hart, E.J., 2007. *Lens of Time: A Repeat Photography of Landscape Change in the Canadian Rockies*. University of Calgary Press, Calgary.

Wilton, A. and Barringer, T., 2002. *American Sublime: Landscape Painting in the United States, 1820–1880*. Tate Publishing, London.

4
STRATEGIES FOR REPRESENTATION (3D MODELS)

> Young people programmed their personal computers to model a middle landscape; one that gave its inhabitants all the benefits of industrialisation with none of the drawbacks. But the social problems of the outside world remained. Utopia stayed inside the computer screen and stubbornly refused to come out.
> (Ceruzzi, 2003, p. 349)

Developing site specificity is important in the representation of landscape character and is an increasing legislative requirement for digital modelling and construction protocols.[1] Digital design is a process and strategy for creating landscape. Arguably the 3D model can be the essential component in the synergy of mapping data (Chapter 1), fieldwork and notation (Chapter 2), perspectives (Chapter 3) and digital fabrication (Chapter 5). Thus, an efficient workflow can emerge in production, and levels of strategy emerge. First, strategies in the discussed representational areas; and second, an overall strategy through which these works connect and move between each other. The dichotomy of digital perspective montages was explored in the previous chapter and the varieties of options for their creation have been discussed. These strategies can be inter-connected; thinking of these technologies and computational processes as enablers of contemporary landscape architecture and the 3D model can be the base that develops strategies but also dictates the strategy between representation and production. The 3D model in building information modelling (BIM) terms can attach both conventional schedules and production information, also known as 4D – the bills of quantities, sequencing and scheduling of a design project. It can also attach less conventional modes, such as mapping data and fieldwork exercises, though this is a research area less explored. 4D is even more interesting as it creates a virtual 3D model as a time-based asset. No doubt the benefits for construction and project delivery are clear, though there is a danger that the design vision is singular and locked in.[2]

As Ceruzzi states in the opening passage, there is a utopian impulse at work in computation that often ignores the realities of spaces. More so, this digital drive can have negative effects as unthought digital strategies apply a utopian binary logic to landscape form, akin to the damage of landscape Picturesque aesthetics. In an architecture context, as Pérez-Goméz and Pelletier state, technology is not a neutral device, but is part of a political or economic domination, repression and control (Pérez-Goméz and Pelletier , 2000, pp. 384–385).

Computation for landscape architecture and urban design may secure and lock-in futures in the recreation of known forms, or be part of a wider dynamic imaginary for future visions, as argued by Pinder (2005, pp. 260–265). While Pinder broadly discusses the decline of utopian thinking after the failures of Western modernist architecture, this imaginary in computational terms does not involve static juxtapositions but fluid complex and wide-ranging data sets derived from heterogeneous sources for the generation of design works that are produced with fidelity to their digital form – the degree of exactness with which something is copied or reproduced. This, however, involves the challenge of the retention of creativity and hybridity alongside the adoption of the new legislated and dominant BIM timeline. Thus, a rationality between virtual

FIGURE 4.1 Ivan Sutherland demonstrating Sketchpad on the TX-2, 1963. Courtesy of the Computer History Museum. Sketchpad marked a specific computer development history. Sketchpad, based on the idea of napkin sketches, refined to create more finished engineering drawings, which formed the idea of the invention of the program. Working with a light pen, a predecessor of the mouse, the user could point with the pen and interact with lines displayed on the screen. Ultimately, Sketchpad developed a graphical user interface that mediated between human and computer with real applications to engineering solutions (Sutherland, 2003, p. 3).

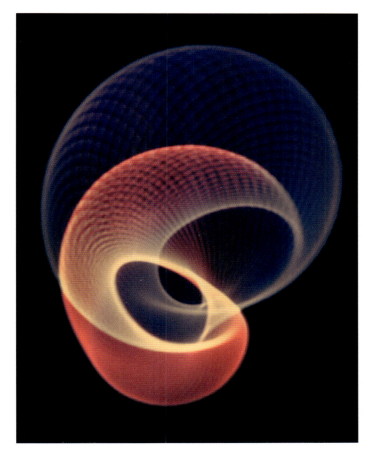

FIGURE 4.2
Ben Laposky, Oscillon #1043, 1952, The Ben Laposky Collection, Sanford Museum and Planetarium, Cherokee, IA, USA. Laposky was a mathematician and artist who created the first computer graphics and electronic art called 'Oscillons' by photographing an oscilloscope screen filled with moving images created by analogue electronics (Reichardt, 1971; Taylor, 2014).

space and built form can lose the revelatory dimension and positive latitude that can emerge during construction (Pérez-Goméz and Pelletier, 2000, p. 390).

The history of computing reveals a continued experimentation and innovation, and it is important to invest in this dialogue and recognise these histories of the future – for example, Ivan Sutherland's Sketch Pad of 1963, which created a user interface and drawing pen to draft on screen and apply constraints to the drawing. Sutherland was part of a rich succession of computer scientists developing hardware and software. One of the earliest successes was to draw a cross which tracked the movements of the light pen (Sutherland, 2003, p. 54). The cross formed the basis of the start of a line. This is what we can see still today in the use of AutoCAD and Bentley MicroStation. The programming involved commands with buttons – for example, pressing a button would fix the cross hair to a selected point to begin drawing a line. Further programming developed points, arcs and lines linked together to form objects (CAD Blocks). These could be stored in a library, and scaled and rotated. This unique interface in CAD drawing is now treated with casualness in comparison to other

FIGURE 4.3 *Byte Magazine*, front cover, illustration by Robert Tinney, January 1977 Vol. 2, No. 1. The technological promise of computer hardware and the generation and simulation of new utopic environments has long been part of computer history, with regular updates and heavy commercial competition for 3D modelling programs, plug-ins, modifications and rendering engines.

software and hardware developments. In 1966–1968 Sutherland and Bob Sproull also developed a head-mounted display called 'The Sword of Damocles', one of the first functional AR and VR machines following earlier prototypes by Morton Heilig (Kipper and Rampolla, 2012; Azuma, 1997). These two inventions and developments point towards a new convergence of technologies as BIM and AR move more to the fore and naturally converge (Wang and Love, 2012). The convergence in automated production has involved new dynamics of working and modes of collaboration using 3D models (Grilo and Jardim-Goncalves, 2010; Moum, 2010).

Ceruzzi (2003) has presented four futurological computing paradigms which are useful to discuss: a digital paradigm, convergence, solid-state electronics and the human interface. These paradigms have by and large held since the publication of Ceruzzi's book. The digital age paradigm is defined as coding and a binary logic forming the basis of human thinking. The convergence paradigm is the merging of devices and functions as previously mentioned. The solid-state paradigm is defined as inventions and innovations in hardware, such as visualisation tables. The final paradigm, the human interface, refers to our increasing relationship and communication with computers (Russell and Norvig, 2013). These paradigms act as drivers for societal

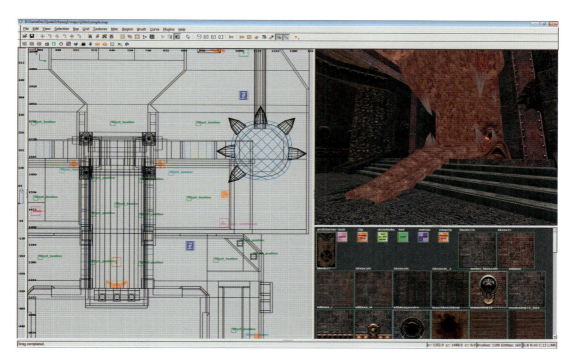

FIGURE 4.4 ID Software, GTK Radiant, Map Level Design Editor. GTK Radiant supported games such as Wolfenstein, Doom, Quake and Call of Duty from 1981. It is now open source. The development of level design software created a wider community to utilise mapping, 3D modelling and texturing for the customisation of their own gaming environments within the limitations of the game engine. This mode of working primed many architects prior to any formal drafting software and the importance of computer games as virtual training environments continues, most notably in the form of Minecraft.

change and by and large can be read as critical to our social imagination (Mahoney and Haigh, 2011); in the context of landscape, our understanding of it.

There is a danger of writing about 3D models and for the knowledge to be automatically relegated and historicised, given the pace of change of processes, hardware, software and strategies. Exploring many 3D modelling software programs' interoperability shows that convergence is increasingly in-built, with 3D printing options and the photogrammetric processing of 2D assets. The pace of change is dramatic, though landscape architecture, and urban design as a discipline, needs to immerse itself in software specification and lead development policy that reflects the profession's needs. Digital advocacy is best evidenced in the toolsets available for architecture, which emerged through experimentation in research/practice units; for example: the first Boston Architectural conference, 'Architecture and the Computer' (1964); William Mitchell's *Computer Aided Architecture* (Mitchell, 1979); or, more recently, the parametrism[3] of Patrik Schumacher and the AA school in 2008, Nox, Lars Spuybroek from 2004 (Spuybroek *et al.*, 2004; Spuybroek, 2016) in the use of algorithmic textures and materials for new architectural expressions and Marcus Novak's liquid architectures (1995), among many others (Carpo, 2012). However, the political implica-

FIGURE 4.5 Myst, 1994. Rand Miller, Robyn Miller, Cyan Games, 1993. The player is immersed in a deserted world with high-resolution rendered stills and landscapes. The player completes a series of puzzles through embedded animations. The game has no pre-story, time limit or set enemies, and has a number of scenarios for its completion.

tions of parametric practice found in BIM advocates and embedded within a neoliberal drive are little discussed (Shvartzberg and Poole, 2015, pp. 3–4). Often a wide representational knowledge and practice is covered in landscape curricula (Parvu and Torres, 2007), though this pedagogy has diverse digital deployment and its relationship to landscape practice are often at odds with wide degrees of 3D modelling capability.

The development of 3D modelling software by and large emerged from graphical software, architecture programs and computer gaming. GIS development ran concurrently and also overlapped. Some notable extracts from this history include SIGGRAPH (Special Interest Group on GRAPHics and Interactive Techniques), which was a conference series from 1974 in which many industry players demonstrated new graphical and animation techniques. This 'digital simulation' (Watt and Policarpo, 1998) in animation and game software generated architectural and environmental scenarios and emerged from software such as the 'Radar CH 1.0' (1984), which was the first virtual block modelling program which later developed into ArchiCAD. Game developments include the 3D commercial game Monster Maze for the Sinclair ZX81 in 1981. Graphic developments include StrataVision 3D, which was one of the first 3D modelling programs for desktop computers in 1989, with raytrace[4] and MacroModel by Macromedia (later Adobe) and post-production in Photoshop 1.0 (1990, raster graphics editor). This software can be seen applied in the creation of surreal landscapes of the imagination in the CD-ROM puzzle adventure computer game Myst (1993) by Cyan Inc., which utilised first-person movement around an 8-bit still-frame world with interactive elements (embedded animation) and ambient sounds. Thus, Myst was indicative of utopian game environments and fictional world generation which allowed terraforming, sky systems and the first-person view (FPV) of these virtual spaces:

> Virtual environments are computer generated domains which create a perception of traversable space and afford the exertion of player agency. They are populated by objects and often human or AI controlled entities with whom players can interact.
>
> (Gordon, 2009, p. 2)

These developments in 3D modelling gained in complexity as the generation of organic and natural forms was difficult given the complex geometry and algorithms needed for their generation. Maintaining a low polygon count has been seen as best practice for a long period in 3D modelling for game design; in wider disciplines hardware limitations have impacted their construction, meaning details and flora are often little considered. Rendering times of naturalised geometry can also be lengthy, with vegetation often being added later, in post-production. There is an increasing mediation between digital naturalism and built form which is gaining ground in game design, an area to which landscape architects and students who are interested in 3D modelling look (see Chang, 2013). This is not hyper-realism, but fidelity. Hyper-realism is a digital enhancement akin to the sublime or pastiche of the eighteenth century; it promises a truth as seen in the previous chapter that is often deceptive. Fidelity, however, is different in the lack of emphasis and a desire for clarity in the model generation. It is also not to say that a creative strategy will be reduced and that its transcription to built form is also possible. It can be seen in crowd simulation software such as MassMotion, with scenario generation for congestion modelling and easing for transport infrastructure (King *et al.*, 2014). It can also be seen in the computer simulation of plants through algorithmic botany; a number of open-source software programs are available to develop such details (Prusinkiewicz and Molt, 1996). Thus, the digital 3D model must be located in a wider cycle of representation agency and valence, make intrinsic connections to reality or clearly distinguish its fictional speculation and exploration. The fictional aspect of a 3D model's agency can be seen in scripting for 3D modelling; mathematical or intuitive manipulation of algorithms of the form become part of the designer's language, and these processes are shaped to connect to reality through digital fabrication or to remain within a virtual space.

In its current position, 3D modelling divides itself into BIM capabilities for project efficiency and the scripted, generational potential of mathematical organic forms as an extension of a designer's language. The two positions are not exclusive, but represent some of the converging paradigms of computational development, the 3D model as thinking, as fidelity of a prototype, as immersive and navigated and as an increasingly available and embedded mode within our lives.

LAYERING COMPLEXITY

Political and social forces are embedded in computational developments and the 3D model has often become a 'hanger' for layered data of various subjects, scales and complexity through geographic computation (Brunsdon, 2015). The 3D model becomes a point of orientation in which to project future landscape, urban and climatic issues. This is termed as big data, large packets of structured or unstructured data which are mined and processed to uncover patterns, theorise from and project futures. Big data situates itself between dystopian fears of centralisation and capital exploitation and utopian modes for new urbanism (Offenhuber and Ratti, 2014). Three-dimensional models become embroiled and scaled up with an ontology that seeks computational models of entire city systems, from capital, transport, energy, culture and many other aspects to model flows and networks (Batty, 2013). Big data could be seen as the hyper-driven desire of the 3D model to attempt fidelity of reality as well as its future. Predominately, this hyper-drive is attached to the process of globalisation concerned with the global competition of systems of cities and economic geographies and the creation of smart cities (Picon, 2015).

Information technologies thus propose 'smart cities' as key to growth and sustainability, though the evaluation of such claims is complex (Townsend, 2014). Smart cities and big data are representations of collective intelligence of whole systems, or our inability to achieve such a goal (Deakin, 2015). This is a very different representational agency and, like many of the forms discussed thus far, has limitations, gaps and voids and can never claim to be a representational form of a collective populace. Arguably big data and smart city hyper-drives are utopic in their position, just as the render of new imaginative landscapes was enabled through computer graphic innovation. Critics are cautious of such claims or see dystopian links in the relationship of big data and capitalism; the antithesis to this position is localised interactivity and a quest for urban happiness which is intrinsically linked to the quality of natural space (Montgomery, 2015).

This is a large and complex subject beyond this book, though the 3D model's role is important to recognise here. The 3D model may be a 3D map, laser scan or other aspect which captures physical features; it is the terrain in which values situate themselves. It is scaled from single sizes to urban blocks, from urban blocks to towns, cities and systems of cities, etc. and layered with various calculations from the identification of permeable surfaces, urban drainage, tree provision, building energy performance, solar, thermal, etc. On top of this layer exists further calculations and simulations such as walkability, service provision and crime maps among other fluid types. These data may change the role of the designer, allowing the testing of scenarios which were previously difficult to compute. This synthesis and the layering of complexity make the virtual model an abstract source which we design from ever more important, though the human element will remain and big data means that this

FIGURE 4.6 Developmental sequence of *Mycelis muralis*, Copyright © 1987 P. Prusinkiewicz and J. Hanan. The development of the wall lettuce is 3D modelled and generated using an L-systems mathematical model which shows the space time developments of plants and their parts, allowing the representation of biologically correct plant growth at various time periods (Prusinkiewicz and Molt, 1996).

STRATEGIES FOR REPRESENTATION

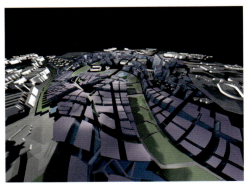
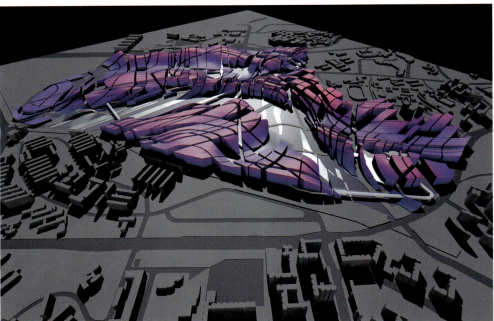

FIGURE 4.7 Zaha Hadid Architects, One North Masterplan, Singapore, 2001–2021. Courtesy of Zaha Hadid Architects. This masterplan for a new mixed-use urban business district in Singapore was the first of a series of radical masterplans by the practice, which led to the concept of parametric urbanism and then to the general concept of 'parametricism' (Schumacher, 2009). The proposal seeks to develop a new type of urban architecture through an evolution of the morphology of natural landscape formations. This is achieved using parametric software, which enables the designers to construct 'deep relationality' between the various elements of the scheme and across different scales, such as streets, blocks, buildings, etc., to produce a combinative, dynamic overall masterplan.

FIGURE 4.8 ASPECT Studios, The Goods Line (Realised), ASPECT Studios (Project Design Lead). Sydney Harbour Foreshore Authority (Client), CHROFI (Design Partner) 2015. The Goods Line, a NSW government initiative, was delivered by Sydney Harbour Foreshore Authority, from an elevated park from a disused rail facility into a multifunctional spine and pedestrian and cycle link. The visualisations were block modelled and vegetation, lighting effects and atmospheres added in post-production.

STRATEGIES FOR REPRESENTATION 141

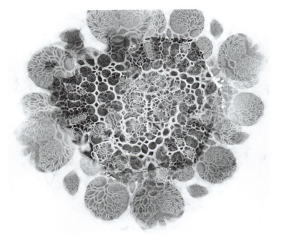

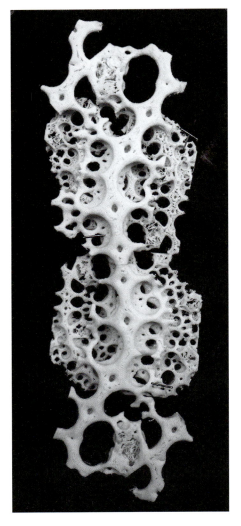
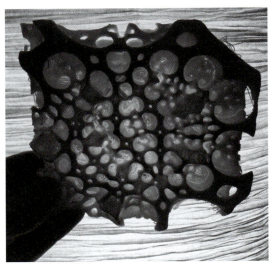

FIGURE 4.9
Alexandra Bergin, Architecture Research Lab, Plastisphere, 2014. Plastisphere is a speculative investigation that projects future visions of animal survival in a world of extensive human impacts, particularly plastic marine environments. Creating a marine research lab supported through a super-massive plastic marine membrane which supports microorganisms (Zettler *et al.*, 2013), Bergin utilises algorithms to generate the membrane and digitally fabricates test structures and surfaces.

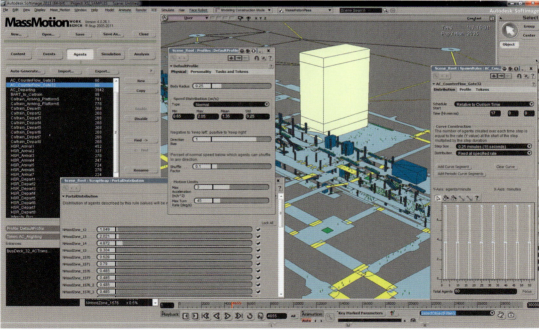

FIGURE 4.10 Visualisation of architecture and simulated pedestrian activity during the evening peak period, Union Station, Toronto, ON © Arup. MassMotion Workbench Interface, Transbay Transit Center, San Francisco, CA © Arup, 2015. The pedestrian software program MassMotion simulates 'agent' movements within a 3D model to calculate flow and capacity. The agents or virtual people can be controlled, have itineraries or utilise certain features like gateways. MassMotion allows the evaluation of both spatial composition and the operational possibility of each design.

FIGURE 4.11 AECOM, Marina Bay and Greater Southern Waterfront, Singapore (realised), 2012. AECOM utilised a Sustainable Systems Integration Model (SSIM(tm)) a whole-systems model, land-planning tool and climate model as a basis for sustainable development. The system uses sustainability metrics as a base for the most optimised design package. The system considers building energy, water services, transportation, public services and renewable energy systems and 'games' these modelled figures and spatial calculations working across disciplines (Sofian et al., 2015).

FIGURE 4.12 Aero3Dpro 3D model of Townsville, picture courtesy of Aerometrex, 2016. Aero3DPro creates geo-referenced, full-textured 3D models for use in a variety of professions – coastal management, urban planning and defence, among others. The virtual environment is navigable via tablets and other media devices, but also Oculus Rift thereby allowing augmented reality, real-time simulation and manipulation of urban factors. Such a simulation creates real-time environments from dawn until dusk.

FIGURE 4.13 Colour Urban Design, BIM for Landscape, 2016. Hartlepool produced in Infraworks at a masterplan scale to express the local vision. The block model creates a spatial typology to include the variety of visions of the town cycle infrastructure and navigation.

FIGURE 4.14
Karl Kullmann utilises 3D modelling as a mode of both deconstructing and working from the ground up. Burns Beach, Perth, Australia explores lifestyle programming in order to envision future landscape and uses utilising 3D modelling as a mode of exploring minimal topographic disturbance, rather than conventions of terracing in building development (Kullmann, 2014a). Kullmann rejects hyper realism as the de-facto mode of landscape modelling and evidences creative representations of data (Kullmann, 2014b).

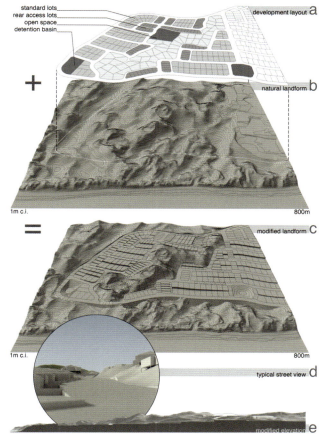

STRATEGIES FOR REPRESENTATION   147

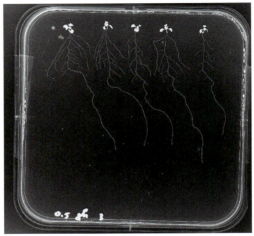

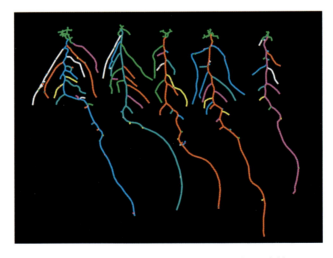

FIGURE 4.15 Rhizo Scan & Plants Scan, INRIA, 2012. Automated acquisition systems of root system architecture (RSA) are now readily available for developmental research and provide high-throughput image data of roots. Existing acquisition systems provide many types of data, from images of dispersed root pieces to full 3D scans of underground root systems (Diener *et al.*, 2013; Lobet *et al.*, 2015).

representational form has a very powerful and persuasive agency and can have big valence – both positive and negative effects. The drive for viewing the arteries of the city and seeing it as a whole can be traced back to Renaissance desires, though many future projections by their agency and valence created highly anxious spaces through a strict and logical order of space found in the work of Le Corbusier. From a technological utopia that purports to sense the whole city, there is a danger of that utopian vision turning very dystopian. Many of these models are based on large computational processes, and as Christine Boyer suggests, there is a sense that out of these iterative procedures new and unpredictable patterns emerge (Boyer, 2005, pp. 165–166). That very abstract manipulation and patterning creates a new paradigm in which we imagine our cities and landscapes.

WORKSTAGES AND STRATEGIES

To create a 3D model a number of workstages (also called pipelines) are required and a number of strategies to enable the models must also be considered. The emphasis of this section is on 3D modelling or 3D BIM. Once the 3D model is produced, a number of additional data sets can be derived or calculated. This could be the line of sight through an urban block, the solar potential of buildings or the flood risk to the site. Thus, the additional and complex data packets attached to the 3D model are not covered in this section. The model may also be used for digital fabrication, and this involves separate strategies and preparation (covered in Chapter 5). A selection of the workstages are covered in the book's companion website, though the purpose of this section is the emphasis on thinking about the overall strategy rather than highly detailed discussion (Christenson, 2015). BIM is a complex layer to the 3D model and further reference is required once these stages are complete. Often these stages are assumed and under-discussed, though it is vital to gauge the production life-cycle to create these models. This is essential in costing modelling time and staff resources in practice and also for students in meeting studio briefs. It is also worth preparing concepts prior to the modelling process to generate an initial outcome.

References (photographs, hand-drawings, mapping data). References are essential for accuracy of your 3D model, both in scale terms but also as indicators of reality. For example, a site sketch may be imported to the workspace to provide an easy reference from which to derive a 3D sketch. Often modellers import four 2D views of objects – say north, south, east, west – in which to develop the model. Another approach is to use perspective-match techniques with site photographs to match the 3D model plane to the 2D plane using reference points – this creates a perspective of the 3D model and design to a site photograph. References can also include BIM objects – parametric objects with attached building specifications supplied by manu-facturers – or BIM resource websites. 3D GIS mapping data may also form the base reference.

Collaboration. Collaboration is an increasing possibility, particularly in BIM projects, in which a central administrator may direct and manage each of the design elements

FIGURE 4.16 (*this page and facing*) Tom Beddard, The Kingdom of Aurullia, 2015. Beddard utilises FractalLab to generate 3D fractals – each part has the same character as the whole and creates complex patterns and recurrences. The search for serendipity forms a big part of Beddard's process exploring 3D fractal algorithms. This case proved very fruitful with the city-scape like structures appearing merely as a side-effect from different combinations of parameters. The sequence could be snapshots of an alien civilisation through time as they grow in complexity to dominate and consume their domain.

STRATEGIES FOR REPRESENTATION

and delegate specific tasks to team members remotely. This collaboration is incredibly important in streamlining production tasks and utilising the team's strengths. For animators, often the modelling, rigging, animation, environment, rendering, effects and post-production are delivered by large teams of specialists with specific designated roles and individual strengths (Evans, 2013).

Modelling. There are different approaches to modelling which involve working from primitives, laser scans or scanning, among other modes (see the 'Modelling modes' section below). The choice of software must also be considered; interoperability is important. If using large GIS data sets, it may be preferable to work in programs such as QGIS, ESRI City Engine or Blender, or if script modelling then Rhino; for complex modelling and animation, perhaps Maya. Researching the software company's development labs is particularly useful as new procedures may save time and reduce the number or processes involved in production. An important and often overlooked aspect is the exploration of the software interface – which file types can be imported and which file types you can export as. This allows you to map the different software and to create a strategy of moving your work between them.

Texturing. There are a number of different ways to texture your 3D model. New approaches include 3D painting – using textures and colours to brush or spray on the sculpted model offer time-saving solutions. UV (U = horizontal; V = vertical) texturing is one of the most common methods, which involves a 2D texture with each pixel assigned to a coordinate of the 3D object, known as vertices. It is best thought of as a flat-pack texture which can be wrapped around the 3D object. Texture mapping is highly complex, though texture packs can be purchased to speed-up production. Any original texture photography or painted material should aim to be as 2D as possible. Bump textures can also assist modelling work and give the illusion of a 3D surface without any additional modelling. Normal mapping is a contemporary technique for the illusion of light and dents on a surface. Displacement maps distort the surface of the model, creating additional geometry.

Lighting and environments. Sky portals can be added to create natural light sources and lighting tags can be added to objects to show landscape lighting design. A sphere can also be added which surrounds the 3D model; the interior of the sphere is then textured with a sky image which gives the effect of a large volume environment in which the 3D model is situated.

FIGURE 4.17 (*facing page*) Atelier Crilio, Oteiza House, 2015. Designed with reference to Jorge Oteiza investigating his 'intention experimental' with simple geometric forms and the notion that all artistic practice surges from a void that eventually reaches a nothing that is everything (Hillargia, n.d.). Atelier Crilio integrate the architectural proposal with its surrounds, meticulously modelling the adjacent stream, woodland and topography. The studio sculpts the terrain and then proceeds to 3D paint, model the structure and place *in situ*. The studio workflow incorporates Speed Tree, allowing careful plant and tree specification and the final stages involve careful compositional choices through clay renders, then rendering at various time zones.

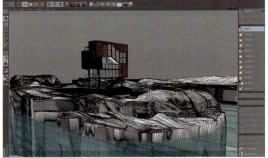

STRATEGIES FOR REPRESENTATION 153

FIGURE 4.18 Marijn Raeven, Natural Environments (Cinema 4D) 2015. In Raeven's animated work, natural environments are generated from a terrain base, terrain texturing, tree modelling, leaves, waterbody, leaf distribution, lighting and environments, shadows and camera viewports.

Atmospheres. Fog, smoke, dust or particles (rain, sparks, etc.) and other atmospherics can be added to the 3D model to create site conditions. Referencing local weather systems and time zones may also assist in the choice of atmosphere created in the 3D space.

Rendering and animation. The rendering process creates a 2D raster image of the 3D model and involves a large amount of computer system resources to achieve the image; the render takes the modelling, texturing, lighting, environments and atmospheres parameters to compute production. Additional steps are required for animation, including the rigging of the 3D objects, dictating movement types by frame, checking joints and the maintenance of textures through movement. Often 'render farms' are particularly useful – dedicated desktops or laptops which process each still or animation frame.

Post-production. Post-production involves the addition of any animated effects, still enhancements using Photoshop, or effects in animation and the emphasis of particular factors.

3D modelling principles and types

There are different workflows for 3D modelling, and a combination of these types can be used or converted into another type. This workflow is not exhaustive and readers should refer to the book's companion website and additional sources cited for extended discussions and tutorials.

- **Polygons**: also known as meshes, these can be 2D or 3D lines of an object that create a wireframe. An example of this is a triangular integrated surface (TIN).
- **NURBS**: using control points, a surface is generated in a 3D space.
- **Subdivision**: a coarser polygon can be smoothed and is preferred for representing organic shapes. It may also be possible to simulate the illusion of a smoother 3D object without the use of subdivision.

Using the modelling types, polygons, NURBS or subdivisions, the following can be created:

- **Wireframe**: a wireframe can be a mesh or polygon which has edges, vertices and faces.
- **Surface model**: a surface or shell is super-thin and represents a 3D object, though it is not solid.
- **Solid model**: a solid model has mass, volume and a gravitational centre.

Modelling modes

When creating design work, a number of modelling options may be utilised and it is important to understand the processes in order to achieve the desired results. This improves modelling efficiency and production time.

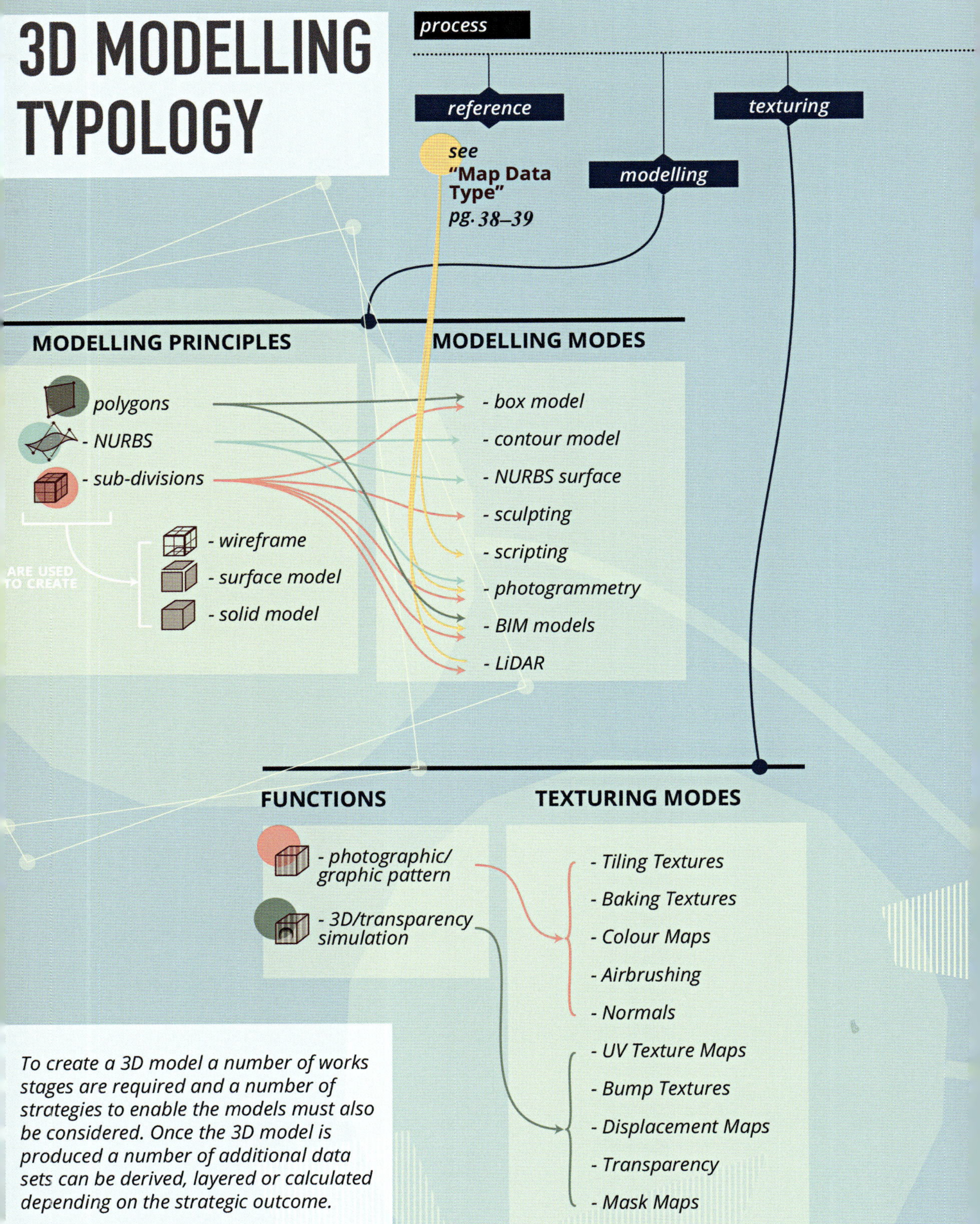

3D MODELLING TYPOLOGY

process

reference — see "Map Data Type" pg. 38–39

modelling

texturing

MODELLING PRINCIPLES

- polygons
- NURBS
- sub-divisions

ARE USED TO CREATE:
- wireframe
- surface model
- solid model

MODELLING MODES

- box model
- contour model
- NURBS surface
- sculpting
- scripting
- photogrammetry
- BIM models
- LiDAR

FUNCTIONS

- photographic/graphic pattern
- 3D/transparency simulation

TEXTURING MODES

- Tiling Textures
- Baking Textures
- Colour Maps
- Airbrushing
- Normals
- UV Texture Maps
- Bump Textures
- Displacement Maps
- Transparency
- Mask Maps

To create a 3D model a number of works stages are required and a number of strategies to enable the models must also be considered. Once the 3D model is produced a number of additional data sets can be derived, layered or calculated depending on the strategic outcome.

FIGURE 4.19 Serena Pollastri, Imagination Lancaster, Lancaster University, 3D Modelling Typology, 2016.

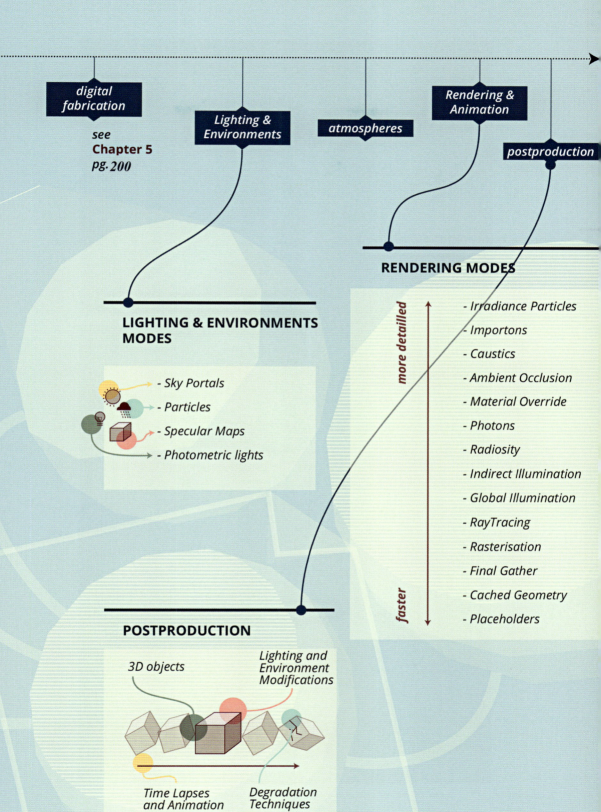

FIGURE 4.20 Christophe Girot, Topology: On Sensing and Conceiving Landscape, 2015. True colour point cloud model (Girot, 2012, 2013).

Box modelling. A simple primitive such as a cone, cube or square is edited to create the desired form. Reference images may be placed next to the primitive and the modeller may have multiple views, and copy the reference, adjusting and editing the form as they progress. The primitive maybe **subdivided**.

Contour modelling. This is the creation of edges of the form desired; the edges are then infilled. This allows greater control than subdividing a primitive.

NURBS surfaces. NURBS (non-uniform rational basis spline) surfaces are edited by manipulating control points or control polygons. Additional points may be added for complexity.

Sculpting. This involves direct manipulation of surfaces, carving, pulling and pushing; it is a newer modelling mode, useful for imaginative speculation of terrains, and is intuitive and tactile creation of meshes from scratch. Additional features allow direct texture painting on the surface mesh, offering quicker modelling processes.

Scripting. Also known as procedural modelling, such as L-Systems, fractals and generative modelling. This procedure involves the instigation of rule- or value-based parameters on a form to control it (Burry, 2011). For example, the application Speed Tree allows specification of vegetation, growth and wind simulation. Scripting may be used at city scale as in ESRI's City Engine for the visualisation and creation of street blocks, for example. Dynamo and Grasshopper are two popular choices.

Photogrammetry. This is the deriving of 3D assets from 2D images to create 3D meshes or photographic point clouds. Distances are measured between the camera position and the object; colour spectrum is also calculated to create a 3D mesh. A number of free software programs allow this creation using cameras, phones and tablets, as well as drones. For complex calculations, GIS preparation is required, involving orthorectification, feature extraction and height calculations.

BIM models. Building information models can be used within the modelling process, from manufacturer's products, to energy performance analysis, mass models or other forms. Stereo pair photography can be used to create 3D building models which have high degrees of accuracy and can be brought into the workflow (Landscape Institute, 2016). The BIM process could be applied from inception if specific products and building specifications are needed, or added to the project at a later stage. The linearity of traditional 3D modelling is changed dramatically in BIM cases, where capital costs are greatly reduced and collaborative working affects traditional specialists (Tennant *et al.*, 2015, pp. 111–112). Visualisation artists and 2D CAD technicians may find their workflows blurred and crossed over, or may find construction projects 'gamified' in interactive navigable games at various stages of production.

Laser scanning. Laser Scanning (LiDAR) is the laser scanning of real-world places or objects to form the bases in which to model. Received as a point cloud, the data requires rasterising, or can be manipulated or repaired. Once rasterised, the surface

FIGURE 4.21 Lee Griggs, particles rendered with Arnold for Maya, 2014.

can be manipulated, solid modelled and digitally fabricated, among other options. Aerial photography may be orthorectified and draped on the LiDAR model, effectively texturing the 3D surface model. A photographic point cloud may be a preferred option, given the cost of LiDAR acquisition (Keranen and Kolvoord, 2015).

Texturing modes

Once the modelling process is developed and the range of strategies applied, the surfaces may be textured – that is, the application of photographic or graphic textures on a 'blank' 3D surface.

- **Tiling textures.** Textures can be tiled if all edges match on repeat; some Photoshop work to site photographs can generate textures used in the 3D model. The tiled textures can be scaled to avoid distortion.
- **Baking textures.** This involves 'baking' an image of some parts of the render ahead of time, for selected objects. For example, a light on a wall can be 'baked' and reapplied to the 3D model, thus saving render time due to fewer lighting calculations.
- **Colour maps.** Colour maps define the surface colour of your texture material without any light or shade factors.

FIGURE 4.22 Paul Cureton, Strategies for Landscape, 50 m LiDAR data with satellite 30 cm ortho-photo drape. Produced with ESRI Arc Map 10.3, Arc Scene, Autodesk 3DS Max 2016, cloud particle system with Fume Fx and post-production with Adobe Photoshop.

- **Airbrushing.** This involves the use of 3D painting tools to apply photo or graphic textures to a 3D surface in software programs such as ZBrush (Lewis, 2016), Mudbox (Jeremy and Patel, 2012) or Blender (Thilakanathan, 2016).
- **Normals.** Normals designate the face on which the texture is applied. Thus, the texture needs to be applied to the front face of a surface. Normal maps are 2D flat-packs on which the user can paint detail without adding to the polygon count.
- **UV texture maps.** A UV texture is a flat-pack of a texture that wraps a model. PTEX is a newer method of modelling, applying textures to the specific mesh without the need for coordinates; it has no seams, unlike UVs.
- **Bump textures.** Bump textures are greyscale images. They are duplicates of a full-colour image, but in greyscale. Both colour and greyscale image are loaded together. The greyscale texture is read by the renderer and gives the impression in the render process that it 'bumps' (raises or recesses) the surface, when it makes no such physical modifications.
- **Displacement maps.** Displacement maps are similar to bump textures, though rather than simulating a raised surface they affect the actual geometry and raise or depress the surface.
- **Transparency.** Some software programs cannot interpret transparency settings; others can take a texture with transparent surfaces and allow that surface to be seen through. This of course can also depend on file type. JPEGs do not have transparent capability, whereas TIFF or PNG files do.
- **Mask maps.** Mask maps allow two textures to be displayed on one surface.

Digital fabrication

Once the model is developed, it may be prepared for digital fabrication as a 2D vector work or 3D object. It may be produced by a CNC miller, laser cutter or 3D printer using additive or subtractive manufacture. See Chapter 5 for a discussion and the companion website for resources.

Lighting and environments

Lighting and rendering can be used to evaluate the design proposal and simulate various conditions; both naturalised lighting and artificial lighting can be used. BIM lighting components may have controllable luminosity and specification, allow a match between virtual and built environments.

- **Specular maps.** Specular maps are the application of light and dark on a texture surface, which can be painted in.
- **Sky portals.** Sky portals define the sky and sun settings within the 3D model. An interior will not render correctly if the sky portal is not in place. Sun positions, strength, size and brightness can all be controlled. Sky portals can sometimes be geo-referenced and seasonal choices and time zones can be applied.
- **Photometric lights.** Photometric lights make reference to manufacturer's lighting specifications and can be used to add precision to the rendering and allow the simulation of different fixture choices on the design proposal.
- **Particles.** Particles can be used to simulate realistic snow, rain and smoke. You can also add physics simulations, like avoidance, gravity and bounce.

Rendering and animation

Rendering involves the creation of a 2D image (or still) from a 3D object in a virtual space. This can be a time-intensive and resource-heavy task, and it is important not to under-estimate the time and resources needed to complete renders. Render farms with networks of computers able to render each frame and cloud rendering may speed up this process. In some software engines you can strip the image – dividing one image into parts and allocating each strip to different computers. Rendering times are dependent on the lighting and material choices, as well as the settings chosen. Strategies in the modelling process should take account of the final output for these works, whether print graphics or motion and effects (Smith, 2011). The range of rendering engines is extensive, with discipline-specific preferences and intentions. Rendering is the summation of the 3D modelling workflow and the choices and range of tools for these outputs are extensive. It is advisable to create a simple interior and exterior terrain to test and explore the dynamics between geometry, materials, lighting and environments and render settings to fully gauge each tool's possibilities. The following typology refers to common elements in the rendering process, though is not exhaustive.

- **Rasterisation.** Rasterisation is a method of rendering which can produce motion effects and converts vector images into raster images.
- **Material override.** Material override applies one material to every element; this is especially useful to evaluate the lighting design in the 3D model, as you can source the colours that lighting choices provide.
- **Cached geometry.** Cached geometry is useful if no further geometrical changes take place as it allows faster computation times.
- **Raytracing.** Raytracing enables indirect illumination, depth of field, refraction and shadows.
- **Placeholders.** These are boxes that surround your geometry as empty boxes to reduce processing time and navigation until rendering takes place.
- **Radiosity.** Radiosity calculates indirect light and is a process which is part of global illumination.
- **Indirect illumination.** Indirect illumination bounces light around the scene.
- **Final gather.** Final gather adds indirect illumination to landscape scenes. You may cache the final gather to speed-up high-resolution render time.
- **Global illumination.** Global illumination can be a separate setting or be part of indirect illumination.
- **Photons.** Photons are closer to what occurs in nature; it is RGB separated colours which react in different ways to permeable and opaque surfaces.
- **Caustics.** Caustics are indirect illumination of concentrated light from transparent objects – refraction and the scattering of light from reflective surfaces (O'Connor, 2010, pp. 220–226).
- **Ambient occlusion.** Ambient occlusion adds naturalism to surfaces through soft shadows and is the opposite of ambient light or global illumination.
- **Importons.** Importons merge together and remove any unnecessary photons.
- **Irradiance particles.** Irradiance particles fire importons into the viewport that locate a surface for their placement. From this point indirect and direct illumination is stored within the particle. This is a useful tool for naturalised objects.

Post-production

Post-production involves final adjustments and finishes to the rendered 3D model or animation. The relationship between perspective composites and 3D modelling is blurred. The post-production process has changed dramatically, allowing the insertion of 3D content in 2D rendered images, animation of stills to create time-lapse pieces and a whole host of toolsets and options for changing the work. The final rendered image may also be traced, and hand-drawn elements may be added through drawing tablets, or printed and drawn upon then re-scanned. Often the artificial quality that can result from the rendering process may require degradation, ageing and damaging surfaces and objects. Post-production may also involve atmospheric effects, lighting enhancements and the populating of views.

SUMMARY

3D modelling is a complex process and its synergistic position between virtual spaces and fabrication is of high importance. The 3D model provides the volume necessary to critically evaluate design spaces. The 3D model can be a speculative agent or the coat hanger on which complex data sets are hung and attached. Thus the 3D model may be the output of imaginative or speculative scripting or the developed base on which to create project efficiency. Importantly, the 3D model forms part of a chain of representational activities to evaluate landscape, from mapping, notation and perspectives. There are no perfect 3D models, though the increasing data-carrying ability and relationship between algorithmic ideational forms and its translation to built-form changes the creative possibilities and outputs of designers. The 3D model and its drive for fidelity of places can be seen at larger scales in big data and smart city agendas, in which the 3D model forms a base of urban calculations.

The 3D model can also be part of the animated and motion-captured world, creating fidelity to environmental atmospheres. Immersive technologies also accelerate this fidelity for tactile first-person manipulation of objects. While the creative terrain is explored, 3D modelling has an increasing importance in collaborative projects, building specifications and project delivery.

NOTES

1. American Institute of Architects (AIA) and BIM Strategy Group in the UK. Australia, Spain, Singapore and Taiwan, among others, place equal emphasis on building information modelling, and this is becoming mandatory for construction projects.
2. 2D BIM can be understood as 2D drawings defining a contractual arrangement. 3D BIM is a virtual model containing parametric objects that make up the project design. 4D BIM is the time-based aspect of the 3D model defining the quantities, schedules and production information. 5D BIM defines the estimates of quantities and manpower. 6D involves the management of the project life-cycle. These increasing levels of attached information can be understood as the true amalgamation between a computer model and the reality of a construction project.

3   Virtual modelling reliant on a stream of constraints and calculations which develops a form.
4   Raytracing computes the paths of light through pixels in a viewport to simulate the effects of light on virtual objects to create a virtual realism.

BIBLIOGRAPHY

Azuma, R.T., 1997. A Survey of Augmented Reality. *Presence: Teleoperators and Virtual Environments*, 6: 355–385. doi: 10.1162/pres.1997.6.4.355.

Batty, M., 2013. *The New Science of Cities*. MIT Press, Cambridge, MA.

Boyer, C., 2005. Playing with Information. In Read, S., Rosemann, J. and Eldijk, J. van (eds), *Future City*, new edition. Routledge, London.

Brunsdon, C., 2015. *Geocomputation*. Sage, Thousand Oaks.

Burry, M., 2011. *Scripting Cultures: Architectural Design and Programming*. John Wiley & Sons, Chichester.

Carpo, M. (ed.), 2012. *The Digital Turn in Architecture 1992–2012*. John Wiley & Sons, Chichester.

Ceruzzi, P.E., 2003. *A History of Modern Computing*, 2nd revised edition. MIT Press, Cambridge, MA.

Chang, A.Y., 2013. *Playing Nature: The Virtual Ecology of Game Environments*. eScholarship.

Christenson, M., 2015. *Beginning Design Technology*. Routledge, New York.

Deakin, M. (ed.), 2015. *Smart Cities*. Routledge, London.

Diener, J., Nacry, P., Périn, C., *et al.*, 2013. An automated image-processing pipeline for high-throughput analysis of root architecture in OpenAlea. FSPM2013 Proceedings.

Evans, D. (ed.), 2013. *Digital Mayhem 3D Landscape Techniques: Where Inspiration, Techniques and Digital Art Meet*. Focal Press, Burlington, MA.

Girot, C., 2012. *Landscape Vision Motion*. Jovis Verlag, Berlin.

Girot, C., 2013. *Topology: Topical Thoughts on the Contemporary Landscape*. Jovis Verlag, Berlin.

Gordon, C., 2009. Experiential Narrative in Game Environments. DiGRA '09 – Proceedings of the 2009 DiGRA International Conference: Breaking New Ground: Innovation in Games, Play, Practice and Theory.

Grilo, A. and Jardim-Goncalves, R., 2010. Building information modeling and collaborative working environments. *Automation in Construction*, 19: 521. doi: 10.1016/j.autcon.2009.11.002.

Hillargia, n.d.. Guggenheim Museum Bilbao. www.guggenheim-bilbao.es/en/works/hillargia-2 (accessed 13 January 2016).

Jeremy, R. and Patel, S., 2012. *Mudbox 2013 Cookbook*. Packt Publishing, Birmingham.

Keranen, K. and Kolvoord, R., 2015. *Making Spatial Decisions Using GIS and LiDAR: A Workbook*, workbook edition. ESRI Press, Redlands.

King, D., Srikukenthiran, S. and Shalaby, A., 2014. Using Simulation to Analyze Crowd Congestion and Mitigation at Canadian Subway Interchanges: Case of Bloor-Yonge Station, Toronto, Ontario. *Transportation Research Record: Journal of the Transportation Research Board*, 2417: 27–36.

Kipper, G. and Rampolla, J., 2012. *Augmented Reality: An Emerging Technologies Guide to AR*. Syngress, Amsterdam.

Kullmann, K., 2014a. The Emergence of Suburban Terracing on Coastal Dunes: Case Studies along the Perth Northern Corridor, Western Australia, 1930–2010. *Journal of Urban Design*, 19: 593–621. doi: 10.1080/13574809.2014.943704.

Kullmann, K., 2014b. Hyper-Realism and Loose-Reality: The Limitations of Digital Realism and Alternative Principles in Landscape Design Visualization. *Journal of Landscape Architecture*, 9: 20–31. doi: 10.1080/18626033.2014.968412.

Landscape Institute, 2016. *BIM for Landscape*. Routledge, London.

Lewis, M., 2016. *Sketching from the Imagination in ZBrush*. 3dtotal Publishing, Worcester.

Lobet, G., Pound, M.P., Diener, J., et al. 2015. Root System Markup Language: Toward a Unified Root Architecture Description Language. *Plant Physiology*, 167: 617–627.

Mahoney, M.S. and Haigh, T., 2011. *Histories of Computing*. Harvard University Press, Cambridge, MA.

Mitchell, W.J., 1979. *Computer Aided Architectural Design*. Van Nostrand Reinhold, New York.

Montgomery, C., 2015. *Happy City: Transforming Our Lives Through Urban Design*. Penguin, New York.

Moum, A., 2010. Design Team Stories: Exploring Interdisciplinary Use of 3D Object Models in Practice. *Automation in Construction*, 19: 554–569. doi: 10.1016/j.autcon.2009.11.007.

O'Connor, J., 2010. *Mastering Mental Ray: Rendering Techniques for 3D and CAD Professionals*, Sybex, Indianapolis.

Offenhuber, D. and Ratti, C., 2014. *Decoding the City: How Big Data Can Change Urbanism*. Birkhauser Verlag AG, Basel.

Parvu, S. and Torres, E., 2007. Landscoping. *Journal of Landscape Architecture*, 2: 20–29. doi: 10.1080/18626033.2007.9723377.

Pérez-Goméz, A. and Pelletier, L. 2000. *Architectural Representation and the Perspective Hinge*, new edition. MIT Press, Cambridge, MA.

Picon, A., 2015. *Smart Cities: A Spatialised Intelligence – AD Primer*. John Wiley & Sons, Chichester.

Pinder, D., 2005. *Visions of the City: Utopianism, Power and Politics in Twentieth-Century Urbanism*. Edinburgh University Press, Edinburgh.

Prusinkiewicz, P. and Molt, W., 1996. *The Algorithmic Beauty of Plants*, paperback reprint. Springer, New York.

Reichardt, J., 1971. *Computer in Art*. Littlehampton Book Services Ltd, London.

Russell, S. and Norvig, P., 2013. *Artificial Intelligence: A Modern Approach*, 3rd edition. Pearson, Harlow.

Schumacher, P., 2009. Parametric Patterns. *Architectural Design: Patterns of Architecture*, 79 (6): 28–41.

Shvartzberg, M.P. and Poole, M., 2015. *The Politics of Parametricism*. Bloomsbury Academic, London.

Smith, B.L., 2011. *3DS Max Design Architectural Visualization: For Intermediate Users*. Focal Press, Waltham, MA.

Sofian, S., Li, X., Kusumawardhani, P. and Widiyani, W., 2015. Sustainable Systems Integration Model: Metrics in Design Process. *Reflections on Creativity: Public Engagement and the Making of Place*, 184: 297–309. doi: 10.1016/j.sbspro.2015.05.094.

Spuybroek, L., 2016. *The Sympathy of Things: Ruskin and the Ecology of Design*, 2nd revised edition. Bloomsbury Academic, London.

Spuybroek, L., Benjamin, A., Delanda, M., et al., 2004. *NOX: Machining Architecture*. Thames and Hudson Ltd, New York.

Sutherland, I., 2003. *Sketchpad: A Man–Machine Graphical Communication System*. University of Cambridge, Cambridge.

Taylor, G.D., 2014. *When the Machine Made Art: The Troubled History of Computer Art*. Bloomsbury Academic, New York.

Tennant, R., Garmory, N. and Winsch, C., 2015. *Professional Practice for Landscape Architects*, 3rd edition. Routledge, London.

Thilakanathan, M.D., 2016. *Blender 3D for Beginners: The Complete Guide. The Complete Beginner's Guide to Getting Started with Navigating, Modeling, Animating, Texturing, Lighting, Compositing and Rendering within Blender*. CreateSpace Independent Publishing Platform.

Townsend, A.M., 2014. *Smart Cities: Big Data, Civic Hackers, and the Quest for a New Utopia*, reprint. W.W. Norton & Company, New York.

Wang, X. and Love, P.E., 2012. BIM + AR: Onsite Information Sharing and Communication Via Advanced Visualization. Presented at the 2012 IEEE 16th International Conference on Computer Supported Cooperative Work in Design (CSCWD), pp. 850–855. doi: 10.1109/CSCWD.2012.6221920.

Watt, D.A. and Policarpo, F., 1998. *The Computer Image*. Addison Wesley, Harlow.

Zettler, E.R., Mincer, T.J. and Amaral-Zettler, L.A., 2013. Life in the 'Plastisphere': Microbial Communities on Plastic Marine Debris. *Environment, Science and Technology*, 47: 7137–7146. doi: 10.1021/es401288x.

FIGURE 5.1 Team 4, The Retreat, 1963. The embedded structure in Cornwall is an example of the agency of model making; carefully executed maquettes derived from sketches develop the structural trapezoid shell and space for that allows panoramic views across an estuary. The maquette helps develop the viewing angle and extent that the model should be dug in and situated within the surrounding landscape.

5
LANDSCAPE MODELLING AND FABRICATION (MODELS)

> When communicating, a model always has the advantage that you are seeing everything at once, that you have an overview and can look at things from different angles ... the model always retains a certain degree of abstraction ... you can't depict the final state of your project since vegetation changes over time. ...
>
> (Günther Vogt, in Bornhauser *et al.*, 2015, pp. 198–199)

> Ubiquitous computing is roughly the opposite of virtual reality. Where virtual reality puts people inside a computer-generated world, ubiquitous computing forces the computer to live out here in the world with people.
>
> (Weiser, 1999, pp. 3–4)

This chapter discusses 3D printing and automated digital fabrication of landscape sites, current limitations and future possibilities. 3D printing can be termed a type of additive manufacture (AM). AM refers to several different modes of production which add material to create a 3D object. 3D printing is the computer control and extrusion of material into a 3D object. This chapter is not an exhaustive exploration of landscape architecture and urban design model making, but connects the previous chapters and representational modes and focuses on the 3D printing of 3D data and strategies for model types. The model is a type of abstract for something else; it reproduces future or historical conditions at varying scales. The model is representational in essence, as Günther Vogt reflects, also noting the difficulties of representing time, succession and vegetation in the landscape architecture physical model.

Mark Weiser's opening futurological comments on computational possibilities also have relevance to contemporary model making. Computer processes have embedded themselves within everyday life, and to Weiser they have become invisible or ubiquitous. This can be applied to the landscape representational arena where, to an extent, 3D printing has already embedded itself in home markets. Projects such as Rep Rap are open community projects that supply cost-effective kits and allow self-replicating parts to create home-made 3D printers and make resources even more accessible. Aside from this, the ability to model, both digitally and physically, feedback, manipulate, respond and have embedded sensory capabilities is coming more to the fore.

The potential for a certain fidelity and accurate description of landscape conditions through digital fabrication is an emerging avenue for landscape architecture model making. The previous chapter discussed 3D modelling as a basis for connecting various representational strands to create an overall strategy. Following the previous chapter, various models can be derived from the 3D data (Menges, 2015). The ability to create physical models to communicate landscape and urban conditions as well as proposals still remains a vital strategic tool for landscape representation, and there is a wealth of sources, particularly in architectural model making, with wide coverage of the subject (Smith, 2004; Knoll and Hechinger, 2007). Creating landscape physical models changes the agency of representation; it provides a tangible resource and 3D output for audiences.

The agency of physical model making is their tangible physical qualities, as Nick Dunn states. The language of the model provides a different type of encoding, allowing a greater readability and understanding (Dunn, 2014, p. 6). Landscape modelling can be completed in a variety of modes; it has until recently largely revolved around abstraction of reality, emphasising certain qualities or elements particular to the landscape brief rather than strict accuracies derived from remote-sensing in the natural sciences or earlier techniques of survey. While these techniques are not necessarily new, model making still has a role in attempting to explain the complexity of the earth's surface, designs, spaces and changes at multiple scales. This agency is also part of the design process; the physical model is generative at the conceptual stage, but also presentational and interactive with its digital state.

The design work may be executed with many different models from concepts to set scales. Some of these scales may not allow manually crafted details to be added and this has remained a limiting factor in production, especially at scales above 1:1,000. Digital fabrication is on the agenda and within the scope of knowledge of students or practices, though it may be an expensive mode of production beyond a project budget for large pieces. A hybrid approach of digital fabrication combined with handcraft techniques offers a mode to address both challenges to retain a range of creative expression (Dunn, 2012, p. 20).

This form of model making and abstraction is changing dramatically given the abundance of new toolsets and future directions. The synergy between computer-generated digital models and computer-controlled production is closer than ever, as is the ability to feedback to the virtual or create processes and algorithms for self-replication. Model making has remained a core component of representation and it is intertwined with the digital 3D model, creating intrinsic, often obsessive patterns and forms (Schmal, 2015). Three-dimensional printing affords a certain fidelity to landscape if the digital file is correctly modelled and a number of techniques employed. This means connection to mapping (Chapter 1) and 3D modelling (Chapter 4), creating an overall strategy that connects different representational aspects. The 3D model may also involve a perspective relief derived from Chapter 3, or the data projection of fieldwork findings and community consultation (Chapter 2). The direction of landscape model making runs tangentially to architectural model making and derives from many techniques in production. Architectural model making has embraced digital agency to physical outputs, exploring mathematical scripts to contour, tessellate, section and form prototypes (Iwamoto, 2009). This agency takes scripting and form finding, modelling and sculpting of landscapes and moves to create this work in physical models; the digital agency transports between media, it translates ideas across forms. Architectural model making research has also explored the material aspect of such outputs, looking at its integration, structural and organic possibilities (Beorkrem, 2012). These two aspects, digital agency and material research, are strong components of work as seen in the work of Fran Castillo, EcoLogic Studio and Yuichiro Takeuchi.

Model making has a rich history of explanation, as the Renaissance architect Leon Battista Alberti famously observed:

> I have often conceived of projects in the mind that seemed quite commendable at the time; but when I translated them into drawings, I found several errors in the very parts that delighted me the most, and quite serious ones; again, when I return to drawings, and measure the dimensions, I recognise and lament my carelessness; finally, when I pass from drawings to the model, I sometimes notice further mistakes in the individual parts, even over number.
>
> (Alberti, 1988, book IX, chapter X, p. 317)

While modern landscape and architectural design does not necessarily follow such a strict design process as Alberti describes, the highlighting of errors is an important point. As Pari Riahi remarks, Alberti creates a threefold division: an idea, its representation and adjustment, the heuristic stemming from the model (Riahi, 2015, p. 60). Digital errors can be corrected to an extent, but still rely on model making fundamentals and structural accountability – for example, LiDAR surveys can detect birds and create data spikes and simple translation to 3D prints results in strange vertices. Following this, digital fabrication affords a certain improvement. Material imperfections may also emerge, meaning hand finishing and repairs are necessary. Thus, the model is intrinsic to design practice; for example, Buckminster-Fuller arguably could not have realised geodesic structures without a model making stage (Buckminster-Fuller and Snyder, 2009). This intrinsic quality arguably comes from the haptic essence of model making, of the testing of material possibilities as well as the development of presentation models.

The haptic is the sense of touch resulting from the direct working of model materials; often the model is interacted with even if no contact is stipulated. During the construction process, the relationship between materials can be sensed; through that juxtaposition reflections can emerge for the material specification. This material working also provides a sense of duration and time, for example by ageing iron and using this in works. The primal qualities of these materials can be explored; certain stonework that may be specified can be used in the model making stage to gauge its tactile quality. Ultimately, through haptics and materiality, the sense of embodying the space can be forecast, as Juhani Pallasmaa writes, 'vision reveals what the touch already knows' (Pallasmaa, 2005, p. 42).

This also has pedagogical implications, meaning model making is a reflective tool on design concepts between students and tutors, between office departments and practice teams. The model is also the most tangible stage before a project becomes realised (Dunn, 2007, pp. 30–33). Research into phenomenology of landscape experience is an extremely rich area of enquiry for fieldwork; in the case of model making, haptics has equal weight. The feedback from touch and working of materials and the responses it provides has a particular agency and heuristic; a way of learning through making.

Haptics as the sense of touch becomes complex with digital fabrication, however; the process of handcraft is replaced by computer control and there are dangers that the sense of 'thinking through' as the model is crafted, a certain heuristics, is lost (Paterson, 2007). Digital haptic technology is thus required, such as AR systems and software toolsets mimicking manual techniques or real-time laser scanning or eye-tracking manipulation. The ontology of model making is reconfigured, even more so in interactive models and responsive systems (Dade-Robertson, 2011). This can be seen in the archaeological use by Gary Priestnall of the Mayson Model, in which Victorian plaster models are replicated through CNC milling, some finished with the same traditional painting modes, others augmented.

Three-dimensional printing is not a shortcut for model making or design communication, nor an easy option for those less confident in model making, as errors appear as much as with handcrafted modes. In itself, a 3D-printed design or map may be an interesting artefact, though it is a redundant work given the need for time-based representation in landscape. This issue can by and large be overcome through interactivity with the model; environmental immersion, data projection and device control of modelling, such as lighting displays and data overlays, brings a level of interaction to the work. The augmented model making process

> and the involved action, modelling – in landscape architecture are not only suitable for depiction and understanding of (future) reality, but are also instrumental for manipulation, analysis and expression of ideas, forms and relationships available in two and three-dimensional space.
> (Breen and Stellingwerff, 2011 p. 2)

Again, careful strategies are required and the relationship between digital and physical must be clear and easily transferrable. Steffen Nijhuis, in another article, views GIS in landscape architecture as a heuristic of future landscape realities (Nijhuis, 2014, p. 94), and to that extent 2D and 3D digital models and 3D physical models that share the same geographic projection system and coordinates create feedback loops, scenario testing and real-time projection of diverse and large-scale data packets.

LAYERING INTERACTIVITY

In Calvino's account of the city 'Ersilia' in *Invisible Cities*, the people who live in this city establish various relationships with each other by

> stretch[ing] strings from the corners of the houses, white or black or gray or black-and-white according to whether they mark a relationship of blood, of trade, authority, agency. When the strings become so numerous that you can no longer pass among them, the inhabitants leave: the houses are dismantled; only the strings and their supports remain. . . . Thus, when travelling in the territory of Ersilia, you come upon the ruins of the abandoned cities, without the walls which do not last, without the bones of the dead which the wind rolls away: spider-webs of intricate relationships seeking a form.
>
> (Calvino, 1997, p. 76)

Beyond the fact that the strings that Calvino describes become analogous with model making, the final line of 'Ersilia' – 'spider-webs of intricate relationships seeking a form' – seems to articulate an understanding of potentially what any 'model' attempts to do, especially between digital (concept or process) and physical space of the model. Model making and interactivity are coming more to the fore in responsive robotic and organic systems. For example, in the work of Alison Kundla, who uses a computer-controlled four-axis positioning table to 'print' intricate bio-architectural constructions out of live plant cells which organically create new systems. Thus, in Kundla's work the material and the medium are algorithmic, this means algorithms manifest dynamic and emergent behaviour and states where new unseen patterns emerge. In presentation models, a different interactivity is possible in which big data sources and geocomputation are layered and controlled using media devices, creating these intricate relationships and networks. With increasing open data availability the projection of city data on the physical model presents a work environment to test the suitability of design proposals. For example, a 12.5 m 1:2,000 scale interactive model of Central London by Piper's Model Makers project historical and future development controllable with touchscreens.

In addition to these strategies for works, the model does not have to be the output of a design process, but can also be the analogue production of scientific investigation of landscape process, such as watersheds or sink holes (Castree, 2005, pp. 206–207).

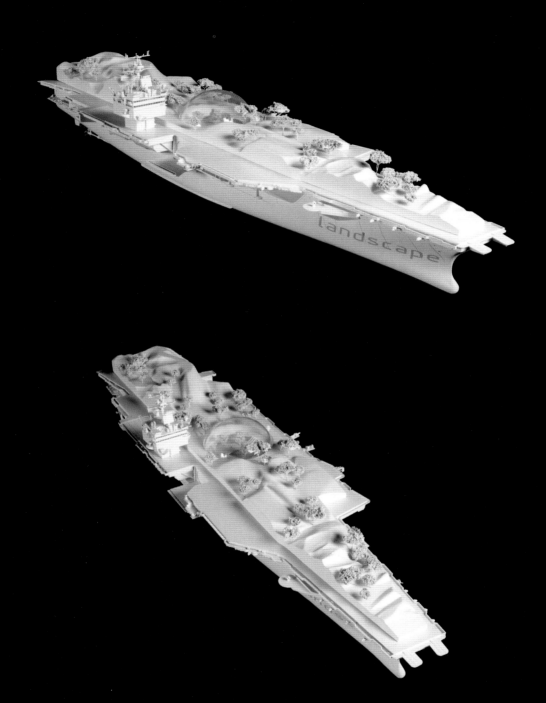

FIGURE 5.2 Ian+, Microutopias, 2003, Housescape. Maquette, plastique, plexiglas, 23 × 100 × 27 cm. Collection Frac Centre, Orléans. The boat is viewed as the perfect rationalisation of space, with reference to Le Corbusier and Hans Hollein, Ian+ proposes extensive retrofitting of super carriers into purposeful recreational spaces creating new operative ecology strategies from our super-massive redundant infrastructure.

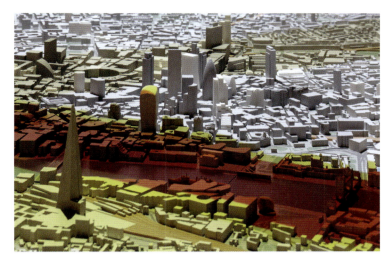

FIGURE 5.3
Piper's Model Makers, New London Architecture Model; photography by Agnese Sanvito and Paul Raftery, 2015. Any design project that has recently been completed, is currently under construction or has planning permission to be built can be highlighted on the model. Projects are highlighted through 3D-printing technology and a projection system linked to an interactive digital display with full project details.

LANDSCAPE MODELLING AND FABRICATION   175

FIGURE 5.4 DR_D (Dagmar Richter), The Wave, Aarhus, 2001, Concours Gigantium, Maquette, Mousse polyurethane, 9 × 90 × 60 cm; photography by Philippe Magnon. Collection Frac Centre, Orléans. The complex interrelated digital fabrication for an Olympic park in Denmark resulted in a complex artificial landscape topography fabricated here and also as 2D surfaces through engraved plexiglas.

While this may be intrinsic to scientific enquiry, such laboratory-based works can also have public appeal in the communication of complexity, and the insight from such enquiry should not be understated (Hesse, 1967). This approach can be seen in the work of the SCAPE Team in the living breakwaters project (see the Introduction). The inquiry or investigation is reasoned on a representation or simulative model, though that position is reinforced through familiarity (Chorley, 1964, p. 127). This familiarity could be the immediate immersive environment, haptics of the model or the immediacy of explanation of large-scale processes using basic elements. Another benefit of such work can come from the time-based description the model addresses – for example, the modelling of the mantle system of Yellowstone National Park (Kincaid, 2013). In another example, if a physical model was created with an impervious straight channel and in that channel a water stream flow was set up, the various effects and importance of meandering could be observed and reflected along with other measures to the public of regulated flood plain development (Smithson *et al.*, 2008, pp. 300–307). Two other benefits of this strategy of working are also possible; the model may be a forward model or an inverse model. A forward model starts with the

FIGURE 5.5 (*facing page*) Terreform 1, Urbaneering Brooklyn 2110, City of the Future, 2014. Project team: Mitchell Joachim, Maria Aiolova, Melanie Fessel, Dan O'Connor, Celina Yee, Alpna Gupta, Sishir Varghese, Aaron Lim, Greg Mulholland, Derek Ziemer, Thilani Rajarathna, John Nelson and Natalie DeLuca. In this future model Terreform 1 have designed an intensified version of Brooklyn that supplies all vital needs for its population. In the city, food, water, air, energy, waste, mobility and shelter are radically restructured to support life in every form. The strategy includes the replacement of dilapidated structures with vertical agriculture and housing merged with its infrastructure. Using the former street grid as a basis for new ecologically active networks and arteries, the model has a masterplan aesthetic executed with a high-quality finish, though it is intended as a vehicle for further discussion on the form of the future city. The model's agency is to encourage future visions and pathways towards it.

LANDSCAPE MODELLING AND FABRICATION 177

FIGURE 5.6 Louis De Soissons, Architect, Welwyn Garden City Masterplan, 1920, Cachemaille-Day, Nugent Francis artist/photographer, RIBA Collection. The garden city has remained one of the most dominant categories of UK city form throughout the concept's history, which has seen extensive literature written on the subject; the garden city idea has remained in the popular conscious. In transport terms, Fredrick Osborn, Ebenezer Howard's second lieutenant, member of the UK Garden City Movement and chairman of the Town and County Planning Association, continued Howard's vision, ensuring landscape wedges, segregated traffic and pedestrian movement in the sketch proposal of 1919. Courtenay Crickmer developed the second sketch layout, developing the industrial east, though de Soissons' plan was preferred and the second garden city was realised.

effects and ends with the results (data > model parameters). An inverse model starts with the results and looks for its effects (model parameters > data). Both modes of working across time have been realised in analogue models and this is a unique representational agency in model making.

3D PRINTING MODELS AND AUGMENTATION

There are many avenues of augmentation and 3D-printing applications; in this case a functional analysis of the garden city idea of Ebenezer Howard (Ward, 2011), from its utopian diagram to its built form. This project explored the particular heuristic of model making of a garden city as a device to evaluate the city's original drawn masterplan, to view landscape over time and its current urban matrix. A comparison between the 1920 Louis de Soissons plan[1] of Welwyn Garden City to later formations and time periods through data projection and a contemporary 3D-printed model afforded evaluations and findings of how the city has changed over time. Welwyn Garden was designed to house its business and industrial base in the locality built from private enterprise, but by and large this has changed due to its agrarian vision and a contradictory globalised economy. Howard wanted a maximum population of 32,000 to 1,000 acres of land, surrounded by 5,000 acres of greenbelt. Four of the eight new towns after the Abercrombie plan for London[2] landed in Hertfordshire (Stevenage, Welwyn Garden City, Hatfield, Letchworth) (Hall, 2014, pp. 113–115). Each city space surrounds itself with green belt, separated communities spaced by agricultural land joined by the 'Inter-Municipal Railway' that Ebenezer Howard envisaged (Hall and Ward, 1998). However, the social use, of course, has changed and the government intervention post-war of establishing garden cities and new towns changed the original vision of Howard of private entrepreneurship enabling a city. Likewise, participatory governance and planning of the city has devolved to technocrats and specialists and the city has naturally changed its urban form.

As 3D-printing technology continues to advance, certain processes now offer the capability to produce accurate, large-scale city models and data sets. The model produced in this case, to the author's knowledge, is the first 3D-printed garden city and the model forms a base in which various data sets are projected and correlated from deprivation maps and census data to transport provision. The model functions as a surface on which many diverse maps of the city can be analysed, layered and visualised, and is hung vertically, whereby a data projector can then be aligned and calibrated to the model. The use of unmanned aerial vehicles (UAVs), car-mounted scanners and handheld devices mean that data capture and production are only set to be streamlined, meaning such future city visions and the creation of high-fidelity works are coming closer to realisation. Three-dimensional printing can provide a surface in which large data sets analysing landscape change over time can be visualised. In the Welwyn Garden City model many of the elements of the de Soissons masterplan can be clearly recognised.

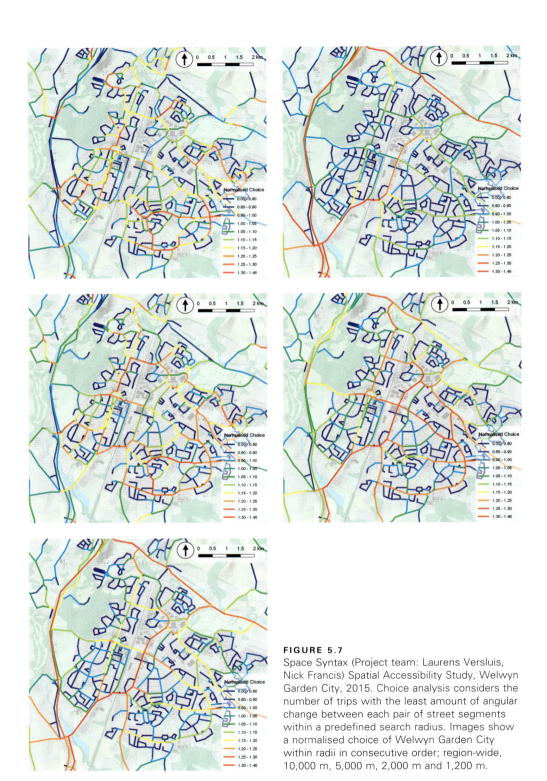

FIGURE 5.7
Space Syntax (Project team: Laurens Versluis, Nick Francis) Spatial Accessibility Study, Welwyn Garden City, 2015. Choice analysis considers the number of trips with the least amount of angular change between each pair of street segments within a predefined search radius. Images show a normalised choice of Welwyn Garden City within radii in consecutive order; region-wide, 10,000 m, 5,000 m, 2,000 m and 1,200 m.

Space Syntax is a set of theories linking space and society and a set of techniques for analysing spatial configuration (Hillier, 1998, 2008). The process is used to assess how the original design concept and the current street layout of Welwyn compares to its original masterplan. Space Syntax was able to interpret the configuration of a spatial network and in doing so measure levels of spatial connectivity that have been shown to influence movement, human encounter and economic opportunities. This animated spatial configuration was digitally projected onto the physical model.

Howard envisioned a low-density suburban environment as a response to large and dense cities such as London (Hall, 2014). Versluis' analysis found that this low level of density has been successfully implemented and still exists today, with a maximum of 12 houses per acre. Howard's vision and de Soissons' masterplan proposed a clear hierarchy of connectivity; central boulevards and quiet cul-de-sacs. The Parkway Boulevard in Welwyn has consistent landscaping along a wide linear axis with 'majestic' features such as fountains. The importance of its design is not reflected by its position within the surrounding spatial network. The cul-de-sac street layout forms a tree like structure. Its branches are separated from each other, limiting movement and activity in their public realm to adjacent residents only. In turn this decreases interaction potential with surrounding residents, natural surveillance and the potential for movement-sensitive land uses such as shops and services. Thus, Welwyn Garden City's landscape infrastructure has a critical role in city performance and spatial movement.

Spaces have a pervasive overlap of local, meso and city-wide centrality that will play a part in the economic, social and environmental sustainability of the neighbourhood through minimising movement and maximising interaction (Hillier, 2008). The clear distinction and separation of residential streets, neighbourhood streets and regional routes of Welwyn shown in this work reflect the different zones and hierarchies envisioned by Howard. The concept of zoning answered to historic issues such as overcrowding; however, it does not respond to today's issues regarding economic vitality, social cohesion and environmental sustainability (Alexander, 2009).

Creating a model and spatial accessibility data demonstrates a particular digital agency and model heuristic, both in processing LiDAR data, evaluating the original drawn plan in comparison to a 3D model and analysing Space Syntax's findings in relation to Louis de Soissons' and contemporary local government plans. Welwyn Garden City is a landed utopia in a unique geographic position, founded on radical ideas; its landscape infrastructure maintains a unique role in mediating transport, ensuring appropriate density and access to green space as originally intended by Howard. Welwyn Garden City has developed over a course of time to a point where its vision and imagination are being questioned more than ever in terms of growth, though paradoxically embraced in terms of Howard's concept. The utopian historian Dennis Hardy wrote that Welwyn 'is a perfect city that was achievable in an imperfect world' (Hardy, 2000, pp. 73–74). Following from this analysis and Hardy's statement, the question emerging from a process of digital fabrication is: are landed utopias timeless?

FIGURE 5.8 Paul Cureton, Welwyn Garden City Model with projected spatial accessibility data from Space Syntax (Project team: Laurens Versluis, Nick Francis), 2015.

FIGURE 5.9 Paul Cureton, Welwyn Garden City, Hertfordshire, prototype, laser sintered 3D polyamide landscape print, Digital Hack Lab & SSAHRI. LiDAR data © Environment Agency. Technical production from Peter Storey. Technical print from Pete Brownhill, Mark Bloomfield and Adam Ladlow. Welwyn Garden City model, full size 1,140 mm width, 1,460 mm length (scale 500 m^2:17.5 cm^2 tile). To create the model, LiDAR data were captured using an ALTM Gemini LiDAR sensor; the 3D data were then processed and 'solid modelled' in sections (tiles) to be joined after printing, as well as being hollowed out in preparation for 3D printing in the most cost-effective manner. Each 3D-printed tile represents a national grid 250 m^2 square. The data accuracy is reduced by the minimum thickness in which the data can be 3D printed (0.12 mm), while the size of each tile is restricted due to physical limits of the 3D printer space, called the 'build envelope'.

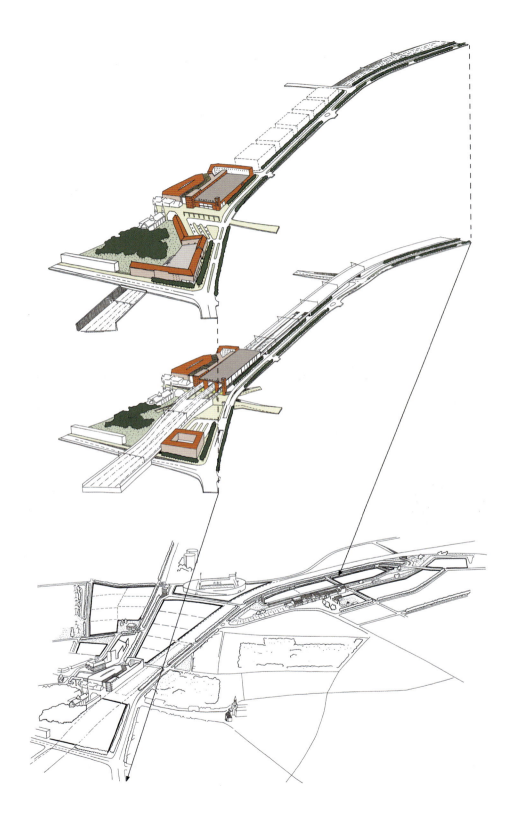

FIGURE 5.10 (*facing page and above*) Palmbout, Roosendaal – Spoorhaven, 2001–2005. The masterplan is for the redevelopment of a railway yard and industrial estate near the centre of Roosendaal, the Netherlands. Palmbout have a unique cross-relational dialogue between drawing and model making in the integration of urban design and railway engineering, demonstrating that the existing barrier formed by the railway line could be removed. As a result, the Spoorhaven area was woven into the network of the town. This network of connections through the agency of drawing and model making enables the development of a new urban area and a new station site.

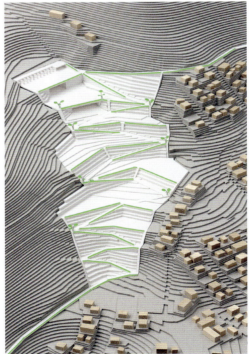

FIGURE 5.11 Marius Ege, Antje Stokman, Primer Lugar Concurso Juan Gunther en Lima, Perú, 2014. After an extensive search and analysis of the problems and potential in a valley located in Lima, Peru, different possible strategies are developed and visualised through model making, proposing urban agriculture, fog catchers and community participation. All are designed to prevent urban growth in the valley and limit illegal settlement by letting the local population benefit from ecotourism and the protection of the natural environment.

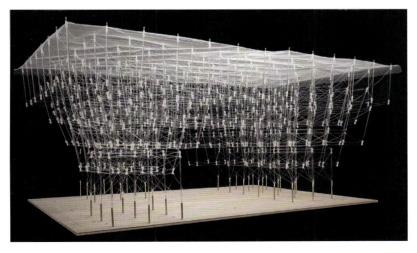

FIGURE 5.12
Drawn in Place, University of Tokyo. Design and Project Management Team: Kevin Clement, Anders Rod, Ratnar Sam, Gilang Arenza. Fabrication Team: Chloe Ying Xu, Takahiro Osaka, Haruka Uchida, Christopher Wilkens, Kenneth Larssen Lønning, Nicky Li, Sion Asada, Takeru Kumagai, Alric Lee, Rodrigo Fortes, Saki Uchida. Professor: Toshi Kiuchi. The large-scale hand-drawn structures are formed when a user manually prints out strings of thermoplastic filament, guided by a digital tracking system which bond with acrylic rods.

Microbial Ecologies. Fabricating Non-Human Ecosystems.

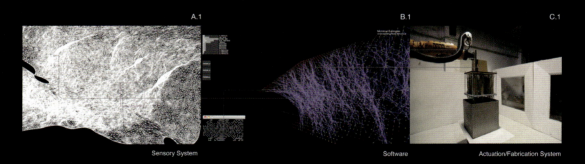

A.1	B.1	C.1
Sensory System	Software	Actuation/Fabrication System

FIGURE 5.13 Fran Castillo, Peter Malaga, Yogesh Karekar and Priyanka Narula, Microbial Ecologies, Research Center, Institute for Advanced Architecture of Catalonia, IAAC, 2015. Microbial Ecologies (ME) is proposing a speculative scenario which is able to explore new robotic fabrication processes as a framework for investigating the generation of (bio)artificial systems. These systems allow the research team to regenerate and protect against soil erosion and encourage healthy plant

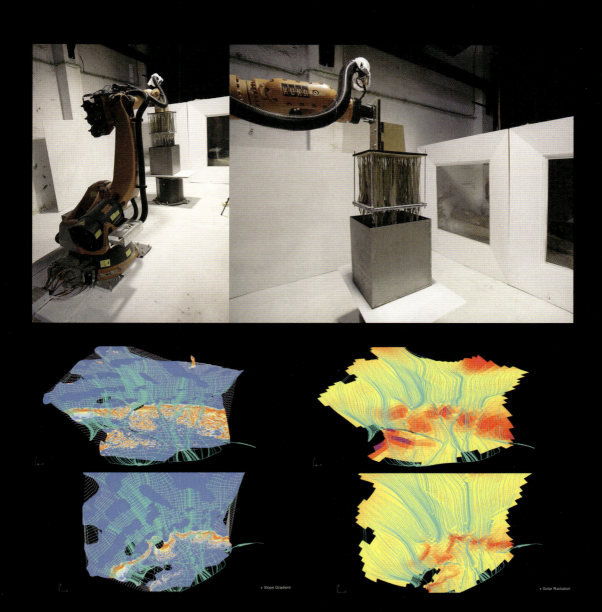

growth using interconnected 3D fibre systems. The research aim was to explore a heterogeneity of fibre structures at a broad range of spatial scales. The heterogeneity and interconnectivity of the 3D fibre system within soil makes it a biodiverse microhabitat for the diverse microbial population and vegetal systems. The system that ME is proposing has a pivotal role in microbial interactions. Therefore, it is able to amplify the biodiversity of ecosystems.

FIGURE 5.14 British Geological Survey (BGS), SARndbox, 2013. Originally designed by Oliver Kreylos, BGS developed an augmented sandbox. As the user digs in the sandbox, the Kinect tracks movements above using a laser light and some basic trigonometry. These changes are then fed back to the SARnbox program, which in turn dynamically remaps the surface image to reflect any changes. BGS has also developed a 3D immersion suite for exploring geological data through GeoVisionary to explore geological information alongside surface studies such as LiDAR. BGS connects its models and data to explore geology in time.

FIGURE 5.15 3D Pitoti, Italy, LiDAR capture Ground Truth Data Acquisition, Valcamonica, and two images of the visualisation tools – magnifying glass and visualisation table, 2015. The 3D-PITOTI project will significantly advance both the state of the art in rock-art research methodology and the 3D recording of rock art in general utilising drone survey, laser scanning, AR and other technologies. The project connects technologies but through the connection enhances and investigates their capabilities. Moreover, it will not only 'take the rock-art to people' for the first time but will disseminate Pitoti (the local term: knowledge) to wide audiences.

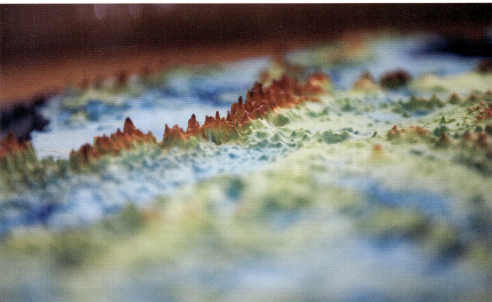

Figure 5.16 British Antarctic Survey (BAS), Bedmap 2, Peter Fretwell, Hamish Pritchard, 2001–2013. CNC resin model produced by Complete Fabrication Modelmakers, Cambridge, UK. The Bedmap 2 project is a detailed model of the past and future evolution of the Antarctic ice sheets. Bedmap 2 describes the surface elevation, ice-thickness and the sea floor and subglacial bed elevation of the Antarctic south of 60°S. BAS derived these products using data from a variety of sources, including many substantial surveys completed since the original Bedmap compilation (Bedmap 1) in 2001. In this case, BAS converted the high-resolution digital elevation model to CAD format, then to STL for 3D printing. The actual model was constructed by a 3D digital milling process from two hard resin blocks using a very fine needle point. The subsequent pieces were then hand-painted to the specifications of the printed map elevation classes.

FIGURE 5.17 Gary Priestnall, School of Geography, University of Nottingham, Mayson Model, 2015. Developed from surviving plaster moulds from an original 15-foot model of the Lake District, in 1875, Keswick, United Kingdom. 'Physical relief models offered visitors unprecedented views of a landscape long before it was common to plan a trip using maps or to have seen an aerial image. Mayson's Ordnance Model of the Lake District was innovative in attempting to provide such an accurate and faithful landscape model as a visitor attraction.' The surviving negative moulds were scanned, and a number of moulds positively CNC milled. An Ordnance Survey base map calibrated to the original model was produced and the replica tiles floated above according to their national grid square. Some tiles were finished with modelling clay and paint, some augmented with projection.

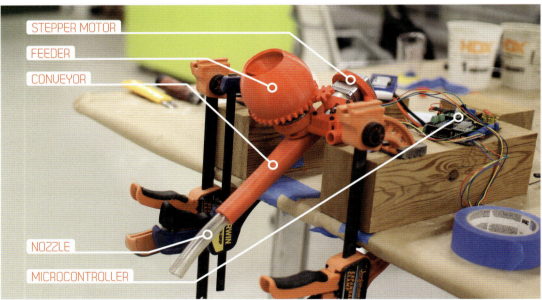

FIGURE 5.18 (*above and facing page*) Gensler, Jared Shier and Tam Tran, MUPPette, 2015. MUPPette (Mobile Unmanned Printing Platform; the -ette suffix designates it as a small version of a scalable vehicle). Extruding cementitious material from a custom nozzle means the MUPPs could be deployed to emergency disaster sites, provide emergency shelter or provide preventative measures such as flood diversion barriers. 3D printed UAV parts can also be readily produced for easy servicing.

LANDSCAPE MODELLING AND FABRICATION

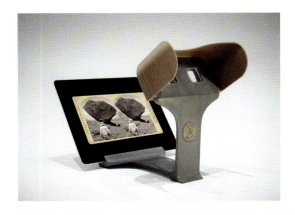

FIGURE 5.19
Kleet & Wolfe, 3D printed stereoscopic iPad viewer printed in stainless steel, coffee and bronze PLA filament. Designed by Ben and Byron Wolfe, 2016. The stereographic viewer allows for continual repeat photography display with three-dimensionality, utilising photogrammetry, deriving control points, creating videos of landscape changes and also digitally fabricating and 3D printing the findings (Senf, 2012, pp. 34–35).

196 LANDSCAPE MODELLING AND FABRICATION

FIGURE 5.20 Tinker Imagineers, Roots Time Travel Experience; photographer: Mike Bink, 2012. From inside a farmer's shed, the environmental immersion company narrate a story about how people and landscape have influenced each other in the North of Limburg, the Netherlands. The project used the walls and the ceiling of an old farmer's shed as the canvas, and so the audience was inside the projection. With the use of props, 14 projectors, morphing techniques and a soundtrack, 5,000 years of history race past in eight minutes. This immersion was further supported by an audio tour across the Floriade grounds.

LANDSCAPE MODELLING AND FABRICATION   197

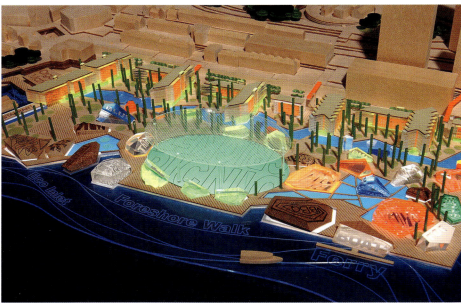

FIGURE 5.21 Marta Swartz and Partners, East Darling Harbour, Client Lend Lease; architect: Richard Rogers Partnership, Sydney, Australia, 2006. The masterplan has three main precincts: the beach, the island and the business district. The beach is a twenty-first century play space for locals, urban professionals and global nomads alike. This unique place has sun, sand, shade and is completely wired, which means you can put down your towel and switch on your laptop. There is a real working harbour in this area which also lends itself to recreational boating. The island includes an island market and a multitude of eco-friendly housing solutions, some of which have been specifically designed for key workers in the East Darling Harbour area. With good transport access, East Darling Harbour provides an ideal location both for global corporations looking for a home in South-east Asia, as well as for an influx of both local and international tourists seeking recreation or respite from day-to-day city life.

DIGITAL FABRICATION

Models may be created using three possible processes from digital files: additive, subtractive or hybrid manufacture. The fabrication process is consistently developing with a host of home-user machines that can be purchased at little cost, to flat-pack kits such as the open-source self-replicating machine RepRAP (http://reprap.org), to liquid resin 3D printers which extract objects from a liquid block. There are also many vested interests in these technologies, many companies espousing a technological innovation, and it is important to exercise caution in selecting a way of working or investing in redundant systems. It may be effective to outsource work to manufacturers with experience and high rates of delivery.

- **Additive manufacture** involves material being applied and added layer by layer to precision coordinates and specifications. This is the creation of a model from the ground up, layer by layer, and is known as 3D printing.
- **Subtractive manufacture** involves the use of block material which is removed through CNC (computer numerical control) machining.
- **Hybrid manufacture** results from machines that have additive and subtractive capability, thus 3D printing and CNC machining.

Principles of 3D printing

Creating a 3D print (3DP) can be limited, digitally error prone, have hardware faults, jams and material inconsistency and also be time-intensive. Digital files must be converted to the most common 3D print format – STL (stereo lithography). For landscape architecture models the major limiting factor in production is the 'build envelope' of common printers. This is the print size that a printer can accommodate. For example, a budget machine may only print 10 cm wide by 10 cm in length to a 10 cm height. This machine may allow rapid prototyping of objects but may not give a large-scale representation unless multiple prints are tiled together. The type of 3DP must also be considered, as there are a variety of 3DP processes needed which match the type of materials used such as SLA, SLS, FDM, EBM, LOM, DLP and SLM.[3] Thus, there are a large number of modes of production with varying costs and outputs. It may be cost-effective to outsource 3DP work to suppliers who can also error-check models and reprint if there is a manufacturing error.

The material choice may also be limited or incur more costs for full-colour 3D printing. The strategy for 3D printing should involve the upscaling and manufacture of 3D data, from rapid prototypes to high-end machines and finishes.

Efficiency. The 3D-printed elements contain no anomalies and can be grouped together, angled or joined as much as possible in the printer build envelope to limit material waste. The build envelope is the maximum area the printer can print and determines how large an object the printer can build.

DIGITAL FABRICATION

model types

- Abstract Model
- Block Model
- Contour Model
- Cross-section Model
- LiDAR/Point Cloud Model
- Material Model
- Augmented Model

digital fabrication processes

- Additive Manufacture
- Subtractive Manufacture
- Hybrid Manufacture

3D PRINTING
CNC MACHINING

3D PRINTING

inputs

DIGITAL
STL file

MATERIALS
- ABS
- PLA
- PVA
- Powder Print
- Resin

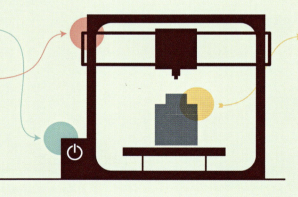

outputs

CHARACTERISTICS OF THE MODEL:

- smaller than the build envelope

- parts can be combined in one model to reduce waste and costs

- can be made from recycle materials

- can't be hollow

The relationship between digital and physical form is complex and the variety of possible model outcomes makes this an important representational mode in a wider representational strategy for landscape architecture. Models may be created using three possible processes from digital files; additive, subtractive or hybrid manufacture.

Economic. 3DP is still an expensive medium; minimise waste and material by shelling any solid areas in the 3D model. The use of recycled material is possible for printing and can reduce costs. The rapid prototyping of smaller machines in initial phases and at smaller scales will assist in the reduction of errors such as missing faces, gaps or thin edges.

Solid. The digital file must be watertight. Any holes or gaps cause difficulties and could result in a failed build and the waste of print material.

3D print materials

3DP materials come in a variety of forms, from chocolate to metal. The materials come as filaments or roles for most desktop printers in varieties of colours, including translucent and neon. The most common types are:

- **ABS**: acrylonitrile butadiene styrene; heat resistant and can be finished and painted and bonded using a variety of glues, though has rough finishes.
- **PLA**: polylactic acid is an environmentally friendly material, has less warping and high strength if cooled while layering, though it can be brittle. PLA can also be sanded and painted after priming.
- **PVA:** polyvinyl alcohol plastic is a water soluble plastic which supports weak parts of a model that are ABS- or PLA-produced.
- **Powder printing** involves laser sintering to fuse parts together; the variety of powders includes polyamide, alumide, titanium and wood.
- **Resin**: materials are printed using a process called stereo lithography and can be transparent, smooth or detailed.

LANDSCAPE ARCHITECTURE AND URBAN DESIGN MODEL TYPES

Model production time, costs and context of output should all be considered in the creation of models. The upscaling of models, from initial card models to fully articulated designs, should also be accommodated in the time estimates. Digital fabrication allows a clear translation of representational scales, meaning digital scales of maps, plans and design can be translated to built form with little calculation. The model types are not exhaustive or extensive, but highlight core model types as well as emerging modes of production. The companion website to the book features tutorials on a number of these modelling types. *The Digital Vernacular* by Stevens and Nelson also provides photographic phases for architecture, which have some application (Stevens and Nelson, 2015).

FIGURE 5.22 (*facing page*) Serena Pollastri, 3D Printing Typology, 2016.

Models' purposes and intentions should be carefully considered. For example, in UK planning applications certain model planning scales may be appropriate 1:100, 1:200, 1:1,250. Various finishes and materials can be utilised and mixed and a typology or representation is a welcome addition to the model types, this could be several classes of grey for building and public space types or clear material separation from wood to ABS.

Abstract. Abstract models may abstract urban conditions in organic or artificially simplified forms, a process of modelling that sidesteps the need and difficulty of the representation of foliage and vegetation, and emphasises conceptual parts of the design brief. The abstract model may lack any particular scale, it may be a form-finding exercise and exploration.

Block model. Block models are urban blocks and heights of the architectural structures of the site. Block models are also known as building height models or mass models. The block model has a key role in large-scale site representation and sustainability calculation. The block model is one of the most fluid modes of translating 3D GIS data into a physical model, through 3D printing or handcraft techniques.

Contour model. Contour modelling can be enabled through GIS layer and production of terrain height values, making a 'stepped' landscape in which further detail may be added. Commonly the contour model can be laser cut and layered as a site base.

Cross-section model. The cross-section model may be an appropriate strategy to represent water courses and sub-surface elements, utilising geological and hydrological data.

LiDAR/point cloud model. A digital surface model (DSM) can be 3D printed; this provides an accurate scaled landscape model of the site surface. This process involves the solid modelling of the surface to enable 3D-printed production. The DSM can be designed in, where the designer creates their proposal in the 3D digital model, reworking the DSM where necessary.

Material model. The material model can be a 1:1 scale model of an object or street furniture, an organic compound that supports plant and root structures, or directly constructed of components from National Building Specifications.

Augmented. Augmented models may be complete virtual models or retain a physical aspect with projection and interaction. The augmented model will need exactness in production to match GIS data assets, or programmed interfaces for control of visualisation tables or digital projections on model surfaces.

FIGURE 5.23 Vahide Kulhas, graduate, University of Hertfordshire, Vyner Street, London Block Model, 2015. Laser-etched slate with sprayed blue foam. The model utilised Ordinance Survey building height data, processed and exported to Trimble Sketch up; the data were scaled then virtually measured for physical reproduction.

FIGURE 5.24 Yuichiro Takeuchi, Sony Computer Science Laboratories Inc. and Japan Science and Technology Agency (JST) PRESTO. Takeuchi proposes a 3D printed garden roof and smaller-scale freeform hydroponic microgardens. The work changes the agency of model making to a supportive living system artefact.

FIGURE 5.25
MCor Technologies IRIS Model, images courtesy of MCor Technologies. True-colour 3D printing allows GIS data to be accurately translated. A tile is produced and aligned with others to make larger models (left) or whole sites are created (right).

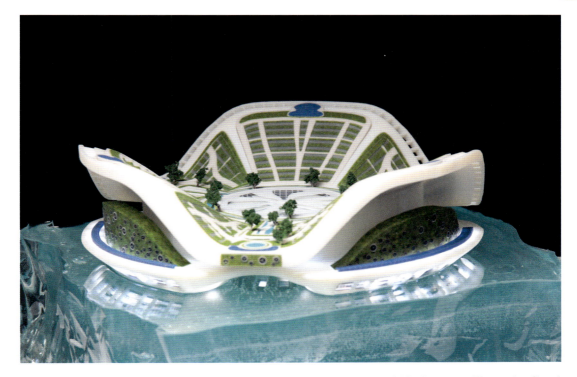

FIGURE 5.26 White Clouds, 3D-Printed Futuristic Architectural Concepts, CES (Consumer Electronics Show) exhibition, 2014. Designers: Kyle Gifford, Kelly Root and Anthony Horsley. The models were printed with a ProJet 660 by 3D Systems and the Connex 500 by Stratasys. The ProJet prints in full colour, producing a brittle sandstone-like material. The Connex machine printed in many different materials including transparent UV-cured resins and hard plastics.

SUMMARY

The relationship between digital and physical form is complex and the variety of model making we have seen makes this an important communication mode in a wider representational strategy for landscape architecture. The model has unique qualities in its ability to provide haptic sensations in making, pedagogic lessons in the accounting of errors and an increasing fidelity to landscape form enabled by 3D printing. The model will, of course, be an abstraction of reality, though this conception is becoming more complex as 3D printed organic systems create new patterns and new algorithms. Interactivity is coming more to the fore over static models, allowing the control and manipulation of urban data and designs and the testing of a number of scenarios. Models may be forward models or inverse models in their method, and their role in scientific explanation of natural processes evidences the model's ability to be part of an analytical landscape stage as well as functioning as a design element in itself. The familiarity and direct experience cannot be overstated and the use of analogue models for community consultation is also beneficial. Following from these discussions, an investigation of the second garden city, Welwyn, and the evaluation of the original masterplan and utopian vision juxtaposed with its contemporary urban state took place. The time-based analysis of the spatial movements of its layout was then decoded through the Space Syntax method. Thus, the 3D print in itself functioned as a tabula rasa in which a series of urban investigations could be undertaken. The 3DP also functioned as a heuristic in the evaluation of the original masterplan of 1920.

Three-dimensional printing is not a panacea for model making, though the expansion of printable material offers options for the development of biological landscape products as well as the construction of traditional landscape models. The strategies for printing were discussed, including possible digitally fabricated model types. This is not exhaustive and is intended as a catalyst for readers to form new or emergent strategies, creating connections between media and the representation of perceptions of place.

A structure of relations, each containing several strategies, has been discussed from mapping, fieldwork and notation, composites and 3D modelling. Between these elements an overall strategy may emerge that attempts to create a plan of action to achieve a number of outcomes and directions, as well as to define the scope of this action. To represent landscape requires careful consideration to representing time in landscape, accuracy of representation or fidelity and participation and evaluation. Novel use of techniques may produce such and such an outcome; however, a truer representation of landscape architecture involves uniting all the elements of landscape practice as well as uniting natural and human requirements. Representation of landscape occurs on many different time points, at its generative base from design conception to future projection. Future projection is perhaps one of the most vital aspects of the strategies of landscape representation, which the concluding chapter will discuss.

NOTES

1. Howard purchased the land in the summer of 1919, acquiring 1,458 acres; he then created a new company, Second Garden City Limited. The first plan was created by Courtenay M. Crickmer, though Soissons was preferred. Louis de Soissons was a French-Canadian who trained at the Royal Academy and the Ecole De Baux Arts in Paris. He was appointed consultant architect in April 1920 and presented the masterplan in June 2010 (Miller, 2010, p. 31).
2. The Greater London Plan of 1944 was developed by Patrick Abercrombie. The plan was directly related to the County of London Plan written by Abercrombie in 1943, with contributions by John Henry Forshaw. The ideas of the plan were to address the perceived failings of unplanned and haphazard development that had occurred as a result of rapid industrialisation in the nineteenth century. Welwyn Garden City and Hatfield (to the south of the city) were designated as UK New Towns in 1948 following the government programme.
3. SLA: stereo lithography, SLS: selective laser sintering, FDM: fused deposition modelling, EBM: electronic beam melting, LOM: laminated object manufacturing, DLP: digital light processing, SLM: selective laser melting.

BIBLIOGRAPHY

Alberti, Leon Battista 1988. *On the Art of Building in Ten Books*, MIT Press, Cambridge, MA.

Alexander, A., 2009. *Britain's New Towns: Garden Cities to Sustainable Communities*. Routledge, London.

Beorkrem, C., 2012. *Material Strategies in Digital Fabrication*. Routledge, New York.

Bornhauser, R., Kissling, T. and Vogt, C., 2015. *Günther Vogt: Landscape as a Cabinet of Curiosities – In Search of a Position*. Lars Müller, Ennetbaden.

Breen, J. and Stellingwerf, M., 2011. 3D Models in Landscape Architecture. European Envisioning Architecture Association, 14–17 Septmber, Delft University of Technology.

Buckminster-Fuller, R. and Snyder, J., 2009. *Education Automation: Comprehensive Learning for Emergent Humanity*, new edition. Lars Muller Publishers, Baden.

Calvino, I., 1997. *Invisible Cities*. Vintage, London.

Castree, N. (ed.), 2005. *Questioning Geography: Fundamental Debates*. Blackwell, Malden, MA.

Chorley, R.J., 1964. Geography and Analogue Theory. *Annals of the Association of American Geographers*, 54: 127–137. doi: 10.1111/j.1467-8306.1964.tb00478.x.

Dade-Robertson, M., 2011. *The Architecture of Information: Architecture, Interaction Design and the Patterning of Digital Information*. Routledge, Abingdon.

Dunn, N., 2007. *The Ecology of the Architectural Model*. Peter Lang, Oxford.

Dunn, N., 2012. *Digital Fabrication in Architecture*. Laurence King, London.

Dunn, N., 2014. *Architectural Modelmaking*, 2nd edition. Laurence King, London.

Hall, P., 2014. *Cities of Tomorrow: An Intellectual History of Urban Planning and Design Since 1880*, 4th edition. Wiley-Blackwell, Hoboken.

Hall, P. and Ward, C., 1998. *Sociable Cities: Legacy of Ebenezer Howard*. John Wiley & Sons, Chichester.

Hardy, D., 2000. *Utopian England: Community Experiments 1900–1945*. Routledge, London.

Hesse, M.B., 1967. *Models and Analogies in Science*. University of Notre Dame Press, Notre Dame.

Hillier, B., 1998. *Space is the Machine: A Configurational Theory of Architecture*, new edition. Cambridge University Press, Cambridge.

Hillier, B., 2008. *The Social Logic of Space*, reprint Cambridge University Press, Cambridge.

Iwamoto, L., 2009. *Digital Fabrications: Architectural and Material Techniques*. Princeton Architectural Press, New York.

Kincaid, K.A.D., 2013. Bifurcation of the Yellowstone plume driven by subduction-induced mantle flow. *Nature Geoscience*, 6: 395–399. doi: 10.1038/NGEO1774.

Knoll, W. and Hechinger, M., 2007. *Architectural Models: Construction Techniques*, 2nd revised edition. J. Ross Publishing, Ft. Lauderdale.

Menges, A. (ed.), 2015. *Material Synthesis: Fusing the Physical and the Computational*. John Wiley & Sons, Chichester.

Nijhuis, S., 2014. GIS-based Landscape Design Research: Exploring Aspects of Visibility in Landscape Architectonic Compositions. In: D.J. Lee, E. Dias and H.J. Scholten (eds), *Geodesign by Integrating Design and Geospatial Sciences*, Springer, New York, pp. 193–217.

Pallasmaa, J., 2005. *The Eyes of the Skin: Architecture and the Senses*, 2nd edition. John Wiley & Sons, Chichester.

Paterson, D.M., 2007. *The Senses of Touch: Haptics, Affects and Technologies*. Berg Publishers, Oxford.

Riahi, P., 2015. *Ars Et Ingenium: The Embodiment of Imagination in Francesco Di Giorgio Martini's Drawings*. Routledge, London.

Schmal, P., 2015. *The Architectural Model: Tool, Fetish, Small Utopia*. Verlag Scheidegger & Spiess AG, Zürich.

Senf, R., 2012. *Reconstructing the View: The Grand Canyon Photographs of Mark Klett and Byron Wolfe*. University of California Press, Berkeley.

Smith, A., 2004. *Architectural Model as Machine: A New View of Models from Antiquity to the Present Day*. Routledge, London.

Smithson, P., Addison, K. and Atkinson, K., 2008. *Fundamentals of the Physical Environment*, 4th edition. Routledge, London.

Stevens, J. and Nelson, R., 2015. *Digital Vernacular: Architectural Principles, Tools, and Processes*. Routledge, New York.

Ward, S. (ed.), 2011. *The Garden City*. Routledge, London.

Weiser, M., 1999. The Computer for the 21st Century. *SIGMOBILE Mobile Computing and Communications Review*, 3: 3–11. doi: 10.1145/329124.329126.

6
CONCLUSION
Future landscapes

> The Future Cities we envisage will offer an unusual variety of sensations in this realm, and unforeseen games will become possible through the inventive use of material conditions.
> (Constant in McDonough, 2004, p. 99)

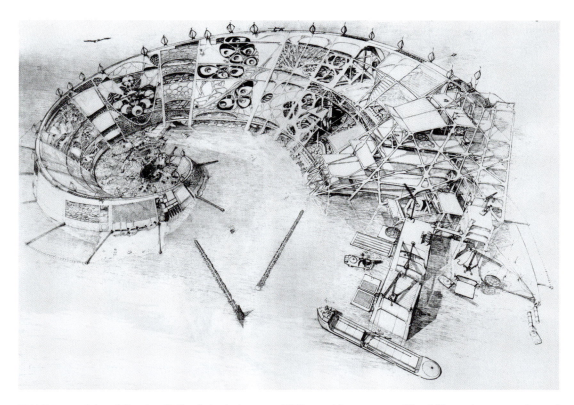

FIGURE 6.1 (*above*) Newton Fallis, Autopia Ampere, 1978, graphite on paper, 92 × 145 cm. Image courtesy of Newton Fallis. Autopia Ampere was the idea of the late seascape architect Wolf Hilbertz, with the coral scientist Dr Thomas Goreau, who invented Biorock™), a mineral accretion technology which quick-grows coral and repairs damaged reefs (Goreau et al., 2005). Given the technological potential, Autopia was seen as a city grown from the sea which utilised cybernetics to evolutionarily expand and support its inhabitants (Cureton, 2013).

These concluding remarks focus on the representational issues of time-based presentation, real-time accuracy and participation within the representation process and our future landscapes. The ability to create a synergetic relationship between digital and physical production streamlines the agency of landscape. This agency changes design processes but also has implications for users of designed landscape space. Essentially, new and emergent workflows are altering the conceptual design process and the ability to conceive new landscape imaginations. For example, the landscape physical and analogue model provides a tangible object with tactility and interactivity, as we have seen in the previous chapter. Modelling can incorporate a variety of processes from fabricating conceptual models, presentation models, as well as intended structural components, among many different modes of making. Model making is not a linear process as it can use inverse model and forward model design strategies, working back and forth between computational algorithms and physical layers.

It is from this basis of emergent workflows that an emerging strategy, action and pattern could be mapped from the chapter themes of this book. Interoperability is the crux of the matter; for example, how does the diagram not only evaluate site conditions but also conceptualise design strategies for it? How does the diagram relate to mapping, to 3D modelling, to model making? While the types of making and designing from maps to perspectives may seem a small output if evaluating the number of processes and resources needed to realise a whole design scheme, the agency and valence[1] of landscape representation comes to a pinch point in projection; what is to become, its future?

Or through a reverse projection, representation may be the evaluation of a place. Thus, two modes of operation are in effect, the first is strategies for landscape representation in the working with media, the connecting and weaving of thought pieces. This involves connecting and moving between media, a sort of hybrid approach is thus required. The second operation is the representation of places, by the designer and its inhabitants. Both modes of operation are connected and intrinsic to each other and both have agency and valence.

To further unpack these operations, future thinking and design evidences the scope of representation and its critical importance. The scope of future thinking falls beyond landscape architecture, involving many other disciplines and media; to evidence futurological landscapes involves assessment of the plurality of futurological thinking reflecting and returning to source. As Winy Maas comments, image production of future cities has moved into an active phase of determination of our future cities (Maas, 2009, pp. 196–197). Maas recognises the agency and valence at play and three issues are discussed here: the capacity of our future landscape imagination or *landscape imaginary*, the scales of these projections; *future scales*, and the representational forms that seek to describe landscape; and *future metabolisms*.

LANDSCAPE IMAGINARIES

Our future landscape imagination can relate to utopian and dystopian thinking, which project visions of types of living in landscapes and urban landscapes, and as an evaluative response to futures soon to be adopted. The dystopian aspect arguably arises from a social anxiety of the wrecks of previous utopic visions on rural and urban spaces which sought regularity and logic that was directly at odds with social change (Read et al., 2005, pp. 3–11). In other words, many landed and realised utopian designs quickly inverted to dystopian places through the everyday social, economic and cultural ways of life. Thus, the vision can in effect be the catalyst for environmental degradation. The landscape imaginary may be individual, though it also has a social force and it is important to consider this factor; the projections often imply a collective or inclusive ability. The ability of a single vision to filter into the popular conscious and a shared representation is a unique and under-discussed function. Gyorgy Kepes comments that in order for a sense of place, 'sensed forms, images and symbols are as essential to us as palpable reality in exploring nature for human ends'; to that effect, Kepes called for new symbolic transformations and images of the processes of experience of spaces (Kepes, 1956, pp. 18–22). As Kepes and Kevin Lynch's work demonstrated in 'Image of the City', it functions through a capacity to internally model and imagine large-scale city space. In effect, this study evidenced alongside many others the imaginative capacity of mapping media which as a device functions fundamentally as a surface on which new navigational and spatial configurations materialise.

This is but one example of a landscape imaginary impulse at work in an urban setting. To this end, Daniel Brook proposes a question: 'to truly orient ourselves in our new century – to answer the question, where are we? In time, not just space – we must know the histories of the St. Petersbergs and Shanghais of the world as well as we know the histories of the Londons and New Yorks' (Brook, 2013, p. 12). Brook's study evidences the need for the discussion of the histories of future cities involving architecture, landscape and many other disciplines, but more importantly demonstrates that in order to undertake such a mode of enquiry it has to be transnational and global in order to gauge the aspects and processes of representation and the social imaginations in force.

As previously stated in the Introduction, there is a need to map two interdependent operations of media and making and people's response to this making, which is to view landscape representation in its historical and future direction, not as a linear mapping of time, but as a more cyclic sequence. The present is often the basis on which historical and future landscapes are projected, often deriving meaning with reference to current conditions. These enquiries ultimately rely on the decoding of meaning in landscape, which is of course a complex topic, as Kirsten Merete and Stefan Winter, state, seeing meaning in landscape as historical, stating that 'landscape's traditional meaning profiles have been projections perceived within society or culture as a factual and comprehensive system where human beings could orientate and locate themselves' (Schroder, 2013, p. 63). They argue that globalised forces create new landscape meanings in addition, and thus a competing set of 'composite meanings' are in force. However, this representational position can be decoded with the evaluation of past future projection which disrupts this 'presentism' and, being a composite, it maps across time the creative scope and direction in which landscape is conceived and reassembles it so it can be evaluated, compared and assessed for its significance. While this text has discussed the function and effect of agency and valence in landscape representation, or media and making, it has done so because these are critical factors in the landscape imaginary capacity.

Such histories of landscape futures provide evidence of the capacity and level of agency for landscape architecture and our imaginative ability. Such histories reflect back our conceptions of nature and our relationship with it. This imaginative ability is both creative and scientific. This mode of looking involves a more expansive outlook for landscape representation which incorporates the fluidity of work and its failures and success across time. A number of writers have produced work on modernism and utopic impulses and are briefly discussed below;[2] this area can assist in developing the issues of landscape imagination and design.

David Pinder views the closure of utopian thinking after modernist architecture as a crisis in which imaginative and alternative capabilities become constrained, when utopian thinking may challenge contemporary dominant conceptions and engage with spaces (Pinder, 2005, pp. 20–23). Pinder's careful account of Guy Debord and the Situationist International (SI) traces attempts at defining and instigating new futures which the SI perceived were necessary from the 'owners of society' and modernist planning practice. The SI believed the 'owners of society' were eradicating meaning of social spaces and replacing it with neo-regulated blocks. Pinder notes that some of these oppressive utopias (e.g. Le Corbusier) should be abandoned, but the space for an emancipatory utopianism as found in the work of Guy Debord and the SI have a greater agency in the disruption of dominant urban futures (Pinder, 2005, p. 243). Thus, following Pinder's line of argument and applying it to the context of future landscapes, they are the sources of evidence by which to measure the contemporary diversity of vision in operation. On this vision in operation, Franco Bifo Berardi suggests that imagination has lost its hold on the future, revolutionary future visions of early modernism are succeeded by heavily futurised financial capitalism (Berardi, 2011, p. 6). There is a lot at stake and many practitioners seek to address this landscape imaginary capacity through future projection, but to the degree that it works with global capitalist visions is open for further critical work. One such landscape example can be viewed in the work of Agnes Denes, where her Pyramids are created for new worlds, utopian to an extent, but buildable and utilitarian, not following capitalist dynamics but ancient Egyptian geometry in realised form, following its own ecological time (Denes, 2008, pp. 248–249).

There is a sense of historical reframing of our urban history at work when reading utopian literature and criticism on the built environment, and this can be seen in Fredric Jameson's text, in which there is an identification of a dominant cultural logic over modernism in which there is only perpetuation of existing urban form (Jameson, 1992, ch. 1). This could be understood physically in the continual repetition of shopping malls and out-of-town centres. This is evidenced on Jameson review of the work of the Harvard School of Design's city project, led by Rem Koolhas in 2001, where students explored not just architectural intervention but diagnosed a series of urban conditions:

> The problem is then how to locate radical difference; how to jumpstart the sense of history so that it begins again to transmit feeble signals of time, of otherness, of change, of Utopia. The problem to be solved is that of breaking out of the windless present of the postmodern back into real historical time, and a history made by human beings. I think this writing is a way of doing that or at least of trying to.
>
> (Jameson 2003, p. 76)

The textual preference as a mode for alternative representation and difference is symptomatic of Jameson's work, though the concern with aesthetic range and the view of design and architectural imagination as a commodity results in Jameson calling for change. Beyond the arguments of Pinder, Bifo and Jameson, further discussion of the design imagination and its capacity and ability falls outside the scope of this book, although the urban aspect of landscape futures should also be noted; many projects visualise urbanisation as inevitable. We cannot think of the world but as a totalising urban form. Notions of inevitability can be seen in the work of Henri Lefebvre, who suggests a complete planetary urbanisation is in effect, citing Issac Asimov's story 'Black Friar of the Flame' and the metropolis of Trantor, which covers a complete land surface. Andy Merrifield interprets this small citation of Asimov by Lefebvre to reconsider the city term: 'let us try to identify a new theoretical and virtual object that is in the process of becoming. Urban fabric does not narrowly define the built environment of cities, but, says Lefebvre, indicates all manifestations of the dominance of the city over the countryside' (Merrifield, 2013, p. 911). Lefebvre's concern with the decline of rural life projects an idea in which the world is conceived as a totalised urban fabric; therefore this suggests a critical importance of the interpretation of our future urban and city forms. Lefebvre is not alone in his concern over urban sprawl. It is not to say that Lefebvre's theory is self-fulfilling, but indicates concerns over future city directions in the types of images we make as well as the future of urban life they represent. The two modes are not exclusive; representation, as I hope I have shown, is a cyclical process between maker and reader, designer and public, agent and effect.

There is, however, an ecological city paradigm that has emerged in representational practice which evidences increasing concerns about the longevity of the city, adaptability to climate change, resource management and the resilience of changing social dynamics and populations drawn from the evaluation of a thousand design

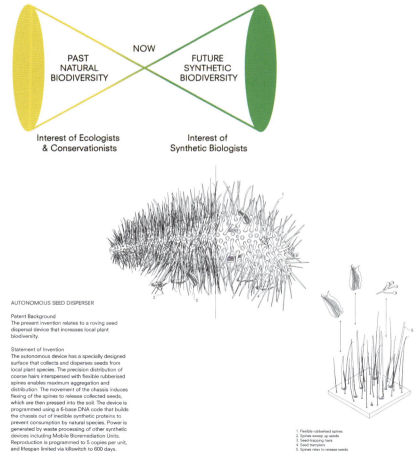

AUTONOMOUS SEED DISPERSER

Patent Background
The present invention relates to a roving seed dispersal device that increases local plant biodiversity.

Statement of Invention
The autonomous device has a specially designed surface that collects and disperses seeds from local plant species. The precision distribution of coarse hairs interspersed with flexible rubberised spines enables maximum aggregation and distribution. The movement of the chassis induces flexing of the spines to release collected seeds, which are then pressed into the soil. The device is programmed using a 6-base DNA code that builds the chassis out of inedible synthetic proteins to prevent consumption by natural species. Power is generated by waste processing of other synthetic devices including Mobile Bioremediation Units. Reproduction is programmed to 5 copies per unit, and lifespan limited via killswitch to 600 days.

1. Flexible rubberised spines
2. Spines sweep up seeds
3. Seed-trapping hairs
4. Seed tramplers
5. Spines relax to release seeds

FIGURE 6.2
Alexandra Daisy Ginsberg, Designing for the Sixth Extinction, 2013. Synthetic biologists seek to transform biology into an engineering discipline, designing with DNA to make biology more 'useful' (see *Synthetic Aesthetics*, Ginsberg et al., 2014). Ginsberg triggers social, ethical and scientific debate over real proposals from synthetic biologists and conservationists to design specialist organisms for solving environmental problems. Ginsberg's fictional bio-remediation ecosystem includes four living devices, developed and patented as corporate products as part of a future corporate biodiversity offsetting scheme.

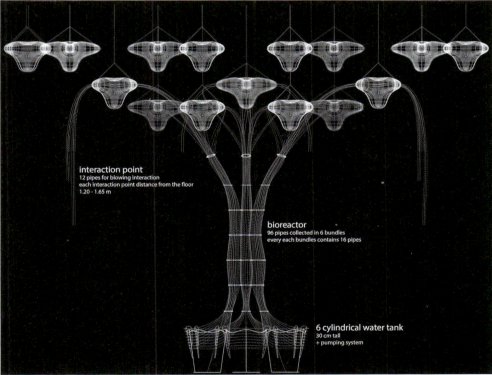

FIGURE 6.3 Ecologic, Hortus Paris, 2013. This bio-architectural hybrid is designed to stimulate the emergence of novel material practices and related spatial narratives; in this sense Hortus Paris proposes an experimental, hands-on engagement with the notion of self-sufficiency, radicalising its applicability to the planning of large urban or architectural landscapes.

works. The paradigm infers a synergy of disciplines with stakes in the city (Dunn *et al.*, 2014). While this is a welcome sign to the landscape imaginary capacity, it should be noted that the landscape representation is part of the century-old futurological profession with vested interests in 'propagandising the future', furthering corporate narratives or ideologies, particularly the techno-utopia of smart cities (Cosgrove, 1999, p. 190). A similar sentiment is found by Mark Augé, who states:

> Technological innovations exploited by financial capitalism have replaced yesterday's myths in the definition of happiness for all, and are promoting an ideology of the present, an ideology of the future now, which in turn paralyses all thought about the future.
>
> (Augé, 2015 p. 3)

FIGURE 6.4 Commonwealth Association of Architects and RIBA, Visualising the Future of the City, student competition, 2015. Resuscitating Dhaka, Bin Sayeed Bakhti and Manal Anis – Bangladesh University of Engineering and Technology (BUET), Dhaka, Bangladesh. Being oblivious to the consequences of squandering away the country's resources for urbanisation, Dhaka apparently is heading towards a point of saturation. However, time and again Bengalis have been capable of coming around from the verge of cynicism and desperation only to survive. Therefore, it is only after this point has been reached that people, endowed with true awareness, will come together, bringing about an influx of positive change. Dhaka, 50 years from now, shall be in the epicentre of such regeneration and armed with her own uniqueness will pull through stronger than ever before. The city will, ultimately, witness a harmony between legalised slums and contemporary architecture; loops of flyovers, roads and restored water channels; globalisation and age-old cultural norms. The aftermath will be an exhilarating oriental triumph breathing new life into a nearly depleted city. Through such inevitable growth, Bengalis will, eventually, emerge with a truly developed South Asian tropical city.

Marc Augé suggests that a technological driver has become the definition of happiness, promoting an ideology of the future now, which in turn paralyses all thought about the future. Augé suggests a dual mode of analysis to escape from this presentism, both analysis of futures as successors and the inauguration of new futures. This futurological techno-utopia refers to computational convergence and liberalisation of communication, though it does not necessarily incorporate the futurological scales in which landscape operations and its tactics are formed.

Future directionality can be worked by incorporating the histories of futures as well as present conditions. This ensures that such dominant modes of thought and representation are carefully evaluated. Digital development in landscape architecture creates new levels of complexity and response; it provides real-time views of the earth

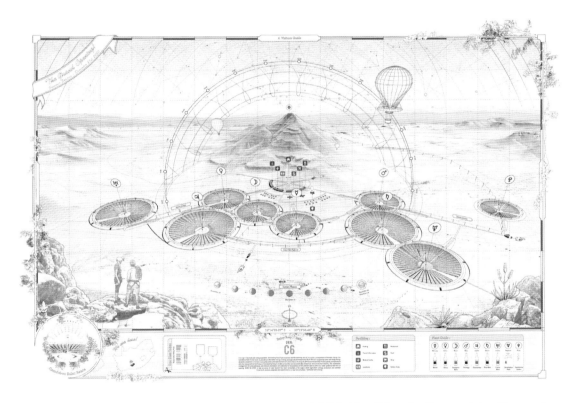

FIGURE 6.5 Commonwealth Association of Architects and RIBA, Visualising the Future of the City, student competition, 2015. Cambedoo Solar Estate, John Cook – University of Westminster, London, United Kingdom. In an age of dramatically rising population, diminishing fossil fuel resources and the alarming and all too visible consequences of climate change, the Camdeboo Solar Estate looks to provide an alternative energy strategy and agricultural resource for South Africa's burgeoning cities and rising energy demands. Located in a remote municipality in the semi-arid environment of the Karoo, its array of CSP (concentrated solar power) plants are hybridised with the long-practised technique of terraced farming to enable a bountiful and economically prosperous wine production industry. The masterplan arrangement, its axial pathways and internal orientations, are calibrated to the positions of the celestial objects within our solar system at the time of opening, 2050. By 2065, a new economy of solar tourism has been embedded in the region, where agriculture, energy production and celestial movements become entwined and experienced as a new form of urban/territorial restructuring.

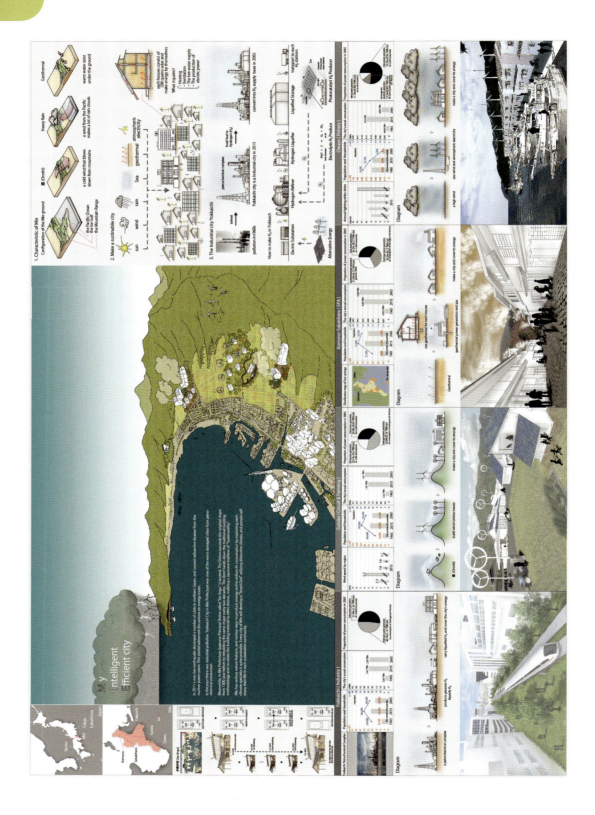

layered with processing, algorithms and calculations of the place in question. This digital ontology has fidelity only if the quality of human input is also sourced. Terrain is mapped but human dynamics can be less understood. Thus, landscape representation and its agency are in essence a reflection of the quality of thoughts and capacity of evaluations of such places between presentation, accuracy and participation. Agency is process and influence and valence is the reaction with cultural and political ramifications. Landscape architecture cannot be a discipline if it does not have an agency in this representation; if it cannot provide narratives and evidence of the types of spaces or their meanings and significance. Valence must also be accounted for, the accounting of mistakes or the perpetuation of unsuitable conditions and ways of living. There is a lot at stake as climatic effects require the depiction of current conditions and immediate responses as well as the real-time modelling of these climatic effects.

FUTURE SCALES

Future projections can emerge from everyday practices as they provide insights into processes. The notion of everyday life as a possibility to reconfigure the city can be found in the vision of the neo-Marxist Henri Lefebvre, who viewed the fragmentation of cities and places as caused by capitalist dynamics and the fragmentation of rural and urban relationships (Lefebvre, 1995, p. 158). This was later developed by Edward Soja (Soja, 1996, 2011) and David Harvey (Harvey, 1989, 1991). Lefebvre, Soja and Harvey's work cannot be covered to any great extent in this text, but are useful sources for further plotting of the positions in which landscape, urban futures, their challenges and paradigms and contradictions can be viewed.

Lefebvre developed the popular term 'right to the city', which he states 'cannot be conceived of as simple visiting right or as a return to traditional cities. It can only be formulated as a transformed and renewed right to urban life' (Lefebvre, 1995, p. 158). Such a social change manifests itself in many forms and it is difficult to evaluate Lefebvre's terms as the pragmatic aspect of his project, Rhythmanalysis, which evaluated urban presences,[3] remained incomplete (Lefebvre, 2013). Though fundamentally

FIGURE 6.6 (*facing page*) Commonwealth Association of Architects and RIBA, Visualising the Future of the City, student competition, 2015. My Intelligent City, Ryohei Fukuhara, Yuki Abe, Kuniatsu Ishihara, Hiroki Oshima, Kohei Osako, Shonnsuke Seki, Kana Morioka, Zhang Yandong – Mie University, Mie, Japan. In 2011 a massive earthquake destroyed a number of cities in northern Japan and caused a radioactive disaster at the nuclear power plant. This started advanced discussions on energy issues. In the past there was industrial pollution. Yokkaichi City in Mie Prefecture was one of the worst damaged cities by petro-chemical production. Meanwhile, in Mie Prefecture the Japanese Principal Shrine, called 'Ise Jingu', is located. The Shrine succeeds the original shape from 1,300 years earlier by rebuilding the same shape every two decades. The deed hands down the traditional building methodology and circulates the building material to other shrines, realizing a Japanese tradition of 'sustainability'. Mie has various natural features, and options to produce energy and to reduce its consumption by exploiting each climate speciality are quite good. Every city of Mie will develop a 'Smart Grid' utilising its distinctive climate, and people will enjoy their life in each sustainable community.

FIGURE 6.7 Commonwealth Association of Architects and RIBA, Visualising the Future of the City, student competition, 2015. London, The Floating Square Mile, Assia Stefanova – Newcastle University, United Kingdom. London is often referred to as 'one of the biggest tax evasion islands'. Here, it becomes the site for a tax haven, constructed in the airspace over the Square Mile, London's financial centre. The new island drains the resources of the city below, while giving back the abandoned land to ordinary citizens. The project is a critique of the growing gap between the wealthiest 0.1 per cent and the rest of the world's population, and the role that technology plays in the monopolisation of power and resources. As the housing problem within big cities continues to grow, the towers on the island are rarely inhabited by their owners yet must be constantly maintained by a disproportionate number of staff. The architectural language is a distorted version of Christopher Wren's architecture and his unrealised, utopian proposal for the masterplan of London. Value is questioned as the buildings are a 3D-printed camouflage, concealing a steel lattice structure.

Lefebvre's social heterotopic (other space)[4] remodelling has direct implications for future landscapes, as Harvey states:

> Of what kind of city we want cannot be divorced from the question of what kind of people we want to be, what kinds of social relations we seek, what relations to nature we cherish, what style of daily life we desire, what kinds of technologies we deem appropriate, what aesthetic values we hold. The right to the city is, therefore, far more than a right of individual access to the resources that the city embodies: it is a right to change ourselves by changing the city more after our heart's desire.
>
> (Harvey, 2013, p. 4)

Harvey, following Lefebvre, is calling for a 'shaping' power or method of control in processes of urbanisation. The implication for landscape architecture in the visioning of social and political spaces rests on its agency, that working with landscapes has a shaping power in making community spaces. The scale of this work may not attract much commercial interest or derived profits, it is a human scale of agency. Representation in true operation can be participatory beyond the current terms of operation of capitalist dynamics. Processes are time-dependent; designs are affected by the agency of these processes and affect processes by their valence. While this is a cyclical force, the assessment of such social shaping is difficult, though it is particularly necessary. This shaping and its assessment can be seen in the illegible urban ecology that Randy Hester's work sought to overturn. With communities he and his team worked through the identification of sacred spaces and the practice of representational ecological democracy (Hester, 2010, pp. 325–331). Hester's work identifies with Stuart Pickett's observation of the metaphoric aspect of ecology, its fragility, and as a representation of people's assumptions and values (Pickett, 2012). The documentation work of Claire Cumberlidge and Lucy Musgrave also demonstrates the role that a designer can have in new social and cultural shaping of landscapes and spaces (Cumberlidge and Musgrave, 2007).

Engagement with this future scale and design agency rests on a participatory model, as found in the thesis of the Civic Systems Lab, where a city's future is 'determined by hundreds of actions taken daily by thousands of people based on what they believe about a city's future and their role in it' (Civic Systems Lab, 2015, p. 6). Participants are seen as contributors and producers to the city that they inhabit. Representation involves new forms of governance in which design agency plays a part. The participatory vision is at odds with the prevailing urban diagnosis of Jan Gehl of disenfranchised social states, though Gehl's promotion of urban plazas seeks a similar renewed urban life (Gehl, 2011). Future projections emerge with a level of validity from representational schemes that include the scope of sensing and experience of places by its inhabitants. For Jonathan Raban, the city is soft, it requires an identity which you must provide and tether to it (Raban, 1974, pp. 1–2). Considering this tethering that Raban suggests, Juhani Pallasmaa has also poetically observed of the socio-urban relationship: 'I experience myself in the city, and the city exists through my embodied experience. The city and my body supplement and define each other. I dwell in the city and the city dwells in me' (Pallasmaa, 2005, p. 40). This individual experience and scale also attaches to the cultural social layer a larger scale of operation in which future projections and projects materialise. As Sharon Zukin states:

> Culture is a powerful means of controlling cities. As a source of images and memories, it symbolises 'who belongs' in specific places. As a set of architectural themes it plays a leading role in urban redevelopment strategies.
>
> (Zukin, 1996 p. 1)

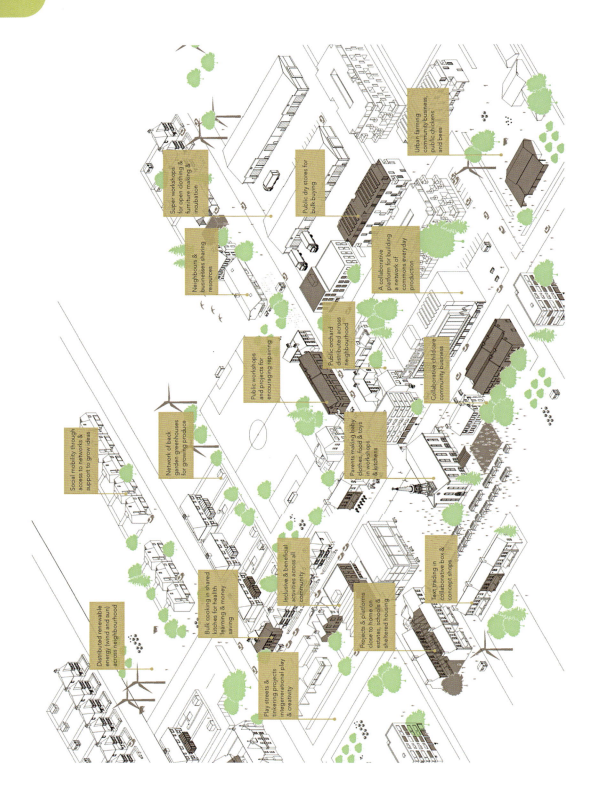

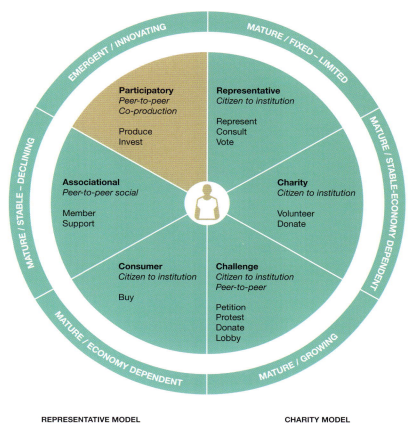

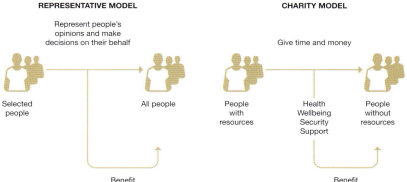

FIGURE 6.8 (*facing page and above*) Civic Systems Lab, Designed to Scale: Mass Participation to Build Resilient Neighbourhoods, 2015. The idea that a dense ecology of this type of micro and macro activity, built into the fabric of everyday life, could generate many positive outcomes is supported by evidence from many smaller projects distributed across the world. People want to live in places where they know and like their neighbours, where they can do things together regularly, where they can help to create welcoming and safe communities in which to raise their children and grow old. Through the participatory ecology described in this report, neighbourhoods could be re-organised, not just for practicality but also to be inspiring and exciting places to live: expanding our horizons, growing ideas and projects, inventing new livelihoods. Examples of this already exist. These new types of neighbourhood will depend on the involvement of the people living there if they are to be the inspiring places we would like. Passive consumption of an environment designed and maintained solely by professional support is neither possible nor sustainable.

CONCLUSION

FIGURE 6.9

MVRDV, The Next Hutong Project. MVRDV has formed a conceptual masterplan that outlines a model for the future development of the Xianyukou Hutong in central Beijing. Located next to Beijing's Tiananmen Square, the district's progress has been delayed in comparison to surrounding sites, creating enormous potential for the area. The studies envision a sustainable economy housed within the existing urban structure, with an aim to both respect and build upon daily life in the historic village. The several spatial tests that have been conceived each explore a specific economic, social or aesthetic potential, and provide an alternative to the Hutong redevelopments that have taken place over the last few decades.

FIGURE 6.10 Agnes Denes, Living Pyramid, Socrates Sculpture Park, New York, 2015. For nearly five decades Denes has used the pyramid both structurally and conceptually to examine environmental priorities and social hierarchies. Every Pyramid Denes creates poses a question. The series began in 1970 and is based on a mathematical theory of probability from which a number system is derived and rendered into visual form for the purpose of exploring its underlying structure (Denes, 2008, pp. 110–128).

CONCLUSION

FIGURE 6.11 Bas Priscen, Marble Quarry, 1998; photograph, Diasec, Endura Photo, 115 × 92 × 4.8 cm © Frac Centre. Bas Priscen explores how the changing Dutch landscape is transformed by users for unscheduled activities.

Future landscape projections may emerge symbiotically, as well as at competing scales from localised to city-wide governance. Participatory modes can also emerge as the antithesis of digital totalisation, as argued in the work of Christine Boyer (Boyer, 1996). Future projections may also emerge from material investigation exploring parameters of mediums, and form generation for new modes of urban living. Questions such as how we live next are fundamental to expanding our landscape imaginary, but also challenge the current conceptions that inhibit work. From the prototype projections these are scaled upwards, adding economic, cultural and social parameters. These modes can be seen, as David Shane states, in a non-linear matrix organisation and set of representational visions which is a networked city or ecological city that is flexible, contracting and expanding (Shane, 2005, pp. 295–297). If we are to gauge both historical and future landscape imaginaries and relate these to people and understand individual and socialised representations of landscape, then perhaps we may be able to fully articulate landscape agency and valence by understanding these fluid operations, then perhaps a different set of spaces may emerge. Futuring as a process is coming more to the fore and it must be fundamental to landscape practice.

FUTURE METABOLISMS

> Most present day cities are based on unsustainable cycles that are open and imbalanced between inputs and outputs, with a relation between inputs and outputs that tends to be linear. In contrast, natural systems have a cyclical course of flows . . . linearity of urban flow systems have to be brought to an end and need to be replaced by a cyclical course.
> (Chrysoulakis *et al.*, 2014, p. 6)

Though a strict metabolic sense is not employed here, the metabolic (see Kennedy *et al.*, 2007) nature of city forms adds new layers to landscape representational agency and valence, in which computational calculations and abstract models represent natural and man-made flows of energy and waste in urban environments for future planning, mitigation and management (Ferrão and Fernández, 2013). Types of urban flow systems include green infrastructure as an infrastructural service and the subsequent management of ecosystem health (Austin, 2014, pp. 5–8). City metabolic studies have certainly emerged for the process of globalisation and the sustainability agenda. The mode and level of metabolic study varies internationally, though in general this ecological research is cross-disciplinary (Baccini and Brunner, 2012). These studies require representation, reading and representing futures. The time frame of metabolic studies projects far-flung futures. Frederick Steiner views landscape as planning which requires reading and presentation to decision makers,

> We need to read landscapes in order to understand where dangers from natural disasters lurk. We need to present that knowledge to decision makers in formats they can understand so they can take the actions necessary to protect human health, safety, and welfare.
>
> (Steiner in Doherty and Waldheim, 2015, p. 142)

Steiner's essay in Doherty and Waldheim's edited book, *Is Landscape . . .* , primarily concerns itself with natural systems, but it is also a representational problem in which the choice of strategies becomes critical. The negative act of representation can be abstract, reductionist or deceitful in its model. The act of making or strategy for representation therefore requires such careful construction, connection and identification of its outcomes and valence, its affectual force. Citing the work of Groundlab and Turenscape, among others, Charles Waldheim sees a positive urbanist force in landscape architecture and application of succinct and positive landscape strategy. Further to this, Waldheim cites the digital model, 'the development of the digital model of associative or relational digital models is at the forefront of landscape urbanist practice, and promises to more precisely calibrate ecological process with the shape of the city' (Doherty and Waldheim, 2015, p. 175). This strategy may emerge from the call from Raoul Bunschoten, Chora, for urban prototypes, models that are both machines and models that connect processes and create pilots (Mostafavi, 2015, p. 616). These observations can be related to the modelling by Space Syntax of London, where the importance of computational calculation becomes ever more real, viewing the infrastructural damage and connectivity of a flood-hit city. These critical data will play an important role in the planning and projection of future urban spaces/landscapes.

In essence some of these environmental or metabolic data models could be considered as urban scenario systems in which the various aspects of city flows and systems are modelled, generated and come more to the fore. As a representation, they provide real-time dynamics, feedback and futures. Though as prototypes and as models the supposed fidelity should be checked and assessed, for no model is complete and never can be, though the digital and metabolic modes of study enable new strategies for landscape representation and support the theory of critical importance of the choice of mode and operation of these fields. Such models may work to mitigate landscape change, as in the case of Helen Meyer and Newton Harrison in Flooded Britain, mapping rising sea levels. Other models may project extreme predictions, as in the work of Terreform 1, who in the Future North project visualise a dystopian mass migration northwards in order to change our current value system. In this vision, projections of sea level rises and desertification mean that world ecotariums move northwards, requiring a complete transplantation of our current cities. Such a futurological projection as an agent reverses its direction back to our present. The audience considers the type of spaces and cities we have now in order to promote a positive valence.

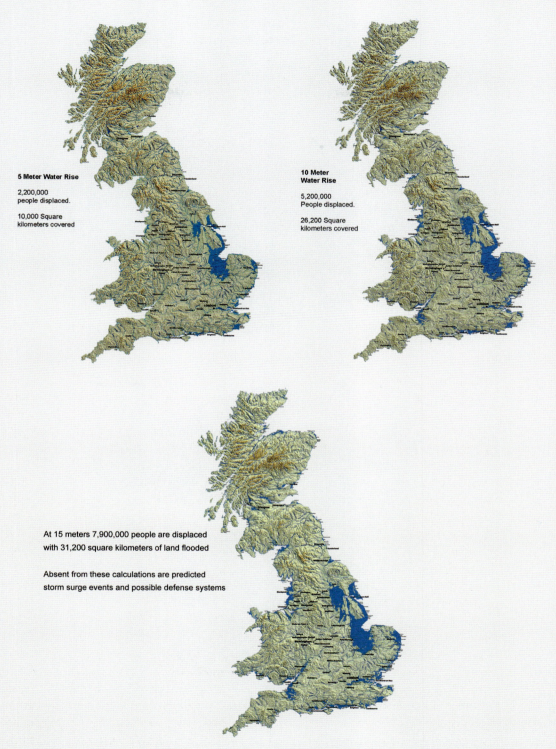

FIGURE 6.12 Helen Mayer Harrison and Newton Harrison and the Harrison Studio & Associates Britain, Greenhouse Britain, 2007–2009. The installation addresses global warming from an artist's perspective. The work proposes an alternative narrative about how people might withdraw as waters rise, what new forms of settlement might look like and what content or properties a new landscape might have in response to the global warming phenomenon. It also demonstrates how a city might be defended.

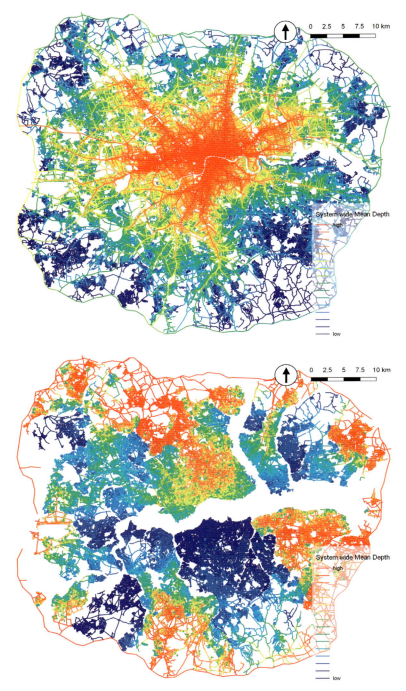

FIGURE 6.13 Space Syntax, Flooded London, 2016. Mean depth analysis considers the total minimum amount of angular change along the path from each segment to all other segments in the system. This effectively highlights how far a place or how deep a place is in relation to all other places. Research done by Jorge Gil on behalf of Space Syntax Limited shows how the impact of infrastructure losses due to flooding changes the hierarchy of mean depth in London.

The work of James Corner, in Field Operations, combines strategic incremental design with interventions in a metabolic study of Rotterdam. The project focuses on the entropy or waste among dynamic urban systems as a point of departure for urban intervention. This work emphasises flows rather than the tangible or static characteristics of the city, and places landscape representation in a time-based sphere of operation, for which two new strategies are required. Representation filters through the process of realising a space from design perception of a site to the public perception of place; what the place stands for at any such time, and then how it changes in time. The working and modelling of media are therefore critical to enable responsive environments and landscape. Future metabolisms rely on a digital agency that works to commutate the complexity of natural phenomena in order for landscape architects to work with it. In that sense, some future metabolisms are utopic, not in the vision but in the method to digitally assimilate natural environments. These are new tools and strategies for landscape which are coming more to the fore and may require a different type of landscape agency, not as author and sole design creator, but as guide and facilitator in the representation of complexity.

FIGURE 6.14 NASA/JSC, US, International Space Station, 'Story of Water' Oman, Kjell Lindgren, Expedition 44 and 45, November 2015.

FIGURE 6.15 (*this page and facing page*) OMA, Eneropa, EuroGrid, Extract from Roadmap 2050: A Practical Guide to a Prosperous, Low-Carbon Europe, 2010. © Image courtesy of the Office for Metropolitan Architecture (OMA). The work of Buckminster-Fuller and his Dymaxion Map (1943)

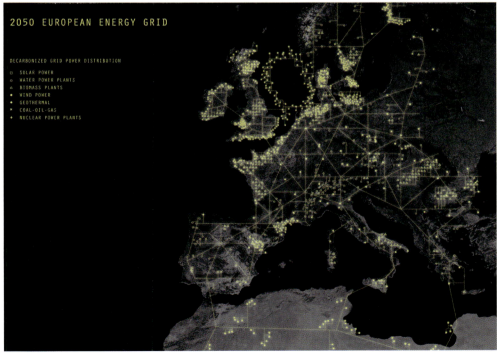

emphasised connectivity of land mass/beyond city/nationalistic readings. These ideas can be seen in the work of OMA and its low-carbon Euro-energy grid, Eneropa (2010). The interconnected city narrative emerges.

FIGURE 6.16 Terreform 1, Future North, Ecotariums in the North Pole. Project Team: Mitchell Joachim, Jane Masching, Makoto Okazaki, Maria Aiolova, Melanie Fessel, Dan O'Connor, 2008. The Future North Ecotarium project is based on the premise that within the next 100 years our climate will be irreversibly altered. Massive migrations of urban populations will move north to escape severe flooding and increased temperatures. Areas inside the Arctic regions will warm up significantly, making their occupation newly desirable. Real-estate values will shift to privilege northern climates that formerly had almost no human inhabitants. To underscore the intensity of such a global shift, we have moved entire cities. The reality of hundreds of millions of people relocating their respective centres of culture, business and life is almost incomprehensible. We anticipate this polemical representation will impact our perception of tomorrow (Markonish and Thompson, 2008).

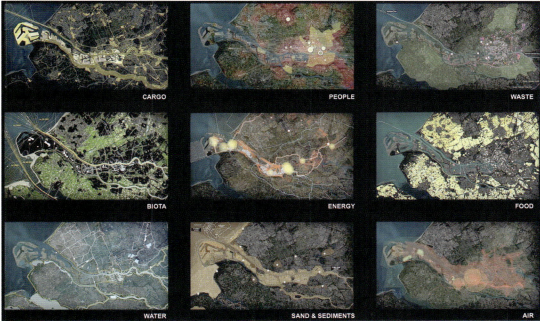

FIGURE 6.17 (*pages 235 and 236*) James Corner Field Operations, Urban Metabolism, 2014 Rotterdam Biennale Research & Exhibition, Netherlands. © James Corner Field Operations with FABRICations. The research moves on to speculate some strategic and programmatic design moves, suggesting and testing scenarios for the twenty-first century port city. Such speculations include a subterranean urban heat network to use waste industrial heat for residences and public spaces, the reintegration of unused port slips into the Rotterdam ecological matrix, sediment capture infrastructure and aquaculture at the mouth of the Rhine, and integration of micro-manufacturing into the city through a newly articulated logistics boulevard.

CONCLUSION   235

CHANNEL HEAT | CONNECT BIOTOPES
COLLECT RESOURCES | CATALYZE INDUSTRY

WALHAAVEN PORT SPONGE PARK

ELECTRIC UTILITIES CORRIDORS | STACKED ELECTRICAL INFRASTRUCTURE | SEDIMENT ACCRUES AROUND VACANT PIER

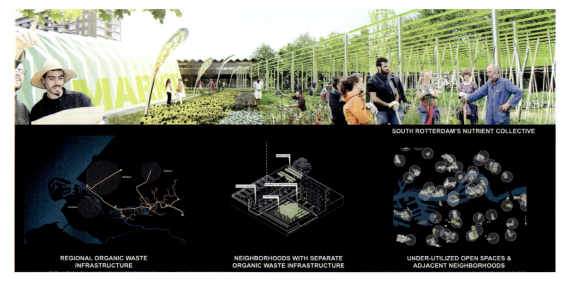

SOUTH ROTTERDAM'S NUTRIENT COLLECTIVE

REGIONAL ORGANIC WASTE INFRASTRUCTURE | NEIGHBORHOODS WITH SEPARATE ORGANIC WASTE INFRASTRUCTURE | UNDER-UTILIZED OPEN SPACES & ADJACENT NEIGHBORHOODS

SUMMARY

A strategy is a point of action, a directive towards an outcome, but as a student or practitioner the forming of outcomes may be difficult. It involves projecting a result working in a future tense and referring back, for often working backwards can help form the direction towards the outcome. The strategy may result from experience or familiarity with media, though many possibilities exist which can be mapped in this book, chapter by chapter or as a connected workflow meant as interoperability which is also interdependent. By making connections, a larger strategy for landscape may emerge with a future tense. This book aimed to connect to other disciplines and launch deeper reading, while providing direct tutorials and instruction.

Representation and landscape have been termed in a holistic sense as a greater range of sources provide new evidence for strategies. Mapping creates a space in which to re-map conditions; the understanding of this process is as equally important as understanding the findings presented. A new mapping 'hover' space enabled by drones provides a readily available aerial/perspective capture that not only provides data on environmental conditions, but can be used archaeologically and futurologically. This mapping space exists between ground and average legal limits of 400 ft. It is neither a god-like eye nor a human perspective.

The agency of mapping and its primal place makes reference to fieldwork and the habitation of spaces; notation provides an immediate feedback loop as it seeks to provide a time-based analysis of a person in landscape. This mapping, fieldwork and notation may refer to two modes of operation – perspectival composites of imagination and perspective composites that form visual evidence for the basis of an environmental study assessing landscape character in the form of repeat photography. The same mode may provide visual evidence for the assessment of a design proposal. The nature of perspective composites and technology mean that 2D and 3D planes can easily be switched; the perspective may be derived from a 3D model or a 3D model may be placed on a 2D plane. The 3D model and the variety of sources point towards four convergence points and developments as defined by Paul Ceruzzi (Ceruzzi, 2003); on this basis two strategic modes are possible, the scripted aspect of strict or creatively generated forms, or the fidelity of building information modelling (BIM), which seeks to enable a parametrically controlled prototype in which all the features of a project are layered. These two operations are not exclusive, though the layering of data is their shared feature. Many big data models and scenarios hang from the basis of the 3D model in order to create calculations. The Smart City and big data agenda provide computational models which to date provide a virtual tabula rasa in which to explore city dynamics, metabolisms and mobility, among other aspects. This is a new strategy for landscape production, but also its valence must be considered. The 3D model and the physical model are intertwined, and digital fabrication enables new modes of landscape model that can look forward or inversely model. Increasing interactivity allows analogue testing of design, dynamics networks and flows of landscape with referable materials. These relations between media can be explored in the future landscapes that are being generated.

While these strategies for landscape cover most media relationships in representational terms, the wider field of representing conceptions of landscape is evidenced in the variety of contributors assembled across disciplines that are projected and realised, simulated and modelled, fabricated and refabricated. These works by and large have been completed in a time-based lens, seeking to address the issues of time in landscape representation. The requirement to analyse our landscape past, current position and future direction is essential to our landscape imaginary capacity. This is not an academic position seeking theoretical reframing, but has direct implications for practice and our relationship with natural spaces and the human relationship with them. The sooner the range of landscape strategies are connected, intertwined and practised, the sooner the directions with landscape are understood, the more we could understand about how we ourselves truly work with the landscapes of past and future.

NOTES

1. Valence is defined in this case as the means and capacity of a design to unite, react or interact with something else. Representation therefore has agency and both negative and positive valence; for example, the propagation of utopian or dystopian futures.
2. Further reading should be undertaken if these sources are unfamiliar; the purpose of the discussion is to map the various intellectual positions in operation.
3. Rhythmanalysis transforms everything into presences, including the present, grasped and perceived as such . . . temporalities and their relations within wholes (Lefebvre, 2004, pp. 22–25).
4. Heterotopia follows Michel Foucault as a space that is utopian, but contains complexity and undesirable elements, an 'other space' (Dehaene and Cauter, 2008).

BIBLIOGRAPHY

Auge, M., 2015. *The Future*. Verso, London.
Austin, G., 2014. *Green Infrastructure for Landscape Planning: Integrating Human and Natural Systems*. Routledge, Abingdon.
Baccini, P. and Brunner, P., 2012. *Metabolism of the Anthroposphere*, 2nd edition. MIT Press, Cambridge, MA.
Berardi, B., 2011, *After the Future*. AK Press, Oakland, CA.
Boyer, M.C., 1996. *Cyber Cities: Visual Perception in the Age of Electronic Communication*. Princeton Architectural Press, New York.
Brook, D., 2013, *A History of Future Cities*. Norton & Company, New York.
Ceruzzi, P.E., 2003. *A History of Modern Computing*, 2nd revised edition. MIT Press, Cambridge, MA.
Chrysoulakis, N., Castro, E.A. de and Moors, E.J. (eds), 2014. *Understanding Urban Metabolism: A Tool for Urban Planning*. Routledge, Abingdon.
Civic Systems Lab (2015) Designed to scale mass participation to build resilient neighbourhoods. Open Works Foundation. www.participatorycity.org/report-the-research (accessed 19 December 2015).

Cosgrove, D., 1999. *Mappings*. Reaktion Books, London.

Cumberlidge, C. and Musgrave, L., 2007. *Design and Landscape for People: New Approaches to Renewal*. Thames & Hudson, London.

Cureton, P., 2013. Videre: Drawing and Evolutionary Architectures, *M.A.D.E. Journal*, 7: 18–27.

Dehaene, M. and Cauter, L.D. (eds), 2008. *Heterotopia and the City: Public Space in a Postcivil Society*. Routledge, London.

Denes, A., 2008. *The Human Argument: The Writings of Agnes Denes*. Spring Publications, Putnam.

Doherty, G. and Waldheim, C. (eds.), 2015. *Is Landscape . . . ?: Essays on the Identity of Landscape*. Routledge, Abingdon.

Dunn, N., Cureton, P. and Pollastri, S., 2014. *A Visual History of the Future*, Government Office for Science, London.

Ferrão, P. and Fernández, J., 2013. *Sustainable Urban Metabolism*. MIT Press, Cambridge, MA.

Gehl, J., 2011. *Life Between Buildings: Using Public Space*, 6th edition. Island Press, Washington.

Ginsberg, A.D., Calvert, J., Schyfter, P., Elfick, A. and Endy, D., 2014. *Synthetic Aesthetics: Investigating Synthetic Biology's Designs on Nature*. MIT Press, Cambridge, MA.

Goreau, T., Hilbertz, W. and Global Coral Reef Alliance, 2005. 'Marine Ecosystem Restoration: Costs and Benefits for Coral Reefs', *World Resource Review*, 17 (3): 375–409.

Harvey, D., 1991. *The Condition of Postmodernity: An Enquiry into the Origins of Cultural Change*. Wiley-Blackwell, Oxford.

Harvey, D., 2013. *Rebel Cities: From the Right to the City to the Urban Revolution*, 2nd edition. Verso, London.

Harvey, P.D., 1989. *The Urban Experience*, reprint, Johns Hopkins University Press, Baltimore.

Hester, R.T., 2010. *Design for Ecological Democracy*. MIT Press, Cambridge, MA.

Jameson, F., 1992. *Postmodernism: Or, the Cultural Logic of Late Capitalism*. Verso, London.

Jameson, J., 2003. Future City. *New Left Review*, 21.

Kepes, G., 1956. *The New Landscape in Art and Science*. Paul Theobald & Company, Chicago, IL.

Kennedy, C., Cuddihy, J. and Engel-Yan, J., 2007. The Changing Metabolism of Cities. *Journal of Industrial Ecology*, 11: 43–59. doi: 10.1162/jie.2007.1107.

Lefebvre, H., 1995. *Writings on Cities*. Wiley-Blackwell, Oxford.

Lefebvre, H., 2013. *Rhythmanalysis: Space, Time and Everyday Life*. Bloomsbury Academic, New York.

Maas, W. Sverdlov, A. and Waugh, E., 2009. *Visionary Cities*. NAi Publishers, Rotterdam.

Markonish, D. and Thompson, J., 2008. *Badlands: New Horizons in Landscape*. MIT Press, Cambridge, MA.

McDonough, T., 2004. *Guy Debord and the Situationist International: Texts and Documents*, new edition. MIT Press, Cambridge, MA.

Merrifield, A., 2013. The Urban Question Under Planetary Urbanization. *International Journal of Urban and Regional Research*. doi: 10.1111/j.1468–2427.2012.01189.x.

Mostafavi, M., 2015. *Ecological Urbanism*, 4th revised edition. Lars Muller, Baden.

Pallasmaa, J., 2005. *The Eyes of the Skin: Architecture and the Senses*, 2nd edition. John Wiley & Sons, Chichester.

Pickett, S.T.A., 2012. Ecology of the City: A Perspective from Science. In B.P. McGrath (ed.), *Urban Design Ecologies*. John Wiley & Sons, Chichester.

Pinder, D., 2005. *Visions of the City: Utopianism, Power and Politics in Twentieth-Century Urbanism*. Edinburgh University Press, Edinburgh.

Raban, J., 1974. *Soft City*. Harvill Press, Glasgow.

Read, S., Rosemann, J. and Eldijk, J.v., eds, 2005. *Future City*. Routledge, Oxford.

Schroder, T., 2013. *City by Landscape: The Landscape Architecture of Rainer Schmidt*. Birkhauser Verlag AG, Basel.

Shane, D.G., 2005. *Recombinant Urbanism: Conceptual Modeling in Architecture, Urban Design and City Theory*. John Wiley & Sons, Chichester.

Soja, E.W., 1996. *Thirdspace: Journeys to Los Angeles and Other Real-and-Imagined Places*. Wiley-Blackwell, Cambridge, MA.

Soja, E.W., 2011. *Postmodern Geographies*, 2nd edition. Verso, London.

Zukin, S., 1996. *Cultures of Cities*. Wiley-Blackwell, London.

INDEX

ABS *see* acrylonitrile butadiene
abstract models 202
abstract time concepts 100
acrylonitrile butadiene (ABS) 201
action paintings 104
additive manufacture (AM) 169, 199
AECOM 144
aerial imagery 49
Aero3Dpro modelling 145
AF *see* autonomous flight
agency: 3D modelling 138, 149, 168; future 210, 219, 221, 227, 231; mapping 10–12, 26–31, 237; model making 170, 171; representation 1, 3, 19; time-based 2D imagery 127–8; visual representation 61
airbrushing 162
algorithms 137, 138, 164, 173
AM *see* additive manufacture
ambient occlusions 163
American Sublime 109–10
America's Most Wanted 4
analogue approaches 26, 205
Andreani, Giona 122
animation 155, 157, 163
Antarctic ice sheets 192
aperture 123–4
Appleton, Jay 64–5
AR *see* augmented reality (AR)
artistic perspectives 123
ASPECT Studios 141
Atelier Bow-Wow 16
atmospheres 155, 157
Augé, Mark 216–17
augmentation 179–98, 202
augmented reality (AR) 76–9, 135
Aurullia 150–1
Australia 147
autonomous flight (AF) 54
Autopia Ampere 209
avant-garde 66, 70
aviation authorities 55

Bahnhofstrasse, Lucerne, Switzerland 79
baking textures 161
Balmori Associates 15
Balmori, Diana 1, 10
bathymetry 41
Battista Alberti, Leon 171
beaches 147
Beddard, Tom 150–1
Bedmep 2 project, BAS 192
behavioural mappings 73
Beijing 108, 224
Bennik, Astrid 96
Bergin, Alexandra 142
Bernstein, Phillip 19
Bifo Beradi, Franco 212
big data 138–49, 173, 237
Big Skies, Big Thinking 7
BIM *see* building information modelling
bio-architectural hybrids 215
bio-remediation 214
biological preferences 65
bird's eye views 84
Birmingham City Centre, UK 42
block models 202, 203
Bluesky International Limited 40
boat design 174
bodily movement 71
Borges, J.L. 23
Boston, Massachusetts 62
botanical gardens 14
box modelling 159
Boyer, Christine 149, 227
Boyle, Mark 68
Brook, Daniel 211
Brooklyn, New York 176–7
Buckminster-Fuller, Richard 27, 171
building heights 44, 45, 203
building information modelling (BIM): delivery of 19; objects 45; strategies 131, 132, 135, 138, 146, 159, 237, *see also* three-dimensional modelling
built-form 164

241

bump textures 162
Bunschoten, Raoul 228
Burckhardt, Lucius 70–1
Burns Beach, Perth, Australia 147
Byte Magazine 134

cached geometry 163
CAD *see* computer-aided design
Cairngorms National Park, Aberdeenshire, Scotland 125
calligraphic visual language 108
Calvino, I. 173
Campbell Park, Milton Keynes 107
capitalism 67, 125, 139, 212, 216, 219
cardboard devices 79
Castillo, Fran 188–9
caustics 163
census maps 37
Ceruzzi, Paul 16, 131–2, 135, 237
Chimento, Valentina 96
Church, Edwin 105, 109
circulation 81, 85
cities: 3D approaches 46–7, data capture 179; future 210, 216–21; garden 178, 179, 180–3, 205–6; metabolism 227–36; perceptions 62, 66; smart 138–49, 237, *see also* urban level
city-planning games 30
Ciudad Empressarial Angulo, Bogotá, Columbia 15
Civic Systems Lab 222–3
climate 114, 234
climate change 103, 217
clipping 128
Coates, Nigel 70
Coire Etchachan Burn, Cairngorms National Park, Scotland 125
collaboration 149–52
collage 103–23
colour 48, 146
colour maps 161
common data sets 32–6
Common Ground 29
Commonwealth Association of Architects 216, 217, 218, 219, 220
community maps 29
community participation 12, 61–96
composites 97–130, 212
computation 16–19, 26, 131–49, 169, 237
see also digital approaches
computer-aided design (CAD) 48, 133–4
concert venues 2
configuration 81
Connex printing 205
contour maps/modelling 43, 45, 159, 202
convergence 135
Corner, James 16, 126, 231

Crilio, Atelier 152–3
cross-section models 202
Cullen, Gordon 63, 64, 66
cultural factors 100, 126, 186, 221
Cumberlidge, Claire 221
Cureton, Paul 7, 89, 90, 92, 125, 161, 182, 183
Cyan Inc. 136, 137
CyberCity 3D Inc. 46–7
Czaky, John 2

3D *see* three-dimensional approaches
2D *see* two-dimensional approaches
3D-Pitoti, Italy 191
data mapping 23–60
De Certeau, Michel 25, 98
De Soissons, Louis 178, 179, 181
Debord, Guy 66, 67, 212
Dee, Catherine 48
Delaware river watershed 53
DEM *see* digital elevation models
democratisation 5, 25, 31, 58, 85
Denali National Park 102
Denes, Agnes 1, 11, 100, 212, 225
Denmark 176
derived models 19
design 48–52, 62, 64, 98
Detroit, US 119
Dhaka, Bangladesh 216
diagrams 12, 81–8, 93
digital approaches: 3D modelling 16–19; agency, mapping 26; design 131; fabrication 19, 157, 162, 169–208, 206; future agency 231; haptic technology 172; instruction 30; paradigms 135; perspective montages 16, 103–9, 110, 128, 129; physical relationships 205; simulation 137; tracking systems 187, *see also* computation
digital elevation models (DEM) 41, 57
digital surface models (DSM) 37, 44, 45, 57, 202
digital terrain models (DTM) 41, 44, 45, 57
displacement maps 162
district planning 119
divided time 100
drawing 26, 50–1, 62, 71–3, 77, 113, 149, 187
Dreyfuss, Henry 61
drift 67
Drone Air, Reykjavik, Iceland 54
drones 12, 18, 103, 128, *see also* unmanned aerial vehicles
DSM *see* digital surface models
DTM *see* digital terrain models
Duempelmann, Sonja 100
Dunn, Nick 170
Dupont, Lien 78

Dymaxion Projection method 27
dystopian approaches 138, 139, 211

Earth's surface 27
earthworks 100
East Darling Harbour, Sydney, Australia 198
The Eastern Ranch, Lubricity, London 6
Ebury Square, London 63
ecological aspects 71–6, 101, 112–13, 213–16, 221, *see also* environmental aspects
economic factors 101, 201
ecotariums 234
edges 81
effects 128
efficiency 199
EIAs *see* Environmental Impact Assessments
emphasis 50
en plein air painting 109
energy efficiency 217, 218, 219
Eneropa 232–3
engagement 12, 50
Ernst, Max 106
environmental aspects: 3D modelling 152, 157, 162; bio-remediation 214; future 227–36; immersion 197; navigation 68–9; planning 110; preferences 65, *see also* ecological aspects
Environmental Impact Assessments (EIAs) 110, 128
equitable development 74
errors, digital 171
Ersilia 173
ethnicity 37, 116, 119
Europe After the Rain 106
Europos Parkas, Lithuania 122
Evans, Robin 3
experience 98, 221
experiential landscapes 65–6
eye-level perceptions 80
eye-tracking devices 76, 77, 78, 79

fibre structures 188–9
fabrication *see* digital fabrication
fieldwork 12, 61–96, 237
figure ground 85
filters 128
final gather 163
final production 128
fixed wing drones 54, 57
flooding 228, 230, 234
flora and fauna 8, 15
Florinsky, I. 25
focal point diagrams 85
Footmeadow Urban Island Park Tree Strategy, Northampton, UK 84
forward models 176–9
Fosters & Partners 168, 186

four futurological computing paradigms 131, 135–6, 237
FractalLab 150–1
fragmented landscapes 67, 219
framing 123
French Lettrism 66–7
FS *see* fabrication systems
future aspects: 2D imagery 126–7, 132; 3D printing 169, 176–7; four computational paradigms 16; projections 205, 206, 209–40

gaming 8, 135, 137
Gamma Tokyo 70
garden cities 178, 179, 180–3, 205–6
garden roofs 203
Gehl, Jan 221
generalisation 50
generational perspective composites 126–7
geo-referencing 50
geocomputation 138, 173
geographic information systems (GIS) 28, 31, 48, 58, 173, 204
geographic segregation 32, 33
geological information 190
geometry 137
Geuze, Adriaan 107
Gibson, William 52
Gifford, Don 8
Gifford, Kyle 205
Gil, Jorge 230
Ginsberg, Alexandra Daisy 214
Girot, Christophe 158
GIS *see* geographic information systems
glaciology 8
global illumination 163
global positioning systems (GPS) 52, 54, 55
global warming 229
Google Cardboard 79
governmental level 19, 33
GPS *see* global positioning systems
grades 81
Grand Canyon, US 100–1
graphic development 137
graphic thinking 81
Greater Southern Waterfront, Singapore 144
Greenhouse Britain 229
Greenwich Peninsula, UK 99
Griffiths, Isabel 79
Griggs, Lee 160
Gross Max 108
Groundlab 120

Hahn, H. 110
Halprin, Lawrence 3, 9, 10, 12, 71, 86–7, 88
Hamilton, Richard 126

INDEX   243

hand-drawings 26, 50–1, 62, 113, 149, 187
Hansen, Andrea 124
haptic essence 171–2
harbours 17, 141, 144, 176, 198
hardware development 131–8
Harrison, Newton 228, 229
Hartlepool 146
Harvey, D. 220–1
Herrington, Susan 100
Hester, Randolph 71–6, 221
heterogeneous spaces 98
heuristic approaches 19, 172–3, 179
hidden landscapes 36–7
Hilbertz, Wolf 209
hill shading 52
historical aspects 100–1, 211, 212, 213, 217
Hoffman, Johanna 82
Holland Park Study 68
Hong Kong 186
Honolulu, Hawaii 46–7
Hopkins, Don 30
horizontal tracking 91
Horsley, Anthony 205
hover space 12, 52
Howard, Ebenezer 179, 181
hue 48
human intellect 11
hybrid approaches 30–1, 170, 199
hyper-realism 137–8
hyperdrives 138–9
hypergraphics 66–7

Ian+ 174
ID software 135
illegible urban ecology 221
image interpretation issues 36
imagination, future 211–19
immersion 197
importons 163
inclusive development 74
Incremental Development 82
indirect illumination 163
interactivity 172–3, 173–9, 205, 237–8
International Space Station 231
interoperability 28–30, 210, 237
inverse models 179
inverted glass pyramid 13
IRIS models 204
irradiance particles 163

Jacoby, Helmut 107
James Corner Field Operations 235–6
Jameson, Fredric 213
Janulis, Karolis 18
Japan 218, 219
Jeffrey Open Space Trail 72, 73
Jorn, Asger 66

Kaplan, Rachel 65
Karekar, Yogesh 188–9
Kepes, Gyorgy 211
Kingery-Page, K. 110
kitsch 116, 128
Kleet & Wolfe 196
Klett, Mark 100–1
knowledge relativism 23
Komar and Melamid, America's Most Wanted 4
Koolhas, Rem 213
Korea 118
Kulhas, Vahide 203
Kullmann, Karl 82, 110, 147
Kundla, Alison 173

Lake District, UK 193
landscape gardening 111
landscape prospect/refuge theories 64–5
landscape and visual impact assessments (LVIAs) 127
Landstat, United States Geological Survey 32–3, 34
Laposky, Ben 133
Las Vegas 34
laser imaging, detection and ranging (LiDAR): 3D models 7, 159–61; data 42, 44, 191; models 202; orthorectification 7; point clouds 5, 49, 57
layer cake method 26–8
layering 127, 138–49, 173–9, 237
layout 50
Lefebvre, Henri 67–70, 76, 213, 219–20
legislation 114
Lemaître, Maurice 66–7
Lennon, Thomas 53
Lettrism 66–7
level design software 135
Li, Jonathan 49
Library of Babel 23
licences 55
LiDAR *see* laser imaging, detection and ranging
lighting 128, 152, 157, 162
Limburg, the Netherlands 197
living breakwaters project 17, 176
Living Breakwaters project, Staten Island, New York 17
Living Pyramid, Socrates Sculpture Park, New York 225
localised flora and fauna 8
London, UK 203, 220, 228, 230
low-carbon Europe 232–3
low-density suburban environments 181
Lubricity proposal 6
Lucas, Ray 68–9

LVIAs *see* landscape and visual impact assessments
Lynch, Kevin 61, 62, 110, 128–9, 211

Maas, Winy 210
Mcgrath, Brian 19
McHarg, Ian 26, 57–8
magnifying glasses 191
Malaga, Peter 188–9
Manteo, North Carolina 73, 75
Mapbox 33
mapping: agency and valence 10–11, 237; behavioural 73; data 23–60, 149; future 237; mask 162; psychogeography 66, 67; symbols 61
maquettes 168
marble quarries 226
Marina Bay, Singapore 144
marine environments 142
Marmot Rock, Denali National Park 102
Marta Swartz and Partners 198
mask maps 162
massing studies 45, 51
material models 202
materials 163, 171–2, 201
MAUD 121
Mayson's Ordinance Model of the Lake District 193
MCor Technologies 204
ME *see* microbial ecologies
Meiji Shrine, Tokyo 68–9
Meirama Mine Tryptich 98
Meldrum, Iona 99
Méliès, Georges 106
Merete, Kirsten 211–12
Merrifield, Andy 213
metabolisms 227–36
metaphoric modes 101
metaphorical aims 85
Meyer Harrison, Helen 229
Meyer, Helen 228
micro-environments 16
microbial ecologies (ME) 188–9
Microutopias 174
Mie, Japan 219
migration 228, 234
Miller, Rand 136
Miller, Robyn 136
mines 98
Minneapolis Riverfront 114–15
mobile unmanned printing platform (MUPPette) 194–5
modelling: 3D 131–68, 210; fabrication 19, 169–208; future 228; perspectives 123–4
modernism 212–13
molecular biology 214
moon landing 106

Moore, Kathryn 7
Moscow 116, 117, 120
motation *see* movement notation
movement 79, 83 *see also* walking
movement notation 9, 10, 12, 71, 88–92
Muir, Richard 26
municipal parks 14
MUPPette *see* mobile unmanned printing platform
Musgrave, Lucy 221
MVRDV 224
Mycelis muralis 139
Myst 136, 137

Narula, Priyanka 188–9
NASA 231
National Bowl Concert Venue, Milton Keynes 2
national parks 102, 125 *see also* parks
natural disasters 228
nature 11
navigation, 2D 61
NDVI *see* normalised difference vegetation index
the Netherlands 185, 235–6
New York 225
Newton Fallis 209
nightsky data 40
Nijhuis, Steffan 173
non-uniform rational basis splines (NURBS) 155, 159
normalised difference vegetation index (NDVI) 40
normals 162
North Pole 234
North Warwickshire, UK 43
notation 12, 61–96, 237
NURBS *see* non-uniform rational basis splines

Office for Metropolitan Architecture (OMA) 232–3
Olin Studio 14, 74
Olympic Parks 5, 176
OMA *see* Office for Metropolitan Architecture
One North Masterplan, Singapore 140
O'Neil-Dunne, Jarlath 56
ONYX collective 28
Orillard, Clement 66
ornamental squares 63
Orpheus, Boughton House, Northamptonshire, UK 13
ortho-photo drapes 161
orthorectification 7, 50–1
Oscillons 133
Oteiza House 152–3

Palamassa, Juhani 76, 221
Palmbout, Roosendaal, the Netherlands 185
parametrism 136–7
Paris 66, 67
Paris, Hortus 215
Parish Maps 29
Parker-Loftus, Sophie 84
Parkour Symbol System 89
parks 74, 84, 107, 120, 122, 225 *see also* national parks
participatory approaches 12, 61–96, 221, 222–7
particles 160, 162
pattern diagrams 88
Paysant, Michel 77
pedestrian activity 143
Pelletier, L. 132
People, Paths, Purposes 80
perceptions, community 61–96
personal viewpoints 124
perspective 4, 103–24, 128, 164, 237
Perth, Australia 147
phase diagrams 88
phasing 98
photogrammetry 41, 56, 57, 159
photography 8, 149
photometric lights 162
photomontages 16, 103, 110, 124
photons 163
physical models 44, 170, 171, 173, 176, 190, 237
physical relief models 193
physical–digital relationships 205, 237
Pickett, Stewart 101
Pickett, Stuart 221
picturesque aspects 8, 64, 71, 128
Pinder, David 132, 212
Piper's Model Makers 175
PLA *see* polyactic acid
placeholders 163
plants 139, 148
planting diagrams 88
Plastisphere 142
play areas 14
Pleiades 35
point clouds 5, 41, 49, 56, 57, 202
Point Sublime, Grand Canyon, US 100–1
political factors 136–7
polyactic acid (PLA) 201
polygons 155
polyvinyl alcohol plastic (PVA) 201
Portland Open Sequence 86–7
post-production 155, 157, 164
post-war apocalyptic landscapes 106
poverty 32
powder printing 201
power stations 112–13

presentational works 3–4
presentism 217
Priestnall, Gary 172, 193
printing, 3D 169–208
Priscen, Bas 226
prospect dominance 65
prototypes 228
psychogeography 37, 66, 67
public aesthetics 4
public square 15
PVA *see* polyvinyl alcohol plastic
pyramids 225

Raban, Jonathan 221
racial segregation 32
radical mapping practices 67
radiosity 163
Raeven, Marijn 154
railway development 184–5
Rankin, Bill 32, 33
rasterisation 163
raytracing 163
reality computing 26
reef street 17
references 127, 149, 156
refuge dominance 65
Regan, Oliver 85
regulations 55
relational digital models 228
relativism, knowledge 23
relief, maps 25
remote ecological power stations 112–13
remote-sensing 12, 23–60, 55
remotely piloted craft (RPA) 54
rendering 155, 157, 163
Rep Rap 169
repeat photography 8, 12–16, 101–3, 128, 237
Repton, Humphry 110, 111
resilient neighbourhoods 222–3
resin 201
response diagrams 85
reverse directionality 3
Reykjavik, Iceland 54
Rhizo scans 148
rhythm 67–70
Riahi, Pari 171
Richter, Dagmar 176
right to the city 219
rivers 53, 114–15
Romice, Ombretta 65–6
Roosendaal, the Netherlands 185
Root, Kelly 205
root systems 148
Rotterdam, the Netherlands 107, 231, 235–6
Rowe, Colin 64
RPA *see* remotely piloted craft
RSVP cycles 71

sacred spaces 73, 75, 221
sandboxes 190
SARndbox 190
satellite imaging 34, 35, 38, 41
Sausalito to San Francisco 9
Savage Rock, Denali National Park 102
scales 170, 202, 219–27
SCAPE Team 176
schematic landscape diagrams 72, 73
Schouwburgplein, Rotterdam 107
Schubert, Hannah 96
Schumacher, Patrik 136
scores 9, 71–3, 82, 88–9, 90, 92
Scotland 125
scripting 159
sculpting 159
sculpture parks 225
seascapes 209
seasonal changes 117–23
Seoul, Korea 118
sequential strategies 117–23
serial vision, urban design 64
Seunsangga Citywalk, Seoul, Korea 118
Shane, David 227
Shier, Jared 194–5
shorelines 17
shrines 68–9
SimCity, Micropolis 30
Simkins, Ian 65–6
simulation 26, 145
see also modelling
Singapore 140, 144
site access 81
site inventory diagrams 85
site specificity 131
Situationists 67, 212
sketchpad 132, 133
sky portals 162
smart cities 138–49, 237
social factors 37, 38, 76, 93, 180–3
social heterotopic remodelling 220
Socrates Sculpture Park, New York 225
software developments 131–8
software interfaces 152
Sokolniki Park Territory, Moscow 120
solid-state electronics 135
sources 124
South Africa 217
space photography 28
space shuttle launch 104
Space Syntax 19, 180, 181, 206, 228, 230
spatial accessibility 37, 180–3
specular maps 162
spot elevations 43, 45
Sproull, Bob 135
station areas 121, 143
Steiner, Frederick 227–8

Steniz, Carl 26–8
stereo lithography (STL) 199
stereographic iPad viewers 196
STL *see* stereo lithography
Stonehenge Hidden Landscape 36–7
Stoss Landscape, Minneapolis Riverfront 114–15
streamlines 114–15
street bridge parks 74
strollology 70–1
sub surface 38–9
subdivision 155
Sublime aesthetics 109–10
sublimity 125
subtractive manufacture 199
succession effects 100, 103, 114
sun shading 52
superimposed assets 114
surface models 155
sustainability 227–36
Sutherland, Ivan 132, 133, 135
Swiss Maps, Digirama Delux 24
Sydney, Australia 141, 198
symbols 48, 61, 71, 88–91

Tainan, Taiwan 121
Takeuchi, Yuichiro 203
Taktyk 98
Tansey, Mark 104, 114
tax havens 220
technology 131–2
Terreform 1 176–7, 234
texturing 128, 152, 156, 161–2
Thames, London 6
The Naked City 66
thermal data sets 41
thermoplastic filaments 187
Thiel, Phillip 80, 81
Thornton Abbey, UK 55
three-dimensional (3D) approaches: cities 46–7; models 131–68; perspective composites 237; perspectives 123; printing 169–208, 206; time-based 2D imagery 128
Thurrock, Essex 7
Thwaites, Kevin 65–6
tidal movements 99
tiling textures 161
time-based approaches 12–16, 93, 96, 97–130, 131, 176, 238
Tinker Imagineers 197
Tinney, Robert 134
Tokyo 69, 70
toolsets 136
topographical sets 37, 38
topology 27, 158
Toronto 143
Townsville 145

INDEX   247

tracking 76, 91
Tran, Tam 194–5
transparency 162
trees 11, 42, 84
Turbine, Elektrenai, Lietuva 18
Turenscape 116, 117
two-dimensional (2D) approaches 61, 117–23, 124–8, 237

UAS\UAV *see* unmanned aerial systems\vehicles
Union Station, Toronto 143
University of Tokyo 187
unmanned aerial systems\vehicles (UAS\UAV) 10–12, 52–7, 79
upscaling 199, 201
urban level: 3D modelling 19; data 39, 45; design 64, 66; development 15, 140; future 216, 217; living 6, 7; parks 120; perpetuation of form 213; prototypes 228; sections 51, *see also* cities
urbanisation 220–1
utopian approaches: 3D modelling 131–2, 134, 138, 149; fabrication 179, 181; future thinking 211, 212–13; game environments 137
UV texture maps 162

valence: 3D modelling 138, 149; future 210, 219, 227; mapping 10–12, 31; representation 2, 3, 237; time-based 2D imagery 127; visual representation 61
vegetation 8, 15, 137, 138
vertical tracking 91
viewshed 51, 52
Villar, Alex 65
violence 33
virtual block modelling programs 137
virtual space 132–3
visions, future 212
visual communication 81–8
visual field diagrams 88
visual impacts: studies 110; time-based 2D imagery 127–8
visual perceptual models 64–5

visual representation 61
visual site analysis 64
visualisation 3–4, 19, 191
Vogt, Günther 19, 169
VR technology 77, 135

Waldheim, Charles 124, 228
walkability studies 37
walking 61, 70–1, 91
see also movement
Washington DC 32, 33
waste 231
waste heat 235–6
Water Carpet and Cone Area, Campbell Park, Milton Keynes 107
waterfronts 144
Watson, David 51
Watters, JJ 83
weather systems 77
Weiser, Mark 169
Welwyn Garden City, UK 178, 179, 180–3, 205–6
West Kowloon Cultural District, Hong Kong 186
Whiston Spirn, Anne 20
White Clouds 205
wilderness 100, 105
Wilkie, Kim 13
windflow 52
Winter Road, Vilnius, Lithuania 18
Winter, Stefan 211–12
wireframes 155
Wolfe, Byron 100–1
workstages 62, 149–64
World Map 28
Wright, Will 30

Xianyukou Hutong, Beijing 224

Zaha Hadid Architects 140
Zaryadye Park, Moscow 116, 117
zone of theoretical visibility (ZTV) 51, 52
zoning 181
ZTV *see* zone of theoretical visibility
Zukin, Sharon 221